The
Witch
as Teacher in Fairy Tales

Discovering the
Esoteric Truth Hidden
in Ancient Fairy Tales

Nuria Daly

Illustrations by Hannah Baek Wha

BALBOA.
PRESS

A DIVISION OF HAY HOUSE

Balboa Press books may be ordered through booksellers or by contacting:

Balboa Press
A Division of Hay House
1663 Liberty Drive
Bloomington, IN 47403
www.balboapress.com.au
1 (877) 407-4847

Because of the dynamic nature of the Internet, any web addresses or links contained in this book may have changed since publication and may no longer be valid. The views expressed in this work are solely those of the author and do not necessarily reflect the views of the publisher, and the publisher hereby disclaims any responsibility for them.

The author of this book does not dispense medical advice or prescribe the use of any technique as a form of treatment for physical, emotional, or medical problems without the advice of a physician, either directly or indirectly. The intent of the author is only to offer information of a general nature to help you in your quest for emotional and spiritual well-being. In the event you use any of the information in this book for yourself, which is your constitutional right, the author and the publisher assume no responsibility for your actions.

Any people depicted in stock imagery provided by Thinkstock are models, and such images are being used for illustrative purposes only. Certain stock imagery © Thinkstock.

Print information available on the last page.

ISBN: 978-1-5043-0643-0 (sc)
ISBN: 978-1-5043-0644-7 (e)

Balboa Press rev. date: 03/09/2017

Where is the ship sailing?

Oh Seeker,
did you know that the 'inner awakening' is like being on a ship,
sailing on the great waters of love, harmony and beauty,
guided by the compass of the Spirit of Guidance,
and driven by the energy of Spiritual Liberty;
while heading toward the Goal of the annihilation of the ego,
where one may begin to realise that the Sailor is in reality
a ray of the Divine presence, sailing in
the Past, Present and Future, on the infinite waves of illusion.

Hidayat Inayat-Khan

With immense gratitude to my Teacher and Guide,
Murshid Nawab Pasnak, who 'gave' me these stories

ABOUT THE AUTHOR

The only child of Jewish parents who fled Vienna in 1939, Irene was born into a small community of refugees who found sanctuary in Londonderry, Northern Ireland. Growing up in a sectarian society such as Northern Ireland, was confusing for someone brought up as Presbyterian of Jewish parents and so she found herself on a search for a spirituality that she could believe in. At fourteen, Irene spent an afternoon in the library looking for a 'new' religion. She thought that perhaps Buddhism would fit the bill.

Irene first trained as a radiographer and worked in England where she met her first husband before emigrating to South Africa with him - while pregnant with her twin sons. Twins! She didn't know this at the time.

Irene spent eleven years in South Africa, divorced her husband there and migrated to Melbourne, Australia with her sons. It was in Melbourne that she discovered Jung and became a member of the C.G. Jung Society. This opened a whole new world for her and led to her doing a Psychology degree as a mature age student, part time, while working in IT and bringing up her teenage sons. This took her eleven years. During this time, Irene underwent almost seven years of analysis with a Jungian analyst and became a hypnotherapist. She was a long-time member of the Jung Society in Melbourne and later gave several talks there.

It was while on a visit to Londonderry that Irene re-connected with Roddy, who worked for her parents in their grocery shop (from when he left school at fourteen). After Irene married and went to live in South

Africa, Roddy stayed connected with Irene's parents and visited them often after they returned to Vienna to live. Her mother had always told her that Roddy was the man for her, but she finally made that connection for herself many years later. After some years of courtship and visits to Australia by Roddy, they had a wonderful Sufi wedding in 2006.

As with many survivors of the Holocaust, Irene's father never spoke about his family (only his mother and sister who had survived). She was aware that the rest of his family had perished, but that was all. There was a childhood memory, of her parents crying bitterly over a letter from her father's cousin, who was being sent east to work. She did not understand that he was being sent to Auschwitz, or what this meant. But she was haunted by that scene and on finding some old documents in her father's papers, went on the search for her father's lost family. She completed this search and had her discoveries published, so that her family can one day understand 'where they came from'.

While still searching for a 'religion' which appealed to her, Irene spent time in Siddha Yoga and Tibetan Buddhism, before finding the Universal Sufism of Hazrat Inayat Khan. After being initiated as a Sufi, she was given the name Nuria. She met her teacher Murshid Nawab Pasnak at one of the first Australian Sufi Summer Schools in 1999. Nawab, like so many Sufis, taught by telling stories, and he was a great story teller! Thus, began Nuria's fascination with the deep and hidden spiritual meaning in many of the old fairy tales. Her first interpretation called 'Giving Life to the Village, Service in the tale of 'Golden Chisel and the Stone Ram' was published in the Sufi journal, *Toward the One* in 2005. This led to four more stories, which have been explored in this book.

Nuria became fascinated with Hazrat Inayat Khan's concept of the mysticism of sound and music, and wrote an article on this called 'Ponderings on the "Unstruck Sound', which was published in *Toward the One*, in the Spring 2007 issue. This is included in this book as an appendix, as it is very relevant to most of the fairy stories she writes about.

Nuria leads a Sufi group in Melbourne and is the National Representative in Australia of the International Sufi Movement. She continues the inner work.

This exploration of the hidden meaning in ancient fairy tales has been a most important outcome of Nuria's spirituality and evolution, where as a psychologist and hypnotherapist, the understanding of consciousness and the mind have been fundamental.

CONTENTS

PREFACE

It was many years ago, at an Australia Sufi Summer School, that my Teacher told us the ancient Han Chinese fairy tale of Golden Chisel and the Stone Ram, in relation to working with the topic of 'Service'. This opened my mind to the understanding that there was an amazing spiritual wisdom in the story, although it came from another culture and another time. I then had the realisation that Sufism was indeed the mystical base of all 'religions' – the Truths were the same. Having been in a Jungian analysis for almost seven years, working with dreams and symbols, I asked my Teacher if he would let me work with the story for myself and thus began a long journey or 'dig' into the inner 'archaeology' of certain fairy tales which my teacher sent me, over the years to work with. Every symbol and idea had to be examined and dusted off. I found myself wondering why and what these symbols represented. My interpretation of the story of Golden Chisel and the Stone Ram was first published in the Sufi journal, 'Toward the One: A Journal of Unity.[1]

There are many common themes hidden in these tales, which is at first surprising considering they come from such diverse sources. One of these themes is the Mysticism of Sound and Music in our spiritual evolution and practice. This has always fascinated me and so I have included my article, *'Ponderings on the Unstruck Sound'* in the Appendix. You may find this useful in understanding this mystical concept.

So, there are indeed vestiges of ancient truths in many fairy tales, some of which are thousands of years old. They have been passed down

---

[1] Volume Six, Spring 2005.

by story tellers in the oral tradition and some have survived to modern times by being written down. Stories have been used for teaching, and for the relating of historical facts and also for entertainment. Sufis have used stories as a mystical teaching tool – it is easier to remember a good story than to take in abstract teachings. There are so many levels of truth to be found in such stories. This wisdom is as relevant now as it was then, and so it is that I have come to understand these fairy tales in the light of the lives we now live. Many truths have been hidden in the symbol and allegory of the stories, but we can uncover these hidden truths.

In support of my contention that fairy tales and myths hold wisdom and truth that has been passed down through the ages, scholars in Lisbon and Durham Universities have discovered that: 'many of the fairy tales --- were rooted in a shared cultural history dating back to the birth of the Indo-European language family. Many stories could be traced back to when Eastern and Western Indo-European languages split more than 5,000 years ago.'[2]

So it can be argued that, if proof were needed, fairy tales, both oral and written, come from a deep, mystical source and are a never-ending source of discovery, joy, wonder, and mystery throughout the history of human (and Fairy) kind. We can still learn from them and apply this learning to our lives, even in these so-called modern times.

Very often folk and fairy tales carry spiritual guidance and esoteric information, preserved down through the ages, not because the successive generations of story tellers necessarily understand those messages, but simply because the oral tradition was scrupulously kept as a link of faith, so to speak; the story is told as it was heard, no more, no less, and that faithful transmission can preserve a surprising amount of detail over thousands of years. For example, many of the descriptions of Troy in Homer's *Iliad*, written around the eighth century BC, but describing events perhaps five hundred years before that, have been shown to be true by modern archaeology.

---

[2] 'Fairy tale origins thousands of years old, researchers say.' in *BBC News*, UK, 20 January 2016, < http://www.bbc.com/news/uk-35358487> at 4 January 2017.

The stories themselves can be read in any order and according to your own leanings, but, as I have discovered for myself, there are some deep truths hidden in them which may only be found on subsequent readings. They need to be mined!

THE WEAVING

The Story and the Dream

My first encounter with the 'witch' was when I was very little and my father read me fairy stories at bedtime. There was one that really frightened me and I didn't want him to read it, even though I suspect that he was fed up with returning to my favourite stories again and again. The tale that terrified me was about a little princess celebrating her fifth birthday. A huge party was planned in the palace for her but when all the guests arrived bearing gifts, the wicked witch appeared in a vicious mood, because she had not been invited to the party. Her gift to the princess was a hailstone for a heart. The princess was left with no heart save one of ice, making her unable to be loved or to love anyone. The effect was immediate. A once warm-hearted princess became cruel. I don't remember what happened in the story after that, because a hailstone for a heart stopped me in my tracks and the memory of the sense of terror is still clear.

Since then myths, fairy tales and dreams have attracted my imagination. The inner life has always seemed more real and exciting to me than the humdrum of the everyday world. I suppose it is no surprise that I later discovered Jung and eventually undertook nearly seven years of Jungian analysis. I thought of this process as a training and hoped one day to become a Jungian analyst myself. This was not to be, as I never found the money or time, to undertake the extensive Jungian qualification but years later, working as a counselling psychologist I was able to integrate Jungian concepts and ideas into my practice.

Having been brought up in Northern Ireland, where the Christianity I experienced was not what I wanted or needed, I had always been on a search for Spiritual Truth. I had heard of Sufism over the years and was attracted to its poets and its focus on the qualities of the heart, but could not discover what it meant in a practical sense and I longed to find a Sufi group and a Sufi teacher. There seemed to be not such a great leap from the Jungian idea of the Collective Unconscious, as the shared depth of our collective being, to the Sufi concept that there is nothing but God, and that God alone exists. In other words, we are all part of the Divine Unity, and this Divine One is part of us. I read that one of the greatest Sufi mystics, Ibn 'Arabi held that there is a *'world of Idea-Images, of archetypal figures, of immaterial matter, which is between the universe that can be apprehended by pure intellectual perception and the universe which is perceptible to the senses. This world is as real and objective, as consistent and subsistent as the intelligible and the sensible worlds; it is an intermediate universe 'where the spiritual takes body and the body becomes spiritual, a world consisting of real matter and real extension. The organ of this universe is the Active Imagination; it is the* **place** *of theophanic visions, the scenes on which visionary events and symbolic histories* **appear** *in their true reality.'*[3]

This intermediary world or realm seems interchangeable with Jung's idea of the Collective Unconscious. It is the place of symbols and archetypes through which we can understand the hidden meaning of things. It is the transmutation of everything visible into symbols, the intuition of an essence or person in an Image which is not part of any universal logic nor of sense perception. Fairy tales are also allegories and are not related to any rational worldly operation. Corbin puts it beautifully when he says that *'The symbol announces a plane of consciousness distinct from that of rational evidence; it is the 'cipher' of a mystery, the only means of saying something that cannot be apprehended in any other way; a symbol is never 'explained once and for all', but must be*

---

[3] H. Corbin, *Alone with the Alone: Creative Imagination in the Sufism of Ibn 'Arabi*, Bollingen Series XC1, Princeton University Press, Princeton, New Jersey, 1997, p.4.

deciphered over and over again, just as a musical score is never deciphered once and for all but calls for ever new execution.' [4]

The Irish would say that we know when we are in Fairy Realm, which is this inner world or collective unconscious or *Alam al-mithal* of Ibn Arabi, when everything looks 'normal' except for one thing, perhaps a magical creature, a witch, or a fairy. These are the symbols that tell us we are in that hidden, mysterious world. In attempting to explain some of these symbols I am possibly doing them a disservice. It is really up to you, the reader, to find your own meaning in each tale. Remember, however, that at another time it may mean something completely different to you. It is the Active Imagination that directly perceives events, figures, and presences, unaided by the senses. This is **not** fantasy, or daydreaming! As a hypnotherapist, I have an understanding of what is called 'trance logic', which is really very literal and does not take the rationale of this world into account. For example, if I asked you to see someone sitting on a chair, while you were in trance, you might see the person on the chair, but also the chair through the person.

In saying earlier that Sufis believe, and come to know, that everything is God and that God is everything, we need to come to an understanding of this huge and all-encompassing statement. For me it began with a dawning realization of what Jung meant when he talked of the 'Collective Unconscious'. I saw us all as a great mountain range, with each mountain being one of us, and yet, as we go deeper down through the centre of our mountain, we come to a place which is shared by all mountains, the depth of the earth, so that as we go ever deeper we come to the core of all Being. The deep unseen part of the mountain range is the 'Collective Unconscious'. It is wonderful and magical, as, not only do we feed and inform this 'Collective Unconscious,' but it nourishes and informs us. This explains spiritual phenomena: telepathy, clairvoyance, clairaudience and so on. When we go deep enough, we have access to everything. We can communicate at this level without words. There is direct knowledge, insight! Our practices help us develop these abilities. Sufis also talk about the drop and the ocean, in that we are the drop and the ocean is the unity

---

[4] Ibid.

of which we are all part. The whole Universe is Divine. It is God and yet more than the sum of its parts. It is so immense that we cannot grasp it with our minds, only with our Heart, which is One Heart. When we experience this we feel 'Intelligence' and great Love.

While I was pondering this mystical realm of Alam al-mithal, I had a dream which perhaps reflects how this mystical realm can function. In the dream I was on an old bus in a very alien place, that I thought might be Japan. It is a culture with which I have had no experience. I was going to meet up with old friends of my family, but did not know where they were or indeed, where I was. I seemed to be in another time and space with no recognisable landmarks. Someone was with me and trying to help me, but I couldn't see him. He offered to lend me his phone, but I knew I didn't have my friends' latest phone number. We came to an open square where the buildings were quaint and painted amber and dull gold, the colours of love and of the element earth. It was pretty and I was calm and interested rather than worried. In real life I would have panicked, as I hate being lost.

Then the scene changed and I was on top of a hill and could see all around me. I was on a very small island, but strangely the ocean came right up to the top of the mountain and I could look way down into the water, as if it was literally under my nose. There was nothing retaining this water, but it was simply there right before me, however I did not touch it. The water was very deep and green, there was abundant vegetation under the water that was a brilliant emerald colour. The water was still, transparently clear, unruffled and I knew that it was fresh water. It was like I was gazing at the source of all life. On my right, far below, I could also see the ocean. It looked quite normal and blue with a beach at its edge. There seemed to be a great wall of rock that 'held' the deep water up to my level from the scene below. It was magical and not rational but very real. My helper told me to be careful, but as he said this, a huge pale coloured creature emerged from the sea, elongating itself and flowing towards me. When its long head reached me, its rear end was still in the ocean, far away. It touched my hand with its paw; a touch so gentle and warm that I felt happy and full of wonder. Love flowed to me.

These are the symbols of that other realm, not to be interpreted, but explored poetically at many levels. One of the things that I experienced in this dream was a deep and tender love that could always reach me, from the depths of the ocean to the top of a mountain. I felt it in my deepest self and can recapture it at will. What we experience inwardly will surely affect our outer life. The dream also reminded me that dreams often use puns to get the message across and they are often funny. It seems 'God' has a sense of humour. In this dream the deep verdant water of life was 'right under my nose'. That was all I needed to know.

So, my journey through the realms continued with my longing to find Sufis and this longing did eventually manifest in a strange way. A comment I made to one of my clients that the Beloved he longed for and saw in his dream, could be an aspect of the Divine (as the Sufis believe it) set him on a search that led him to a book by Hazrat Inayat Khan. I shared in his enquiry and loved Hazrat's teachings but it was not enough for me to just read about the Sufi path, I knew I needed a teacher. Eventually, in that wonderful synchronistic way, I found a Sufi group who amazingly followed the teachings of Hazrat Inayat Khan, and so I eventually found my teacher – Murshid Nawab.

Nawab teaches in many ways, but mostly by example, showing how to be spiritual in a completely natural and authentic way. He tells Sufi stories of course and this completely engaged me. Nawab is also a writer of children's stories and TV programs, but I didn't know this at the time. One year, while leading a Sufi Summer School here in Australia, Murshid talked about a very ancient Han Chinese folk tale with a definite spiritual, even Sufi component. This story was 'Golden Chisel and the Stone Ram'. I was fascinated to find that the basic elements of the mystical path of Sufism were contained within this ancient Chinese story and in other folk stories I have worked with since. This was the beginning of a great journey for me, although I did not realise it at the time.

The universal Sufism of Hazrat Inayat Khan understands that the essence or base of all religions is mysticism and mysticism is Sufism. In our prayer, Salat, we say:

Thy Light is in all Forms, Thy Love in all beings
In a loving mother
in a kind father
in an innocent child
in a helpful friend
in an inspiring teacher.
Allow us to recognise Thee
in all Thy holy names and forms
as Rama, as Krishna
as Shiva, as Buddha.
Let us know Thee
as Abraham, as Solomon
as Zarathustra, as Moses
as Jesus, as Mohammed
and in many other names and forms
Known and unknown to the world.[5]

From a Jungian point of view, a myth or fairy tale can be seen as the journey of one person, the Hero who is our own self, either male or female, and who can be engaged with, much like a personal dream. These stories can also contain the 'dreaming' of a people, and can be explored for knowledge of the collective unconscious. I would say that most fairy tales are also teaching vehicles, much like Sufi stories. Many contain the vestiges of spiritual wisdom and knowledge that is very old, probably pre Christian, and perhaps carry a racial memory from the times of a matriarchal society. For example, scientists have identified that the Aboriginal dreamtime story of the appearance of a palm tree in an isolated valley in central Australia is indeed fact, and not fiction. Palm Valley lies within the Finke Gorge National Park in the Northern Territory (south west of Alice Springs). The Finke River is a very ancient, but now dry river bed, and is the only place in Central Australia where Red Cabbage Palms (Livistona mariae) survive. Aboriginal Legend

---

[5] Hazrat Inayat Khan, *The Dance of the Soul*, Gayan, Vadan, Nirtan, Motilal Banarsidass Publishers, Delhi, 1993.

recorded in 1894 described 'the gods from the north' bringing the seeds to Palm Valley. Scientists now conclude that humans up to 30,000 years ago carried the seeds to the central desert. Traditional stories often hold deep truths, although sometimes the meaning has become lost or obscured in the retelling.

The Rasul – Giving Life to the Village

In the first tale in this book, Golden Chisel and the Stone Ram,[6] there once was a village where there was no fresh water, so that the people did not know the true taste of tea and food. Also in the village there was a tradition that fresh water would one day burst forth as a spring from the mouth of a stone ram.

Golden Chisel was a talented young stone mason who searched long and hard for such a ram. After a night away on a high mountain perhaps meditating, he returns to see a light and digs at this place. This light is the Divine Light, which we see when we are attracted to the spiritual path. As he digs, he finds a bright stone in the rough shape of a ram. The ram in traditional Chinese astrology was understood to be the eighth animal to arrive in the world, and, of course eight, is a very lucky number for the Chinese. The ram is considered artistic and the most feminine of all the signs of the Zodiac. In shaping and sculpturing the ram, Golden Chisel finds the stone very hard and his tools are blunted; it takes a long time for the little stone ram to be completed, and in that moment of completion it comes to life. This ram becomes Golden Chisel's Ideal, his Teacher and also his steed. In Sufi understanding, we too have to forge our Ideal of the Divine, of God, and this is a slow and difficult process. Just as when the sculptor is making his masterpiece, we need to see in our mind's eye the features we want to immortalise, and we can then chisel away what we do not need. With the last stroke on the fore-hoof, the ram came to life. Filled with gratitude, the ram offered Golden Chisel gold and silver, but he only wanted fresh water for his village.

This is real Service. Rather than accepting riches for himself, Golden Chisel chose to have the sacred water, which his community desperately needed. Although this was more difficult, the ram agreed,

---

[6] 'Golden Chisel and the Stone Ram', in *Favourite Folktales of China*, translated by John Minford, Graham Brash, Singapore, 2000. All of the subsequent quotations and references from 'Golden Chisel' are from this source.

but made Golden Chisel promise never to divulge their secret to a soul. If a stranger should spot him and 'tell the world', then that would be the end of the magic. So here we first come across the mystical idea of the 'great secret'. In fact, the word mysticism means 'to conceal'- it is a mystery and mystics see their experience as part of their own journey of transformation. We must never speak of our experiences because they really cannot be communicated – they belong in that other realm – of *Alam Al Mithal*, and each person's experience is so different. We each build our own Divine Ideal or Ideal of God, but to explain this to another is not only impossible, but when we do so, we ourselves loose the power and magic of the Ideal. People who have not had a mystical experience will not understand what has been said, and worse still, will misinterpret what they think they hear. A friend once told me of his professor in Cambridge, who was the author of many books and papers on spirituality and mysticism. Late in life he had his own powerful mystical experience in, of all places a staircase, and he never spoke of it or wrote of spirituality and mysticism again.

This story of Golden Chisel is in three parts, as are all the others in this collection. In the middle section of the process, the little ram helps and advises Golden Chisel so that the villagers have water from the Yellow River that the little stone ram brings to the village every night. The villagers are happy to have fresh water for their tea and food. So it is that with the efforts of one person, quietly and secretly, the spiritual life of a community can be restored.

The journey of spiritual evolution in Sufism is also depicted in three stages. These are Fana Fi-Shaikh, Fana Fi-Rasul and Fana Fi-Allah. Fana is generally translated as annihilation and at first it means merging into the Teacher, then into the Prophet and finally into Allah. I think of fana as a dissolution or dissolving of the small self or ego, into the Teacher, then the Messenger or Prophet and eventually into Allah. My understanding of this is from my own experience with my Murshid. In the beginning I would often ask him what I should do in a certain situation, or how I should behave. A true teacher will seldom tell you what to do, but will guide you on the right path, sometimes in unusual ways. There is a certain magic about it, but it is done with such love, friendliness and support that the small self or ego does not feel threatened but can accept everything calmly. We are not 'killing' the ego but gaining mastery over it. Then there came a time when I did not have to ask my Murshid any more questions, probably much to his relief. I just knew what he would say and I could be like him without even thinking. This is Fana, perhaps you could say an integration of the teacher into my own being.

The next stage is a similar process but involves a dissolving of the small self into the Rasul or Messenger we follow. In our case it is Hazrat Inayat Khan who died in 1927. For me, this took the form of 'hearing' his voice in his teachings and understanding them as he spoke them all those years ago. There comes a time when we make or forge a relationship with our Rasul, so that we can have conversations with him and receive immediate answers. It is of course an inner process. Likewise, there also comes a time, when the wellspring of water flows freely without the intermediary of a teacher or guide. This is the final integration or Fana into the Divine Presence or God. Fana Fi Allah is the outcome of this story in a spiritual sense.

Sufis speak of the Spirit of Guidance which can be seen as an archetype that has been 'fleshed out' by our relationship with our teacher. This guiding spirit can be experienced simultaneously as a person and as an archetype, that is, a 'person archetype'. In Sufism, Khidr is recognised as the archetypal guide and teacher. If you have had archetypal dreams, you will know that these beings are luminous and powerful and very, very real. They exist and are accessible in that wonderful deep level of Alam-Al-Mithal. In Sufi stories, Khidr was the teacher of Moses and of Elijah. In that inner realm there is no time or space, so Khidr is in the eternal present, available to us all if we know how to access him or her. It is interesting that Khidr is described as he who has attained the source of life, and has drunk of the water of immortality. He is the Verdant One and associated with every aspect of Nature's greenness. This could relate back to my dream of the vibrant green vegetation in the depth of the water. Was this an aspect of Khidr? Sufis consider that the hidden Imam, the Lord of Time, dwells on the Green Island in the middle of the sea of Whiteness. As I have said, these 'places' are real and those who have studied Shamanism have learned how to go to each of these known places. The White and Shimmering City, the Green Island, are related to 'centres' and colours. The colour of the supreme centre, the 'mystery of mysteries' is said to be green.

In the case of Golden Chisel, there appears to have been no outer teacher; he was guided from within. In other words, his tradition supported and informed his inner life so that he understood intuitively how to progress and lead his community. Often a great Messenger or Prophet comes into being in this way, having a direct communication with the Divine. This is in fact Fana Fi Allah. It is rare, but I feel that Golden Chisel did become this messenger, or Rasul for his people. He showed them how to access the water of life directly for themselves, without any need for an intermediary.

There is a similar story to Golden Chisel, which Hazrat Inayat Khan tells in Volume 12 of *The Sufi Message*. A woman called Una works for years making a statue in her studio and despite the distractions of her world she spends every possible hour with her creation. When the statue is finally complete, she addresses it as 'the ideal of her soul', the 'outcome of her love' and tells it that she longs to hear it speak to her. First the statue says that *'Yes, I speak, but I speak only when you are silent.'* This is a great lesson, for we can only hear the inner voice of our Beloved Ideal when we are deeply silent. Then the statue tells her that she must first learn what love means and that it involves sacrifice, one continual sacrifice from beginning to end. *'I come to life only when you become dead.'* he says. What is it that becomes dead? It is the small self. Una answers that she would willingly die a thousand deaths, if by dying she could gain his Beloved Presence. He offers her a poisoned cup and in drinking it she falls down as though dead. The statue raises her up into his arms, embraces and kisses her and brings her to life again.

Sufis talk of dying before we die, and this is indeed what Una has done. The statue says: *'You have gone through death but have not died. The sacrifice you made did not rob you of life but has raised you above death. Now you are living with my life. It is your love which has given you the life after death, a life to live for ever.'* Una answers *'Your light has illuminated the dark chambers of my mind. Your love is rooted in the depths of my heart. Your peace alone is my life's repose. Your will is behind my every impulse. Your voice is audible in the words I speak. Your own image is my countenance. My body is but a cover over the soul. My life is your very breath, my Beloved, and my self is your own being.'* So this is Fana: a total becoming and dissolving into the Teacher and Divine Ideal, there is only One Single Being, no longer an I and a Thou. *'How true it is that before one comes to the real conception of God, the first thing is to build Him in one's heart. The word God has the same origin as the word good, but its original in the old Hebrew means 'ideal'.'*[7]

Now using his Stone Ram or Ideal of God as an inner teacher, Golden Chisel and his stone ram brought the fresh water of Life or Sacred Teachings to the village. The community could now be nourished by this precious water in their tea and food. Every night this 'water' was fetched from the mighty Yellow River – the source of all things. I imagine that this happened while Golden Chisel was in the realm of Alam al-Mithal, perhaps inspired by dreams and insights from his meditations. He himself became the spiritual Guide for the village.

But after a long, long time something happened and the Little Stone Ram did not return and the water was not replenished. Golden Chisel went in search of his Little Ram, finding it at last, grievously wounded, along the path to the Yellow River. The God of the Yellow River had become jealous of the ram taking 'his' water every night. So he attacked the ram, cutting off one hoof. The teachings could no longer flow. This can happen to us for many reasons. Perhaps we lose mastery over our spiritual ego, or perhaps it is due to a conflict with a religion, or perhaps a crisis of faith or even a deep depression, which can leave us unable to move. Our inner teacher (the stone ram) can no longer point the way with his 'forepaw' or even move at all; the authentic message, the Water of Life no longer flows. In realising this terrible wounding, Golden Chisel must remake his Ideal of God; he re-forges the ram's foot in the pure gold of Love and Compassion, in the inner realm of Harmony and Beauty. This is profound and difficult work. It takes time, as the very

---

[7] Hazrat Inayat Khan, *The Divinity of the Human Soul*, Sufi Message, volume, 12, Motilal Banarsidass Publishers, Delhi. 1995.

tools we use (our practices) become truly blunted in the process. It is such a struggle to focus on our practice, when doubts, frustration, anger, hurt and perhaps feelings of abandonment push into our awareness. It is a heroic feat.

But now Golden Chisel is angry and wants to avenge the injury to his ram. We too need to be angry sometimes and use the energy of anger so as to take up the fight. As Pir O Murshid Hidayat says, 'It is not spiritual to be a doormat.' I remember at one Summer School, getting angry with some people who wanted to pressure me into an activity which I did not want to do. I felt very uncomfortable and 'invaded' and so I told them very clearly that I would not take part in spite of their pressure. Murshid Nawab overheard the exchange, so I apologised for being angry. His response was that 'It is OK for you to be angry.' I have never forgotten it.

Golden Chisel took the Sun-and-Moon talisman that had been passed down through his family, and confronted the God of the Yellow River who attacked with various weapons such as cold and turtle demons. The turtle is said to be an aspect of the Chinese God of Examinations (referring to the imperial examinations to select the best potential candidates of merit in subjects on society, culture, religion and philosophy), who stands with one foot on a giant turtle (Ao). There is a traditional saying 'to stand on Ao's head' meaning coming first in examinations. So it is clear that there was a mighty debate using cold logic and rationality, in the examination of religion versus mysticism. The God had no answer when Golden Chisel told him that the sacred water flows for everybody and does not belong to any one God. And so the jealous God was defeated by the power of the Sun-and-moon-talisman, where the sun represents the masculine principle, and the moon the feminine, united together they represent the Divine Light - *Nur.* It is this which defeats the jealous god. Begging for mercy, the God of the Yellow River asked Golden Chisel what he wanted, and Golden Chisel and the ram answered with one voice that they wanted fresh water for the village. The God then took from his mouth (another metaphor for that in-between realm), a pearl, saying that when the stone ram would hold it in his mouth, fresh water would flow from it forever. This pearl symbolises the yin or feminine power of the water and all its potentiality. It is this feminine aspect which is so important and was, up to now, so lacking in this tale.

However, the ending of this tale seems to be paradoxical. In returning to the village, the stone ram was 'seen' by a young cowherd, as a light shooting towards him. He cried out for everyone to look at Golden Chisel riding a stone ram, so fulfilling the prophecy. But when the ram heard this he immediately transformed into a heap of rocks, out of which flowed a limpid, sweet spring. When we chisel out our Ideal of God, and indeed mend this from time to time, we have constructed an inner structure of understanding the Truth of the world. We have achieved Fana Fi Rasul, but there is a further and final stage. The Rasul too has to be annihilated into the being of the One, in Fana fi Allah. Once the Light is perceived by the people who are able to see it, like the young cow-herd, then the water constantly flows from the spring pure and sweet without any intermediary.

A little while ago I met a wonderful man who told me his story, which reflects this dissolution of the structure perfectly. He had been part of the Hari Krishna's for 22 years since his youth. He learned so much from this and the inner structure of this religion was formed in him. However, there came a time when he 'saw' the organisation, politics, egos, failures and structure for what it was, and knew that he needed to progress beyond this. It took him ten years to deconstruct and totally smash the structure which had sustained him, so that the sacred knowledge could flow directly to him bereft of the dogmas and structure of the 'religion'. It must be said that we need our Teacher and the teachings, whatever we are drawn to, but as we evolve, we realise that it is all One. This man is a true mystic and we had a wonderful harmonious open sharing of our Truth. This is so rare. His story does remind me of the smashing of the stone ram so that the water could flow.

Once Golden Chisel was seen riding the stone ram, the structure was exposed and thus disintegrated into dust, so that the sacred water of life could flow. This man also told me that when the Hari Krishna's opened a new school in India, they would make a statue of the Goddess Sarasvati (Goddess of learning); all the rituals and prayers in the ceremonies were then directed towards this statue. However, when the ceremonies were over, the statue was thrown into the river, where it dissolved into the mud from which it was made. The statue was only there as a focus of the rituals and then it was no longer needed.

When there is a great need a Prophet will come. As we say in our prayer Salat:

> *O Messenger, Christ, Nabi, the Rasul of God!*
> *Thou Whose heart constantly reacheth upward,*
> *Thou comest on earth with a Message,*
> *as a Dove from above, when Dharma decayeth, and speakest the Word*
> *that is put into Thy mouth,*
> *as the Light filleth the crescent Moon.*[8]

So Golden Chisel becomes the Rasul or Prophet for his people. He has achieved Fana fi Allah and he speaks the message from above. The teachings continue to flow from the One. The teacher can be closer to us after death, than when he was alive. To quote Hazrat Inayat Khan "Those who come after me will have the possibility of being much closer to me than those who know me in the flesh." We know him in a refined or finer way than those who knew him in life. Somehow we have a direct and immediate connection with him and with the message, which is to the whole world, we are open to everyone and welcome all.

This inner process is as important for us now as it was to the ancient Chinese Han people.

---

[8] Hazrat Inayat Khan. *The Dance of the Soul. Gayan, Vadan, Nirtan*, p.76.

The Little Horse – Vehicle and Teacher

After Golden Chisel, my teacher sent me a Russian fairy tale 'The Little Humpbacked Horse' by Pyotr Yershov.[19] This weaves together many ancient fairy tales, including Firebird, into a more modern long epic poem. This is not an ancient teaching tale and there are clearly social and political implications, which have erupted from the poet's deep unconscious.

This is an amazing tale of a quite different inner journey. The situation, we learn, is dire in the kingdom of the Tsar; every night a 'demon' is trampling the golden corn in the peasants' fields. I imagine that if the lands are so troubled, then, like the Fisher King, the Tsar himself is wounded or lacking in some way and this is reflected in his kingdom. Our hero, Ivan, is the youngest son of an old peasant and after his two older brothers attempt to tackle the 'demon' and fail because they are too fearful, he eventually goes out one night to fight the 'Demon' himself. There is one thing I love about Ivan and that is that he is not afraid of anything. The 'rogue' who was causing havoc in the Tsar's fields turns out to be a ferocious white mare who gives Ivan the fight of his life. Ivan jumps on her back and hangs onto her tail for dear life, as she tries desperately to throw him off. Finally, he masters her and in return for her freedom she gives him two magnificent horses and a small steed with two little humps, long ears and coal dark eyes. The mare tells Ivan that he must never part with his little steed under any circumstances and in return he will have a faithful friend, who will care for him, keep him warm in winter, cool in summer and always find him food and drink. I find it significant that the 'demon' whom Ivan has managed to master was female – a mare and I think this gives a hint as to what is wrong in the Tsar's lands; there is no feminine mentioned in the story so far, thus anything repressed, ignored or dishonoured can rise up from the depths of the psyche to destroy the crops, nourishment

---

9   First printed by Progress Publishers, USSR, 1957 and viewed at<http://lib.ru/
LITRA/ERSHOW/horse.txt> at 4 January 2017.

and creativity of the realm. When mastered, the magical feminine gives the hero what he needs to continue in the journey of life. We shall see that this theme of the 'magic' of the feminine being able to sustain us is a recurring thread. This little humpbacked horse, is now Ivan's teacher, guide and also his steed, much like the stone ram in the story of Golden Chisel. What is fascinating is that the little humpbacked horse may well be a historical representation of a Sufi Teacher. It is said often in fairy tales told by Dervishes, that the 'guide' was a dark magician. The Dervishes were actually self-effacing or sending themselves up, not wanting people to get attached to them, (for example, in Rumpelstiltskin the task to 'discover my name' is to discover God).

Given that the people of the more northerly parts of Russia only knew of horses at this time, I imagine their reaction to seeing their first camel would be to call it a humpbacked horse and the little humpbacked horse of the story could well have been the record of a Sufi teacher, who rode a camel. The hero, Ivan is very much an innocent in this story, much like the 'Fool' in the Tarot. Ivan first appears in the story lying on top of a stove, just like the witch Baba Yaga who we shall meet later in the story of the Frog Princess. The Russian stove functions as the heart in the Russian home, both giving off heat and being used for cooking. It therefore symbolises the Heart and centre of our Being in these stories.

Now the little-humpbacked-horse helps Ivan to outwit his wicked brothers and, in so doing he discovers a brilliant Light (without smoke or heat) glowing in the dark of the forest. This description of Light reminds me of the beautiful Sura 35, Nur in chapter XXIV of the Koran.

'Allah is the light of the heavens and the earth; His light is like a niche wherein is a lamp. The lamp encased in glass; the glass is as it were a shining star; From a blessed tree the lamp is kindled, whose oil is neither from the east nor of the west, Whose Light would well-nigh shine out though flame touched it not!, It is light upon light! – Allah guides into His light whom He will; and Allah sets forth parables for men, for Allah is the Knower of all things.'

Ivan's little-humpbacked-horse identifies the brilliant Light as a Firebird's feather and tells him he must not touch it otherwise many sorrows and woes will befall him. But Ivan ignores this advice and instead wraps the glowing feather in a rag and hides it in his hat. Once again the Light must be covered, untouched and hidden. We, too, take up the Light feather in our youth knowing perhaps that it will cause us difficulties in later life, but unable to do anything else. Robert Johnson, in his book, *He* suggests that men experience a deep mystical Unity (the Grail Castle) at some time in their adolescence but as they do not yet know the answer to the Grail question, are not admitted to the Grail Castle. Jung would say that later in middle age they again search for this experience and having found the Grail Castle have a chance to answer the riddle of the Grail. If they get the answer right, they have access to the Holy Grail itself – a Cup which never empties. Johnson further comments that women actually live in the Grail Castle and that their spiritual journey is quite different from that of men. We shall see more of woman's' spiritual journey in The Frog Princess story

So, at the end of the first part of this tale, Ivan has outwitted his two brothers, left his home behind and gained entry into the court of the Tsar, as Master of the Horse, together with the two magnificent horses given him by the white mare to care for, and of course his little-humpbacked-horse.

In the second part of the story, Ivan finds himself tricked, manipulated and threatened into catching the fabled Firebird for the Tsar and, indeed, of likewise 'catching' the Tsar-Maid for the Tsar as well. Ivan's protagonist in court is the previous Master of the Horse, the chamberlain, a nobleman who bitterly resents Ivan and wants to catch him out and see him deposed. As he never sees Ivan actually grooming the horses, yet they are always fabulously turned out, he believes that Ivan must be a wicked infidel who has forsaken the Church (since he eats meat during Lent), and therefore is an evil sprite. The chamberlain spies on Ivan as he enters the stable at night, bars the door, takes off his hat and carefully shakes out the Firebird's feather. Ivan places the Light in the corn-bin and grooms, feeds and waters the horses with mead, all the while singing a merry song. I like to think that this is Ivan's spiritual practice. Music, sound and song are so important for a mystic. Hazrat Inayat Khan states that 'The mystery of sound is mysticism' and he quotes Shams-e-Tabriz that 'the whole mystery of the universe lies in sound.'

'Abstract sound is called sawt-e-sarmad by the Sufis; all space is filled with it. The vibrations of this sound are too fine to be either audible or visible to the material ears or eyes, since it is even difficult for the eyes to see the form and colour of the ethereal vibrations on the external plane.

It was the sawt-e-sarmad, the sound of the abstract plane, which Muhammad heard in the cave of Ghar-e-Hira when he became lost in his divine ideal. The Qur'an refers to this sound in the words: 'Be! And all became'.

Moses heard this sound on Mount Sinai when in communion with God, and the same word was audible to Christ when absorbed in his heavenly Father in the wilderness. Shiva heard the same anahad nada during his Samadhi in the cave of the Himalayas. The flute of Krishna is symbolic of the same sound. This sound is the source of all revelation to the Masters to whom it is revealed from within. It is because of this, that they know and teach one and the same truth.' [10]

Hazrat Inayat Khan was a classical Indian singer and musician who has brought us the singing Zikar and many Wazifas put to music by his son, Pir O Murshid Hidayat Inayat-Khan. These are a major part of our spiritual practice, and his teachings.

To return to the story, caring for his magical horses is Ivan's nightly practice. However, the chamberlain is very frightened by what he sees (Ivan under the Light of the Firebird's feather lovingly caring for his horses) but he stays hidden, watching, and when Ivan is finally asleep, steals the Firebird's feather from under Ivan's hat. He takes it to the Tsar, telling him that Ivan has hidden this magical feather but that Ivan could actually bring a Firebird to the Tsar. What is striking here is that the Tsar clearly does not understand the real value of the Firebird but simply wants it for himself to put under lock and key. He even bites the end of the feather to see if it is genuine! But he does not 'use' it or know its purpose. The lesson here is that when we do have an insight or

---

[10] Hazrat Inayat Khan, *The Mysticism of Sound and Music*, Shambhala, Boston, 1996, p. 170.

realization like the Light feather of the Firebird, we should make use of it. I had a client in therapy many years ago who had beautiful insights – again and again. She never acted on them or was able to use them, so they simply reoccurred time and time again. So we understand that the Tsar is not a 'real' authentic Tsar. He does not embody the Heart or Divine Governance. As the Irish would say – there is a lack in him. Partly, I believe, this is due to the fact that there is still no mention of the feminine in this tale. He is out of balance.

Poor Ivan, not realizing that his Firebird feather has been stolen is dragged before the Tsar, protesting that he was not supposed to be wakened (disturbed in his practices or meditation). This was part of the deal he had made with the Tsar. However, when he sees that the Tsar has the feather, he starts to grovel before him. This made me feel ashamed on behalf of Ivan, but then I realized that he was in fact behaving the only way he could in the circumstances. In the law of reciprocity, we learn to become aware of needing to interact with people according to their level of 'evolution'. When dealing with children we communicate with them as children. When with a person we perceive as at a higher level than us, we should show respect, listen to what they say, rather than promote our own ideas. There is that phrase – casting pearls before swine, which means that we do not espouse ideas to a person who is not able to understand them. They are not valued. We would not or should not teach beyond the level a person is able to comprehend, otherwise great misunderstandings can happen. Some people are very concrete in their thinking and so to speak of abstract concepts can only be alienating for them. Neither should we expect empathy from a narcissist! We cannot, and should not, expect others to be at the same level as we are whatever that is, and yet so many of us do just that. A beggar can be a highly evolved soul, and a tsar can be quite the buffoon, as this one seems to be. A person's position must be respected and we have to deal with each being accordingly. It is a very great lesson. As my Irish husband would say – 'what do you expect from a pig but a grunt?'

I had a client for many years who never quite learned to adjust her expectations of others at work, or in her family. This caused her untold hardship, as she had a rather Victorian set of values. They were the values she was brought up to and she was a good and upright person but she did not recognize that others certainly did not live up to the same values that she held, nor would they want to. Thus when Ivan perceives the situation he is in, as well as recognizing the character of the Tsar, the only thing left for him to do was to grovel. This is part of making our way in the world, as the world is, with the injustices of corrupt systems and authorities.

On threat of impalement, Ivan reluctantly agrees to find and fetch a Firebird for the Tsar. His little humpbacked horse always meets Ivan so happily and tells him not to worry; he will help and they can accomplish this task together! But he does tell Ivan that as he had rejected his advice in taking the Firebird's feather, he now has to pay the price. There is always a price to pay when we do not listen to the inner voice of our teacher! They flew together for seven days – a long, long time, until they came to a deep wood, wherein was a beautiful glade with brilliant emerald grass (the colour related to Kidir), and lovely luminous flowers. In the middle of this glade stands a hill made of silver where the Firebirds come every morning at dawn to drink water from the stream. This is a special and sacred place in the realm of *Alam al-Mithal* – a place known to mystics and shamans. Here Ivan puts out food for the Firebirds; wine from over the sea and grain, a sacrament which they happily feed on. His little horse tells Ivan to ignore the chatter of the birds and seize the nearest one. Again, there is a reference to the language of the birds, so a hint of that mysticism of sound which recurs in these stories. Ivan was not to let himself be lulled by their bird-song. When Ivan actually sees the birds he gazes at them in wonder, but at the same time thinks they look absurd as they did not look anything like chickens, which seems to be the only bird that Ivan was familiar with. This is so often the case that when we are confronted with something totally strange, we do not know how to relate to it and compare it with something that we know. Our minds categorise and compare everything. The description of the Firebirds' tail reminds me of a peacock, but the Firebirds had red feet – clearly solar energies. They seem to be drawn to the feminine silver of the hill. Ivan grabs the nearest Firebird and bags it, but Ivan cannot resist scaring the birds before he leaves, just like a child running at a flock of seagulls on the beach to watch them rise up squawking. His little horse is not impressed – again!

Ivan brings the Firebird to the Tsar, who is as enraptured as the Chamberlain is furious. When the Firebird is let out of the bag, everyone is frightened as they think the palace is on fire, but Ivan tells them it is only the Firebird – a lovely plaything. The divine Light as entertainment! This is the play of divine creation.

Now one evening, the chamberlain looking for more mischief to do to Ivan, comes to the palace kitchen and overhears a story being told about a fabulous Tsar-Maid whose mother is the moon and whose brother is the sun! I find it interesting that a 'servant' is telling a story there in the kitchen and that it is one of a set of five stories. Our own teacher has many sets of five in his teachings – five elements, five element breaths to be done five times each and so on. Perhaps it was a Sufi teacher spreading the Message? But the chamberlain rushes off to the Tsar and tells him that Ivan can catch this Tsar-Maid for him. Once again, the Tsar threatens Ivan with impalement if he does not go immediately to find his Tsar-Maid. So often in life it is our antagonists who spur us on or challenge us to do great things, which we would never even attempt otherwise. Ivan's brothers do this in the first part of this tale and now the Chamberlain in the second part.

Again Ivan and his little-humpbacked horse fly for a very long time and arrive at a dark, dense green wood, from where they can see the ocean and its shore. This is again an in-between place of *Alam al Mithal* where they will find the Tsar-Maid. Here they pitch their tent of gold brocade, lay out a cloth and special dinner service with special sweetmeats to tempt the Tsar Maid. Ivan is warned not to act foolishly, but wait till she enters the tent and partakes of her meal. When she takes up her musical instrument and begins to play, Ivan must immediately go into the tent and grab her. If he keeps his wits about him and does not fall asleep all will be well. When Ivan sees her he does not find her pretty or attractive and is disappointed. He finds her pale and skinny - like the new moon, with legs like a chicken. Strange this analogy with chickens! Where the Firebirds are Solar and Jelal (masculine), the Tsar-Maid is clearly Lunar, and Jamal (feminine). However, while Ivan is thinking how unattractive she is and how glad he is that he need never marry her, the Tsar-Maid starts to play her musical instrument and sing, so lulling the unsuspecting Ivan to sleep.

We too need to be very alert when in a deep meditation, that we do not fall asleep. There is an edge we need to be on which is honed by concentration practice. We cannot hope to meditate until we have learned to concentrate and focus. First we learn to concentrate, then to contemplate, and finally to meditate. Ivan has lost his focus and forgotten to stay alert, so he drifts off to sleep. He is woken by his horse furiously neighing. Ivan is frightened at having failed but his little horse tells him he has one more chance. Notice again the importance of sound in this story. Next day when the Tsar-Maid began to play her music and sing, Ivan gets angry with her for trying to cheat him and so having stayed awake enough to seize her by her hair he yells for his little humpbacked horse to come and fly them to the Tsar.

This time as they arrive at the Palace gates, the Tsar runs fast towards the fair maiden and leads her by the hand to his throne, where he asks her to be his bride. She, however, turns away from him scornfully and refuses to reply. The more she ignores him, the more the Tsar wants her and begs for her to accept him. Finally, she sadly relents but tells the Tsar that she will marry him, - if he can find and bring to her, her signet ring which lies on the bottom of the ocean, and to do this within three days. This signet ring is a symbol of authority – a signature, in fact, unique to the Tsar-Maid, which reflects her power and prestige. For her to rule as a tsar she would have need of this ring of power and authority. It is a seemingly impossible task for the Tsar, who immediately calls for Ivan and this time bribes him to bring him the ring, on the promise of giving him anything he asks for. Ivan protests that he is still very weary from his last quest and asks for time to recover.

This gives us an understanding that this inner works is hard and tiring. Perhaps when we are tired and withdrawn from the world, we are actually 'cooking' something in our inner world. We must respect ourselves and the work that we do. It is difficult when outer life (the Tsar) demands our attention. As Ivan turns to go, the Tsar-Maid calls out to him and gives him some further tasks to do. She knows full well that the Tsar himself is not going to attempt her quest and so speaks directly to Ivan. She asks him to visit her green mansions and ask her mother, the moon, why she conceals her light for three days of the month, and her brother the sun why he hides his face behind the clouds. These are powerful questions about Light and why it is sometimes hidden from us. These are difficult questions for all us and we cannot solve them, or force answers based on our logic. This is a difficult and arduous task for poor Ivan, who despite not knowing what to do, trusts in the quest itself.

In the final part of this story, the quest goes deeper into the depths of the ocean of the unconscious in search for the signet ring. First, he comes across a monster whale who is suffering terribly. The whale asks Ivan to enquire of the moon who is ruler of the oceans, the reason for his suffering and how long he must suffer for. Ivan and his little horse visit the great Moon / Mother Goddess where she receives their news of her daughter. She is very angry to hear that the Tsar wishes to marry her daughter. He is old and decrepit, she says and should never marry a young girl of only fifteen. Most importantly, she says 'see what that nasty toad wants to reap, who never sowed. Why, he's greedy as he's vain'. The moon is ruler of time and the cycles of time, so fifteen is middle of a cycle and a most fertile time. This is also why the old Tsar is very wrong for the young and fertile Tsar-Maid. The moon grants the monster whale his boon, and the whale then helps Ivan in his search for the ring. The whale is like the Tsar of the ocean. First he calls his sturgeons, but they cannot find the ring which we learn is hidden in a chest. They suggest that the feisty and brawling perch may know where the ring is to be found. When they search for the perch he is not at home, but finally is found fighting lustily in a pond and has to be dragged off to appear before the Whale, all the time begging to be allowed to throw another punch at the carp fish he was fighting. This puts me in mind of someone who would be found in a pub and wondered why this type of creature would be the one to know where the ring is to be found. I was told 'You need to know that when you go into a pub like that you are losing your inhibitions, you are completely there in the moment. If somebody insults you, you react. There is no pretence or performance.' He is the lovable rogue who understands life and all the dark places in life. On top of that, the perch is a fish which is not much liked, in fact it is a fighting fish which is feared. What better place to hide the signet right but in a lowly dark place protected by the perch? This is the creature who knows where the Tsar-Maid's ring is to be found! It is that kind of feisty energy who will brook no insult and knows no fear, who knows every nook and cranny of the depths of the ocean bed even in the mud and rock.

There is a wisdom about the perch: he has had to stand up for himself and protect himself in the ocean of life, but he also enjoys himself mightily in the process. He makes me smile when I think of him – a lovable rogue. There is a use for this kind of energy which I find so delightful in many ways. So fearless. The perch very quickly finds the casket and tries to dig it out. Although small it is very heavy and weighs over a ton. This suggests that the casket is made of lead, which in alchemy is the base metal or condition of human existence or the soul, which needs to be transformed and transmuted, by the 'great work'. In other words, the magical ring is contained within the heaviness of gross earthy manifestation, and must be released and transformed by the hero. The perch tries to get help from other fish but they can't shift the casket either. It is only when he calls the sturgeons that they quickly raise the casket which had been stuck in the mud and rocks. After finding the casket with the ring, he tries to kiss some pretty fish on the way out, and punches a few sprats in play. The perch then happily returns to his scrap with the carp!

Meanwhile Ivan is sitting on the sand waiting for the whale's return with the ring and getting more and more disheartened and angry, thinking that he won't come in time, for there is a deadline of course. It is a terrible waiting game. When we give up our need to 'do' and trust that God will provide the support we need, things will unfold as they should. We have no idea of what is happening in the depths of our being; in the nature of the world unseen, especially in the deep collective unconscious. This only comes to us in dreams. Faith, patience and trust are our only means of surviving this time. Finally, at the last minute, the whale appears and dumps the heavy casket on the sand with a thud which rocks the shore. The whale tells Ivan that if he ever needs him just to call. Once we have a loving and respectful connection with the Tsar of the deep, we can always call on him in need. Both Ivan and the little humpback-horse thank the whale for what he has done – we too must be thankful / grateful for everything that we receive. It seems like there is cause and effect here, but in truth it is by Grace that we receive our greatest gifts. However, now the chest is too heavy for Ivan to lift, although he tries many times, but his little horse simply flips it onto his back and away they fly back to the Tsar and the Tsar-Maid. Ivan is not yet able to carry the weight of the lead – the base metal which will be turned into gold by the great work or magnum opus. It can only be managed with the help of our inner Teacher. All our inner work is of Service, which is what his little horse keeps telling Ivan.

'Where's my ring?' says the Tsar as Ivan and his little horse come to the palace gates. He feels that the ring is his and cares nothing for what Ivan has accomplished in finding it! Ivan answers that he 'has it, of course' but that it is very heavy. So the guards are called to carry the casket with the ring. The Tsar now eagerly rushes off to the Tsar-Maid to tell her that there is now no obstacle to their marriage, as he now has her ring. The Tsar-Maid knows this and is quite impatient with the Tsar telling him that there is no way she can, or will, wed him – he is an old man and how can she possibly marry an old man? Despite all his arguments, she remains adamant that she will not marry him. Finally, she seems to relent but says that if he is not afraid of pain he can become young again. This is the great and final test. Early next morning there are to be three cauldrons placed on the courtyard lawn, one filled with cold water, one with boiling water, and one with boiling milk, with a fire to be under the two heated cauldrons. To be young and handsome again the Tsar must plunge naked into the boiling milk, then the boiling water and then the cold water!

This scenario of the three cauldrons needs to be examined carefully: the symbol of milk over the fire, lets us know that this is a powerful process about initiation, transformation and rebirth. It is about the flow of sacred life as related to The Great Mother – an integration or merging with Sophia as feminine wisdom. The fire which burns under the first two vessels symbolizes transformation and purification but also is related to the generative power of the sun and so is masculine. It is the fire of alchemy, where fire and flame belong to the heart. Perhaps we could see the process as a symbolic death by fire into a rebirth to the milk and water of life. Both milk and water are symbolic of the great Mother. To dive into the water really means to search for the secret and sacred meaning of life and to be reborn into it with all its potentialities. This is, in fact, the transformation of base lead into gold. Water and light have the same vibration spiritually. In many of these stories, first a Light (enlightenment) is experienced, which leads the hero to a search for the Water of Life. We will see more of this in the story of the Fairy of the Dawn.

The Tsar, of course, true to form, straightaway calls for Ivan his groom, who protests bitterly that he is still stiff and sore from his last quest, and refuses. Why should he let himself be boiled alive like a pig or the proverbial chicken? The Tsar goes into a towering rage and threatens Ivan with all sorts of torture and painful ways of dying. Ivan as usual is the reluctant hero. It is life – the outer world - which pushes him into his various battles. His little horse once again tells him that if he hadn't picked up the Light feather he would not be in this present fix, but of course the little humpbacked horse will again do what he can. This time he says that all his help and friendship will be needed for Ivan to accomplish his great transformation. This is the final task, although I would say that there being three cauldrons means that this process for us who also undergo it, can actually last for a long time – many years in fact.

In the morning Ivan, as requested, askes for his little horse to be present so as to make his farewell. The little humpbacked-horse then waves his tail over the proceedings signifying the spirit of guidance, perhaps even a blessing. Then he dips his snout into each of the three cauldrons, and sucking up some of the contents of each one, squirts the contents, over Ivan twice. Numbers are so important to Sufis, and the fact that the little horse squirted Ivan twice from each cauldron is crucial. My feeling is that 'two' means the life force, which contains the duality of masculine and feminine principals, perhaps even of wisdom and self-consciousness. It is like a baptism.

Then the little horse whistles loud and long three times. Sound, especially a piercing sound like a whistle, has a profound effect on the psyche. A specific sound has a specific effect on certain centres or chakras. The sound of the whistle, among many other sounds, finally becomes the sound *Hu*, the most sacred of all sounds:

'This sound *Hu* is the beginning and end of all sounds, be they from man, bird, beast or thing.

The word *Hu* is the spirit of all sounds and of all words, and is hidden under them all, as the spirit in the body. It does not belong to any language, but no language can help belonging to it.

The mystery of *Hu* is revealed to the Sufi who journeys through the path of initiation.

The more a Sufi listens to *sawt-e-sarmad*, the sound of the abstract, the more his consciousness becomes free from all limitations of life. The soul floats above the physical and mental plane without any special effort on man's part, ---'[11]

So, when the little horse whistles loud and long three times, it represents the spirit of all sounds, the mystical *Hu;* the trinity of male, female and uniting intelligence. This gives Ivan the ultimate gift on his final test.

Ivan takes a deep long breath which reminds me of our Pranayama practice, and dives in and out of each cauldron. When he emerges, he is completely transformed, beautiful and handsome in every way. He dresses and bows to the Tsar-Maid. The crowd and the Tsar are amazed - so much so, that the Tsar seeing that Ivan is so transformed, crosses himself many times and dives into the cauldrons thinking that he too can be transformed. But in fact he has done no preparation or practice and so he was boiled there on the spot as he dived into the cauldrons. The Tsar-Maid now stands up and calls for silence, lifts her veil, and addresses the crowd - the Tsar is dead! – will they take her in his place instead? Will they accept Ivan as her husband? Because of her,

---

[11] Ibid, p.172.

and for her sake, they agree and so the Tsar-Maid and Ivan are married with great acclaim from the people. She becomes the female Tsar with Ivan as her consort. What a wonderful outcome and ending of this story.

In Sufi stories the King is usually the highest part of the Self or heart, but in this story the Tsar is far from being highly evolved or even a 'King' in fact. I think he represents the patriarchy and he is seen more like a pompous buffoon or even an autocratic and corrupt CEO, or simply outer life with all its irrational demands which distract us, but from which we are forced to learn so much.

This is an intricate and detailed story of a powerful inner process, which can provide insights every time it is read. It deals with the issue of being in the real world, but not of it. Sufis would say it demonstrates the difficulties we encounter and the ways of overcoming them. That which we go towards, makes us change. The small-self disintegrates and we move toward Realisation.

What also delighted me with this tale is that the ultimate goal was the ascension of the real hero, the female Tsar, the Tsar-Maid of the story. She was not a Tsarina or a Queen, as in the wife or consort of a Tsar, but she was a female Tsar in her own right- a complete, evolved and individuated woman. Ivan, the hero was there to help and aid her, but it was not for him in the end to become Tsar but to be her consort.

Pyotr Yershov published his epic poem 'The Little Humpbacked Horse' in 1834 to immediate success. Not an ancient fairy tale or myth, it seems to have erupted from his psyche as a complete tale. It was the only writing of note that he ever produced. It is intriguing and although it differs from other fairy tales in many respects, it still holds a storehouse of fundamental truths.

Ancient Venus as Witch / Teacher

Because of this evolving element of the feminine in the stories, I then asked my teacher, Nawab, if he could find a tale for me that reflected female aspects in the storyline. He sent me 'Fairy of the Dawn', an old Rumanian folk tale, which can be found in *The Violet Fairy Book.*[12] The opening scenario in this tale shows us a mighty Emperor who ruled over an empire so large that no one knew where it began and where it ended. This is a perfect description of the vast inner realm known as the *'Alam al-mithal'*. Everybody in the realm was aware that the Emperor's right eye laughed, whilst his left eye wept. This reminded me of an instructive Sufi story, 'The Miraj of the Prophet'. It is said that the Prophet was to travel from Jerusalem to the Temple of Peace, a journey from the outer to the inner temple. On his way, the Prophet saw Adam, who looking to one side, smiled and then to the other side, he shed tears. This illustrates that the human soul, when it develops the heart quality of love, will rejoice in the progress of humanity while sorrowing over its degeneration.

In this story the problems in the land are reflected in its ruler, much like the previous story. This Emperor had three sons, the youngest of whom was Petru, who like Ivan of the previous tale was happy, laughed and sang and had a more feminine nature. He was also said to be very wise. Petru requests his older two brothers to ask their father why his one eye laughs and the other weeps, but they are too frightened to do this, so Petru goes straight to his father and asks his question. The Emperor is furious and boxes Petru's ears. However, Petru notices that after this his father's left eye seemed to weep less, and the right one to laugh more. He realises that it is worth having his ears boxed to make both his father's eyes laugh, so he continues to ask the question until this happens. This shows that we must suffer and sacrifice so as to

---

[12] Andrew Lang (ed), *The Fairy of the Dawn 'in' The Violet Fairy Book*, Longmans Green & Co. New York, 1901. All subsequent quotations and references are from this source.

heal the inner realm. The Emperor then tells Petru that his right eye laughs when he sees his strong and handsome sons, but that his other eye weeps because he is afraid that when he dies his sons will not be able to keep the empire together, safe, and protect it from its enemies. He then tells Petru that they, his sons, must bring him water from the spring of the Fairy of the Dawn, to bathe his eyes and then they will laugh for evermore. Here again is a quest for fresh spring water. It is an oft-used metaphor that when attaining the Spring of Life, or mystic, esoteric truth, this will free the protagonist from the literality of the world and organised religion. It gives us mastery. This is the next part of the great quest.

The older brothers, who can be seen as aspects of the ego, leave first on the quest, one after the other, until they come to the borders of the empire. Here was a deep, deep trench which girdled the whole realm, but there was only a single bridge by which the trench could be crossed. Guarding the bridge is a monstrous dragon, with three fearsome heads. This bridge is at the edge of our conscious reality and the dragon guarding it is fierce and very scary. It guards the bridge to that other realm, the treasures of inner knowledge and the water of life. Both brothers do not even try to fight the dragon, but flee from it terrified, just as Ivan's brothers did when faced with the demon in the previous tale. I find it fascinating that the dragon is miffed when they run away, and gives a great sigh when they do not put up a fight! We are here to fight our dragons, find the water of life and so find our purpose and when we shirk this task, something in us is unsatisfied. The dragon challenges us to breach that other realm where we can find our genuine self. If it is too easy, we do not value it, or may in fact not even notice. If we do not make the journey to this realm in our lifetime, we cannot hope to go there after our death. We must learn to find our way with confidence and trust 'on the other side'.

Petru now takes up the quest. When he first meets the dragon on the bridge, he does attempt to fight it, but finds that his horse is not steady enough under him to allow him to cut the dragon's head off with his sword. Petru realises that he needs a better steed to do this. This means that his 'horse', or spiritual tradition, or religion is not strong enough to support him in his effort to overcome the dragon. He returns home to be met by his old nurse, the archetypal witch, who had also been his father's teacher.

Petru's old nurse / teacher, Birscha, tells him that he has not gone about things properly. He must find the horse that his Father, the Emperor, rode in his youth. In other words, to discover for himself, the structure of the sacred teachings, which seem to have been lost or gone underground since his father the Emperor was young. In many countries, such as Russia, Sufi teachings, for instance, went underground during the revolution and under communism. These teachings were held privately by devotees in the communities, or in the heart of the people. Currently, mainstream Christianity as a religion is waning in the west, certainly this is the case in Australia. Young people do not have a strong tradition to support them any longer, and so cannot take up the fight with their demons without being desperately wounded in some way. It is a serious problem.

When Petru asks his father about his old horse there seemed to be nothing left of it except the old and rotting scraps of its reins (the outer guidelines and ritual perhaps). These are the remnants of the old traditions, which involve the mastery of the self or ego, as symbolized by the reins. We use reins to guide and restrain our egos. Also, this sense of self-mastery can be seen in the reins that are used to guide and restrain infants when they are first learning to walk, so there is a sense of Petru finding his balance in being guided by the reins. These reins of old tradition once sustained the Emperor, but now he has almost forgotten them. Petru brings the remnants of the oldest, blackest and most decayed pair of reins to his old Teacher. Perhaps we can say that he finds her the oldest and most pure form of these teachings, so that they can be revived. She is able to work with them and she murmurs over the reins, sprinkles incense over them and so revitalizes the teachings which she then hands over to Petru. When she gives Petru the reins, she asks him to strike them against the pillars of the house. This is his way of forming the new structure of his teachings and beliefs, which will sustain him on his quest. As he does this, a beautiful brown horse stands before him – 'a splendid horse, a splendid saddle, and a splendid bridle, ready for a splendid young prince!'

This brown and beautiful horse becomes his inner guide and teacher. As soon as he sits on his steed, he feels his heart braver and his arm stronger and so his brown horse tells him to sit firmly in the saddle and away they go on their great quest. It takes a long time to reach the bridge where the dragon is standing. That place on the borders of our consciousness! This time the dragon is much more fearsome than before and it now has twelve heads! Twelve would seem to indicate a complete cycle, perhaps one for every month of the year. There are so many sets of twelve in the universe – twelve months in the year, twelve hours in the day, twelve disciples, twelve signs of the Zodiac and so on. Petru shows no fear and simply frees his arms for battle. The brown horse now tells Petru exactly what to do, and indeed Petru soon cuts off the largest head of the dragon as he leaps over bridge and dragon on his horse. Sometimes the only way is to simply take out the biggest obstacle to our progress as we make a giant leap across the abyss into the magical realm of *Alam Al Mithal*.

Petru and his horse now enter a place which is strange and wondrous. A place that Petru had never heard of or seen before. He then journeys through three different woods, copper, silver and gold, each indicating a stage of life perhaps: and each time Petru is tempted away from his path. He is warned by his brown horse that he must not become distracted and pick the flowers which offer themselves to him. But in spite of these warnings, he eventually cannot resist and succumbs to the temptation. He so desperately wants to pick these beautiful flowers by the side of the path. So, too, are we distracted from our spiritual path by the beauty and delights of this world we live in. We also want to pick the beautiful flowers at each stage of our lives and we do. It is impossible not to do so if we live in the world.

What I do love about Petru is that he weaves the flowers that he picks into a wreath, first a copper wreath, then a silver one and, finally, a golden one. These wreathes symbolise what he has made out of the flowers he has picked, for example, the beauty of a place, or a feeling, could be made into a poem, or a song, or some form of art work. The achievements of our lives are the wreathes we weave out of the flowers we have picked. These 'achievements' are not material successes, but achievements in the sense of attaining our realization of the divine. Sometimes this can be as simple, and yet profound as our sense of the beauty and oneness of nature and our unity with this sense of being.

This is also a great lesson for us, of not becoming attached to the things of the world. We can appreciate them, even love them, but we must not get attached to or 'pick' them. Each time Petru does this he has to fight a Welwa, which is I think the terrible ego-monster of distraction and of greed and pride, as well as a lack of concentration and focus. One of the many things we must learn on the spiritual path is concentration and it is a very difficult practice. Without the strength and focus of being able to concentrate, we become weak and, in fact, unsuccessful in everything we do in life, be it practical or spiritual. When we do succumb we end up with an even greater battle to fight. This battle with the various Welwas go on for a very long time and are exhausting both for the Welwa and for Petru, but he is warned that he must not let up even for an instant. I find it interesting that sound is used by the Welwas in their battle – they make great sounds especially towards the end of the battle. Particular sounds have particular effects on one's opponent as we saw earlier. As soon as Petru is able to throw a bridle over the head of the monster, thus restraining it, the Welwa turns into a beautiful horse, who thanks him for freeing it from enchantment. This enchantment is really our attachment and ownership of people and things which we actually cannot own. For instance, our children - we love them and want to protect them from the difficulties and challenges of the world. We feel responsible. But this can turn into a control issue. The son or daughter may feel that they are only loved if they do what their parents want them to do. These desires for our children, however benevolent, make them extensions of our egos. We must fight these ego monsters and set them free, and in setting them free, we also free our loved ones. We should always be loving and respectful – non-attachment is a great lesson and difficult to learn, especially for those who see themselves as being helpful. This is very hard for parents, who can only advise, but not control. Once we have overcome this, the released monsters become our guides and advisors on the path, just like the Welwas. Now the Welwa horse advises Petru in his subsequent encounters.

Three times in three aspects of life, copper, silver and gold woods, he overcomes a Welwa until he has three Welwa horses, the third one, and the most fearsome, being female. With his four horses he is now entering deeper and deeper into the inner realms of the feminine: first, into the kingdom of the Goddess Mittwoch (Wednesday in German), the feminine form of Mercury, although this day used to be called after the Norse God, Odin. Mercury is the messenger and communicator of the Gods. It is through her that we can communicate between the outer life and the inner realms. Her realm is of extreme cold, of being frozen out, the very absence of love and human feeling. We see this aspect of icy heartlessness in other fairy tale creatures, such as the Snow Queen who turns everything to ice. It is a very negative aspect of the Goddess, as indeed are the realms of all three Goddesses in this story.

This rigid, hard place is the opposite of the 'fresh' living water, which Petru is searching for in the realm of the Fairy of the Dawn. He is warned not to warm himself at the fires alongside the road. This time, being much stronger he is not distracted and endures the terrible cold, until he comes to the dwelling of Mercury herself. Here he enters her hut and greets her respectfully. She tells him he has borne himself bravely, and so she gives him a box, which will tell him anything he wants to know and also gives him news of his homeland.

It is the ultimate communication and connection device. It is like gaining the intuition and knowingness that comes with practice and understanding; The ability to know what is happening in the outer realm, when we are deep in another. When Petru is a little way from her hut, he uses the casket and asks for news of his father, who, he discovers is furiously angry because his older brothers are trying to rule him and the empire, but they are not fit to do it. This is the ultimate communication, which is an aspect of Mercury. We see this aspect in the teacher.

Now they move on to the kingdom of the Goddess of Thunder, where it is hot enough to melt the marrow of his bones! He is again warned not to succumb to the lure of flowers, cool streams and shade by the side of the road. He cannot even speak it is so hot, but eventually comes to the hut of the Goddess of Thunder (Donnerstag or Thursday). This time when he gets off the horse, the Goddess comes out herself to meet him and he is invited in and asked about his journey. I feel that the feminine aspect of heat and fire relates to the Goddess of the hearth, heart and heat, and this connects with the story of Cenerentola, which we will discuss later. With respect to the mysticism of sound, thunder is related to the plane of the mind, sometimes referred to as the realm of the Jinns. This is the last level of creation and can be understood as the "causal" region, because it is the effective cause of everything that lies below it – being the astral plane, and the world of mankind and the animals below that. The sounds related to this realm are said to be of thunder or the beating of drums. With Thunder comes Lightening – the heat and power of enlightenment, and then often followed by rain, which is the water of life. From a spiritual point of view, light and sound are really one. We can see and hear in our dreams when our physical senses are asleep. Some people can hear light and colour, and also see sound.

This Goddess is, like the others, constrained and seen very negatively, so Petru's journey is about rehabilitating both the feminine within us and in our outer realm also. Without the support of the Goddesses the whole quest is impossible. This rehabilitation is an act of recognition that then enables us to act in an enlightened way to achieve our quest, which is in both the inner and outer realms.

The Goddess of Thunder promises him a gift when he returns from the Fairy of the Dawn, and he is told to warn Venus not to delay him on his way to the Fairy of the Dawn. Perhaps this is a hint for him not to get involved with this great Goddess of Love.

Now he finds himself in a kingdom which is neither too hot nor too cold, where the air is soft like spring. He finds himself in the realm of the Goddess Venus (Freitag, Friday). That these Goddesses have names which go back to Norse mythology, could well mean that the stories themselves have a pre-Christian heritage, but come from a later time where the feminine (as reflected by the Goddesses) was very much relegated to their darker aspect. They are constrained and almost stuck in a negative state. It is from this that Petru must save them and, in saving them, he also saves his father's kingdom. Everything contains its own opposite, so the archetypal 'old hag' is really, in one sense, the destructive, ugly side of the creative, seductive and beautiful Venus. In another sense, the old hag is the way that the patriarchy consigns the power of the feminine, because it fears the wisdom and power of the feminine.

Note that Freitag (Friday), which the story identifies as Venus, would have been the day of the Norse Goddess, Freya, who is similar to Venus as the Goddess of all forms of love, including sensual love, but Freya also loved romantic music and stunning floral arrangements. She had a darker side, of course, and was known as the Goddess of War and Death. Though this captivating Goddess had numerous lovers, she was the wife of the mysterious Norse God, Od whom she deeply loved and was devoted to. They were never separated, even after his death when he was admitted to Valhalla - the 'otherworld'. She comforted the dying and eased their transition into the 'otherworld' serving as guide and companion on the journey. So, in fact, she is the perfect representation of the sublime Feminine Love and Wisdom. Monogamy was not practiced in those ancient times and infidelity was the social norm. Women nowadays have Aristotle, the apostle Paul and Augustine to thank for the 'misogyny that has infected philosophy and theology, with heartbreaking results for women, denying them education, liberty and the chance to develop their minds, their gifts and their art.'[13]

From their misogynistic teachings sexuality was viewed as unclean and shameful, even in marriage. To quote Nightingale again, 'Augustine associated sexuality, directly with original sin. The shame of sexual love, by his reasoning, derives from the fateful disobedience in Genesis, after which Adam and Eve had the first sexual desire (there having been none, according to Augustine, in Eden) ----every child is conceived in sin and is in some way marked at conception, since every man carries the contaminated seed of Adam ...this corruption, expressed in the flesh of every one of us simply by our being born, has an easy identifiable

---

[13] Steven Nightingale,. *The Light of Andalucía*, Nicholas Brealey Publishing, London, 2015, p.170.

cause: the yielding of Eve to the temptations of the Devil in the Garden of Eden.'[14]

Seeing these comments written baldly like this, is extremely unsettling and makes me even more sympathetic to Venus / Freya. 'We can see how such ideas led naturally to the beliefs and practices we would expect: the requirement of celibacy for priests; the insistence upon shame, if not depravity, of sex, even within marriage; the council against sexual pleasure, which alienates us from God; the natural inferiority of women, the exaltation of virginity.'[15]

No wonder the Great Goddesses like Venus / Freya were driven underground, deep into the unconscious. When the glorious feminine has been so repressed, it can erupt in a grotesque and distorted manner. How sad and heartbreaking it is to realise how many people, both male and female, have suffered and are still suffering from these terrible attitudes. Even my husband wondered how it would have been for him if he had been brought up with the loving and accepting outlook of, for instance, the people of Andalucía, before that culture was destroyed by the greedy and power-hungry Ferdinand and Isabella. A culture where mysticism flourished and where Jews, Christians and Muslims lived together in harmony and at peace for 800 years. So many great 'Saints' were born out of this milieu – from Ibn Arabi (Muslim / Sufi), to King Alphonso the Wise (Christian), Maimonides (Jewish), John of the Cross and Theresa of Avila (who were Jews who converted to Christianity), and even Saint Frances, who was said to have spent time there. Imagine the scenario where love and the act of love is sacred. Where the feminine has been completely integrated into the psyche of the culture, when lovers are united openly and trustingly, 'What they feel is far more than pleasure. Their devotion does more than burnish the body; it awakens the soul. The sensual, with such radiance and unity in bed, is more than sensual: it is transcendental. The experience is a special dispensation of God, and it means that sexual love might be understood as ecstatic and initiatory prayer. This gives us directly, and, unmistakably, a foretaste of

---

[14] Ibid, p.172.

[15] Ibid, p.173.

paradise. We move outside time in a benediction of flesh that is natural to human life. ---- erotic love, rightly practiced, can bring us spiritual refinement, and our shared pleasures are both joyful and sacramental.' This is a vision of sensual life, of marriage and of sex, written by a Spaniard in exile in Tunis after being expelled from Andalucía in the 17th century.[16]

The ecstatic prayers of St Theresa, are expressed in terms of a union with the Divine, that is so powerful and integrated with every aspect of being, that it is described in a similar way to sexual union. Here again we see the union of the divine realm with the earthly realm, which is experienced as bliss.

The realm of Venus / Freya is guarded by the whirlwind or the wild elements of nature, so Petru's horse tells him to toss the copper wreath to this whirlwind with a particular saying recognising the fairy souls that make up the whirlwind. It is almost like an incantation to a nature spirit, and it does appease the wind which tears the wreath to pieces. Now the horse teaches Petru the whole ritual of what he must say, and do, to gain access to this very reclusive Goddess Venus. He must offer her the silver wreath that he has made, and he must say that he has made it especially for her. In fact, he has to tell her that the whole difficult journey was made just for her. This is actually the truth, but Petru does not know it.

Venus / Freya asks to see the wreath which Petru has woven, so that she can discern what Petru created in his life with the flowers that he has picked in the silver woods. We too need to assess what we have done with the flowers that we have picked. Everything that has happened to us, all the stories we have lived, are woven into this wreath. One could say that all the experiences I describe in this book, all the stories I tell, are my weaving of the flowers of my life. Everything, even the most terrible, heartbreaking and difficult experiences have a beautiful outcome, even though we cannot always discern this meaning. These things are the compost from which our flowers grow. It is how we deal with the events of our lives that is important, and if we do not

---

[16] Ibid, p.175.

resolve our difficulties, they rise up to face us, again and again in more challenging forms, just like the Welwas in the woods. But when they – the monster Welwas - are overcome they become our guides. We learn from them.

So Petru passes the tests which Venus / Freya gives him, and is invited into her house. He treats her with the utmost respect, just as we should treat our Teacher. I just love feeling into this next scene and can imagine it perfectly. Petru sits near the fire and listens to everything Venus / Freya chooses to talk about. He listens to all her complaints about the world of men, agrees, and empathises with her in her anger and outrage. So Petru is in total harmony with Venus / Freya, and understands her complaints completely because he is totally at one with her. He knows what she, as the receptive Feminine, has suffered. This is the aspect of the Feminine, which has to endure the dark side of the world of men. The Venus / Freya who Petru encounters is ancient, with many wrinkles, like the old crone or witch of many stories, but Petru, 'devours her with his eyes' – he sees her Beauty and feels her love. This makes Venus very joyful in her heart. He mirrors her beauty and her love as she is his soul.

Then Freya goes on to explain who she really is – she has been there right from the beginning of time. "Nothing was that is, and the world was not a world when I was born", she says. She became herself when the world came into being as part of the human experience. She was the most beautiful girl that was ever seen, the archetype of the Beloved, of Love, and of the Lover. Many hated her for it. This is a telling remark regarding the patriarchy's fear of the archetypal feminine. Now she is very, very old!

She goes on to tell Petru that she was the daughter of an Emperor, and that their nearest neighbour was the Fairy of the Dawn, with whom she had a violent quarrel. She is clearly still very angry with the the Fairy of the Dawn, who is of course another great archetype. This archetype has many layers, and in this story we see her as the guardian of the waters of life. And so we learn that the realm of the great Goddess of Love and Beauty is right next to the realm where the water of life is to be found. This is quite extraordinary. It is perhaps giving us a hint as to the 'structure' of the inner realms. Imagine that the whole world is like an onion. Our outer life, manifestation and consciousness could be the outer layers of the onion, and as we go in deeper into ourselves, the various levels of the unconscious right through to the collective unconsciousness or 'mind of God', could be the deeper layers of the onion. Somewhere we come to that divide where there is that bridge which we must cross, overcoming the dragon which guards it. Then, as in this story, we pass through the freezing copper woods, the melting heat of the silver woods and the 'just right' realm of the Golden woods, from each we learn and weave our wreaths, which we then carry deeper into the levels or layers of the Goddesses, from Mercury, as the communicator and messenger between the realms, to Thunder, as the advisor and helper – the knower of the path, to the great Goddess of Love, Venus / Freya. Her realm is right next to the angelic realms - the deepest of which is where the Fairy of the Dawn is to be found. In Sufi thought the planes of existence are the Astral, Jinn, Angelic (Cherubim to Seraphim, Archangels) and deepest and central to all, The Throne of God. In fact, the archangels are believed to surround the Throne of God, which is right at the centre of the World; the centre of the onion. So, Petru is travelling inwardly from outer to the inner realm of the Divine One.

The Goddess continues to teach Petru for a very long time and tells him all about the Kingdom of the Fairy of the Dawn and how it is guarded on all sides by wild and fearsome beasts. Again, we find that the sacred water is guarded by a powerful 'demon or Fairy', just as the God of the Yellow River guarded the sacred water in a previous story. The Goddess tells Petru about the well; whoever drinks from it will blossom again like a rose. Venus / Freya asks Petru to bring her a flagon of this water and she will do anything to prove her gratitude. Petru tells her that he has another task to fulfil at the Fairy of the Dawn and Venus is well pleased with this.

Freya / Venus then gives him a tiny flute, which was inside an iron-bound chest. An old man (her Teacher?) gave it to her in her youth. She tells him that whoever listens to this flute goes to sleep and nothing can waken them, but that he must keep playing it, then he will be safe.

He must play it while he is in the realm of the Fairy of the Dawn. It is interesting that it is the sound of a flute which will put people to sleep. Hazrat Inayat Khan teaches about the effect of sound on the psyche.[17] In many of our practices we use specific sounds to 'open' certain chakras. The inner sound that can be heard in certain practices can be the sound of the harp, veena, flute, or the buzzing of bees. Hazrat Inayat Khan has said that '*The sound of the abstract is always going on within, around, and about man. As a rule, one does not hear it because one's consciousness is entirely centred in material existence-----Those who are able to hear the sawt-e-sarmad and meditate on it are relieved from all worries, anxieties, sorrows, fears and diseases; and the soul is freed from captivity in the senses and in the physical body. The soul of the listener becomes all-pervading consciousness---*'[18]

In the morning Petru feeds and waters his horses, just as Ivan cared for his horses by the light of his Firebird's feather in the previous story. This means that he is doing his practice, I think. For Sufis this can consist of prayers, Pranayama or breathing practice such as the element breath, chanting, singing Zikar, and sounding the chakras. Whatever is required to keep our inner Guides happy and healthy. It is so important to keep up our practices. If we don't, it is like letting a fire go out, and then we have to start up all over again. In alchemy we know that we have to keep the fire burning under the sacred container of our life.

As he is about to leave, Freya / Venus stops him with some more important advice for him. Firstly, he must leave one of his horses with her. This means that he must leave his Beloved Guide, and at this point only take with him, what he has learned from his journey through life, his three Welwa horses. Secondly, he must ride slowly to the Fairy's kingdom, then dismount and go on foot. To go slowly is important advice and so easily overlooked. In life I certainly was in a big hurry when I was younger. There was so much to do, so many adventures to be had - even in love: I had a boyfriend whom I met in school. He was a handsome, and a troubled soul – very attractive to me! When I finished

---

[17] Hazrat Inayat Khan, *The Mysticism of Sound and Music.* p.170.
[18] Ibid, p.170.

my studies, he was starting medical school with many years of study ahead of him. Even though I loved him, I couldn't wait and so moved on, too quickly, into a disastrous marriage with someone else. I married my first husband four months after I met him, knowing nothing of him, who he was and how we would relate to each other. We then emigrated to South Africa, with my being pregnant with twins, although I did not know this at the time. All this within a year - I should have ridden slowly! But, if I had, then I would never have had my twin sons, who are part of the flowers of my life.

Now Petru is completely alone, his magical brown horse has been left behind. There is nothing to support or guide him. Finally, he is told that he must never look the Fairy of the Dawn in the face, for she has eyes that will bewitch him. She is hideous, more hideous than can be imagined. Venus tells him again and again that he must not look at the Fairy. On his return he must walk while his three horses remain on the road. Although the word hideous is used, a more insightful view would be that she is terrible to behold, and too awesome for mortal eyes to take in.

The whole realm of the Fairy is very beautiful – a Light behind the Palace, the white castle so splendid that he is dazzled. This is the inner place which is known by Shamans and mystics, and which is alluded to in some other of these stories. It is a 'real' place and seems to me to be an aspect of the angelic realm. Petru jumped down from his horse and left it to graze on the dewy grass, while he played his tiny flute. The flute is said to be the instrument, or sound associated with the level or realm of the angels. Lord Krishna is always depicted playing the flute. The sound from the flute is a sacred sound that captures the heart. But that sound has no material form – it is pure spiritual sound. And that divine sound descends into this world from the flute of the Lord Krishna. While the little flute is being played every being around falls into a deep sleep. This is what we must do when we go to the depths of the angelic realm; we must listen to the pure sound that is constantly present and find the sacred water of life. As long as we concentrate on the sound, we are held in that space where we can achieve what we need to. In this way, the deep sleep of all the beings in this inner realm is a mystical state that enables Petru to enter and leave the realm without harm. We cannot force entry to this realm in our natural state, only penetrate it in a mystical way that is suspended from the laws of nature.

All the giants who guarded the castle, as well as the monsters and dragons were asleep. Then Petru came to a river of milk which flowed around the castle; at the bottom of the river were precious stones and pearls, all aspects of the feminine. Petru sees the most beautiful gardens imaginable, with fairies sleeping on the flowers and Petru wonders how come the fairies are all so beautiful but the Fairy of the Dawn is supposed to be so ugly? This angelic realm reminds me of picture books of fairies, angels and elves of my childhood, but it also does contain the monsters, dragons and giants from the fairy rales. The angelic realm is beyond the mind, or Jinn realm, beyond the human and even archetypal realm, and so it is outside of time and space, beyond the manifest. A Sufi teacher once told me that angels do not understand discrimination, right from wrong, as they are from a world beyond opposites. The angelic beings have to come to earth to learn these things, and when they do, are faced with their own opposite, which is what we would consider evil.

This is a seriously difficult and dangerous place for Petru to find himself. His only tool so to speak is the little flute. At the dawn of creation there was the 'Word and the Word was God' and that word was Light, and when the Light dawned the whole creation manifested. This Word is ringing in every atom of creation, and it is to 'hear' this word that we do our practices and meditation. It is the *Hu* that we can perhaps hear after Zikar when we close our ears. When we chant, or sing, the sounds we create vibrate through different parts of our body and our soul. The power of the Word is in accordance with the illumination of the soul. So, we play Krishna's flute for ourselves and Petru played it so that all the strange creatures and beings of that world go to sleep and cannot harm or distract him.

The sound made by the Japanese Bonshō bells is thought to have supernatural properties, and it is believed that it can be heard in the underworld. The sound of the bell is made up of three parts and can have many different tones, rich in harmonics. It is used in Buddhist temples where the sound is considered to be calming and to induce a suitable atmosphere for meditation. There is a particular 'great hollow bell', which is hung above a well, and it is believed that the sound of the bell resonates down the well into the underworld, to summon the spirits of the dead. So, we can understand that particular sounds, like the low tone and deep resonance of the bell, rather like the *Hu* sound we have already referred to, function like the 'sound of the universe' that we can hear in deep meditation. In western culture, each of the planets were believed to vibrate with a perfect note. Each note combined into the divine harmony of the spheres.

Now Petru has to cross the river of milk. He tricks and yet still has to fight a giant who is finally forced to agree to lifting Petru across this river. Petru then passes through the amazing gardens into the castle itself which seem like paradise; the most splendid place that one can imagine. "In the stables the horses of the sun were kept." We come to understand that the masculine sun and the feminine are balanced and in harmony here in this realm. This is the ultimate place of perfection, which has at its core the sacred living water of life. Petru quickly goes upstairs and through 48 sumptuous empty rooms, to find the Fairy of the Dawn in the 49th room. This is seven times seven – the magical number of the Universe and of completeness. In the middle of this huge room was the ancient sacred well he had come so far to reach. The Fairy herself was asleep beside the well. On a table nearby was bread made of doe's milk and a flagon of wine – the bread of strength and the wine of youth, we are told. Deer are sacred to the Feminine Moon Goddesses, so bread made from doe's milk is a sacrament of the Goddess and her strength. Wine is the sacrament of the solar, masculine God of youthful action. This is a sacred meal signifying completeness – a celebration of the sacred marriage of the Masculine and the Feminine. Petru longs for this.

In spite of the warning, Petru does look at the Fairy of the Dawn and as he does so, a mist comes down over his senses. Curiously, the Fairy reported as being so hideous, is not described. It is as if Petru sees her on a plane that is beyond words and beyond physical being. He drops the flute and stops playing: so the Fairy opens her eyes and looks at him.

In this look Petru further loses his mind, just as the glance of a Guru, can induce enlightenment, so a glance from the Fairy of the Dawn can pull him down into nothingness. But he remembers the flute, and by playing on it, regains his senses. In this 'seeing' of the Fairy herself, he actually loses his sense of himself and is almost completely overwhelmed. If we use the analogy of each of us being a drop in the great ocean of consciousness, we need to hold onto our 'specific gravity' and sense of 'dropness' (or individual being) when going into that ocean, otherwise we may not be able to hold onto this sense of ourselves when we come out again. Doris Lessing has talked about this in her book, *Briefing for a Descent into Hell*.[19] Many people who are considered insane have really been on this spiritual inner journey and lost themselves somehow. This book is a very disturbing insight into this inner journey when it goes wrong, which intriguingly demonstrates a circular, spiral journey of ascent and descent into totally unknown realms. The hero of Lessing's book has amnesia and so must re-discover himself. When on this quest we must hold ourselves together in union with the One, by concentrating on the sacred sound within the *Hu;* then we can achieve what we need to, without the total otherness of the angelic realm overwhelming us.

The Fairy drifts off to sleep again. He kisses her three times and lays his golden wreath on her forehead. This golden wreath he had previously woven from the flowers in the Golden Wood, is, in effect, the crown of his spiritual life. Gold represents Nur, the uncreated Light of God, enlightenment and immortality. He crowns the Fairy with this wreath, as an ultimate letting go, of detachment from everything, even what is sacred to him. He has complete mastery over himself – in doing this he is nothing and yet everything. His kisses show his love and devotion for the Fairy of the Dawn and all she represents.

He then eats the piece of bread, and drinks a cup of the wine of youth. He does this three times over. He partakes of the sacred sacrament of Bread and Wine and, in so doing, nourishes himself spiritually. Then he fills the flask with water from the well and vanishes. His task is done for now. When he passes through the garden now,

---

[19] Doris Lessing, *Briefing for a Descent into Hell,* Jonathan Cape, London, 1971.

everything seems more beautiful and vibrant. The flowers are lovelier, the streams run quicker, the sunbeams shine brighter and the fairies seemed gayer. All this, as the story says, because of the three kisses he gave the Fairy. When we show our love and devotion to this great Fairy, we are given the same experience. Happiness! Lightness!

I have been wondering why the central character of this story is called the Fairy is of the Dawn. Why the use of the word Dawn? The dawn of creation mentioned in our prayer Rasul, or Messenger of God, is the source or dawning of all creative energy: of light and the water of life. The quest for spring water, which is guarded by the Fairy of the Dawn, is a deeply spiritual quest, as you can see from the prayer below. The Fairy of the Dawn is that creative energy and potentiality, which comes from the dawn of Creation and guards the Water of Life, at the divine Source of All and everything.

Rasul

Warner of coming dangers,
Wakener of the world from sleep, Deliverer of the Message of God,
Thou art our Saviour.
The sun at the dawn of creation,
The light of the whole universe,
The fulfilment of God's purpose,
Thou the life eternal, we seek refuge in thy loving enfoldment.
Spirit of Guidance, Source of all beauty, and Creator of harmony
Love, Lover, and Beloved Lord,
Thou art our divine Ideal.[20]

Who or what is this Fairy who guards the water? 'Fairy' is generally the name given to 'Goddesses', or Teachers from pre-Christian times. I would say that the witch of eastern European fairy tales is of a similar character. Both Fairy and Witch were beings who were strong, magical, and tricky, but helpful to the 'right' people. They guard the boundaries of the inner realms, and of the life-giving water, as we have seen. The

---

[20] Hazrat Inayat Khan, Unpublished prayer.

three Goddesses also take on this role, as teacher and guide for Petru. His horse can only guide him to the goddesses and instruct him how to approach them but then it is up to the goddesses and Petru himself.

But, this is not the end of the story, as you will see. Petru is back in the saddle, speeding back through the levels of the realms to Venus who was waiting for him. She knows he is coming! The Goddess always knows exactly where we are in our journey. He greets her and she welcomes him back. She receives the flask of magic water with joy. Then Petru swiftly visits the Goddess of Thunder as he had promised but, as he is about to leave, she gives him a warning: 'Beware of your life; make friends with no man, do not ride fast, or let the water go out of your hand, believe no one; and flee flattering tongues. Go, take care, for the way is long, the world is bad, and you hold something very precious.' This is advice we can all use!

Again Petru is told again to ride slowly. It is something that I also have had to learn. I always walked fast so that my husband used to joke that I was always three paces in front of him, instead of three paces behind! I remember once we were going out to lunch with my teacher, Nawab, and his wife while we were on retreat, and Nawab actually had to grab me by the arm and hold me back. 'Nuria', he said, 'There is no hurry!'. I had to learn this. Hazrat Inayat Khan always walked slowly and nobly, and there is a story that once he was on a long train journey from the East to the west of America. When he had got off the train to stretch his legs. The train took off without him, but he kept walking slowly, unhurriedly and majestically along the platform, and the train stopped to let him get on. No-one know why this had happened. He would never rush or hurry.

Then the Goddess of Thunder gives Petru an enchanted piece of cloth: whoever carries it will never be struck by lightning, pierced by a lance or smitten with a sword, and arrows will glance off his body. So, he is protected from the weapons of the masculine, weapons which are sharp and which pierce. The Goddess of Thunder knows how to protect her people from being killed by these kind of weapons.

Now Petru takes out his treasure box or communication device and inquires how things are at home. Not good indeed – the Emperor was now completely blind, and Petru's brothers were still demanding that their father give them governance of the kingdom. The Emperor would not allow this, and said he would wait till he had washed his eyes with water from the well of the Fairy of the Dawn. Then the brothers had gone to consult old Brischa, the nurse and witch, who told them that Petru was already on his way home bearing the water. They had set out to meet him, and would try and take the magic water from him, and claim, as their reward, the government of the emperor and the empire. Petru would not believe this, and thought it was a lie. In anger he threw the treasure box on the ground, breaking it. It was so hard for Petru to believe this of his own brothers, or if we look at his brothers as aspects of his ego, then to think of ourselves in this way. So, we have a final lesson to learn. Having won the prize, we need to keep it pure - not to allow the ego to claim it, so that the ego becomes inflated. But as well as that, we do have to beware of everyone, even our own families and most trusted sisters and brothers. For a spiritual being, this is so very difficult. For example, the greed that manifests in some people over a last testament, when a member of the family dies, or is dying, is something that is so horrible and hard to contemplate that we cannot believe it, but we must recognise this, as part of the way of the world.

We can understand that Petru finds this totally unbelievable. Remember too, that we can only see in others what we have in ourselves. It is a re-cognition. If we don't have these traits like greed, for instance, then we cannot recognise them in others. That is why it is so shocking when we are forced to acknowledge something like this in someone we love. Sometimes, we can only be convinced of this when the other does indeed try to 'kill' us or put us down in some fashion. Rumi tells an amusing story about this, in 'When a Madman Smiles at you' In *Delicious Laughter*.[21]

Galen, the great physician, asked one of his assistants to give him a certain medicine. The assistant replied, 'Master, that medicine is only for crazy people! You are far from needing that!'

Galen, 'Yesterday a madman turned and smiled at me, did his eyebrows up and down, and touched my sleeve. He wouldn't have done that if he hadn't recognised in me someone congenial.'

---

[21] in *Delicious Laughter*, interpreted by Coleman Barks, Maypop Books, Atlanta, Georgia, 1990.

Anyone that feels drawn, for however short a time, to anyone else, those two share a common consciousness.'

Rumi tells us that if someone with a negative, even crazy trait, finds you congenial, then we should look for that trait in ourselves. This is different to when another person dumps their own negative traits onto you. This is projection, although I do feel that we should also examine ourselves closely when this occurs.

Petru does not want to acknowledge that his brothers are greedy, and would do him harm. He cannot believe it of them, because there is no greed in him. Soon Petru catches glimpses of his native land and hears his name being called. The closer we get to the outer world, especially after long and arduous inner 'work', the harder it is to remember what we know. It is like forgetting dreams as soon as we wake up. His horse tries to tell Petru to ignore the calls, but he is once again unable to heed this advice. He wants to know who is calling him. The world calls us back to itself again. He turns around and finds himself face to face with his two brothers. He forgets the warning from the Goddess of Thunder and jumps off his horse to embrace them. It is touching and sad. When we are in the world we do not always notice the inner voice or intuition, especially when it goes against our dearly held beliefs. His brothers praise and flatter him. Petru is still an innocent when it comes to the world and I think that most mystics really are innocents at heart. When our inner horse and guide sees us doing this, it can only sadly hang its head, as did Petru's brown horse.

The brothers offer to carry the precious water for Petru, but he refuses and tells them what the Goddess of Thunder had told him about the cloth she had given him. Oh, how trusting and oblivious is Petru, but this is how we are with our much loved family, friends and inner circle, and even with parts of ourselves, our ego. We continue to trust ourselves implicitly. Perhaps we sabotage ourselves? The brothers immediately understand that the only way that Petru can be got rid of, is by water – by drowning. He is, of course, not immune to the element which he has won, and which he carries and protects. So, when they come to a fast flowing stream with clear pools, they suggest that that they drink from the pool before they ride home. What a good thing, they say, that he has them to protect him. Another way of understanding this part of the story, is to think of the stream of water as life – the water of life. To drown in this water could mean to let oneself become totally immersed in the everyday life of the world and forget the journey that he has been on. To simply use his prize water, and lose himself.

His horse neighs a warning and this time Petru understands what this means. He heeds his inner voice and does not go with his brothers. Petru goes home to his father, and cures his blindness. This is the end of the story. The brothers are never heard of again. In this we learn that Petru can see through the material reality of himself and others. He is a complete, enlightened and individuated being.

So, the story teaches that each aspect of the feminine archetype must be dealt with in a courteous manner and with deep respect. It demonstrates the difficulties of being in the feminine realm when on the heroic quest. Without the particular feminine or Jemal qualities of being receptive, open, loving, gentle, inner focused and also wise, the quest cannot be fulfilled. These qualities must be honoured and integrated.

The Frog Skin and the Witch

After working with these stories for a long time, I realised the importance of the feminine in fairy tales, and in our spiritual lives, and so I asked my teacher to find me another story with a female hero. *The Frog Princess*[22] was his response and it was here that I saw how the fearsome Baba Yaga, or witch, was a fabulous (in all senses of the word) teacher for a young hero. This story is a favourite of Nawab's wife, Nirtan, who is Russian, and I am indebted to her for her insights and understanding of the symbols used.

In this story, the Tsar wants his three sons to find appropriate wives, so that he can have a true heir. This is a quest for the truly evolved feminine 'wife' or soul of the 'next' Tsar or ruler of the kingdom. The truly evolved feminine principle rules the evolved being, so the Frog Princess also shows us the harmony and perfection that comes when she is given her proper place as ruling consort. It is very important that each of the princes finds a wife who is at the same level of evolution as they are, but the wife that they each choose is also a reflection of their own evolution. As Jung has written, a prince must marry a princess. At an inner level our masculine and feminine side should be matched. Once again, the two older brothers shoot their arrows and find wives who are appropriate for them, but not for a future king. They are not princesses. And, once again, it is the youngest son, Prince Ivan, who shoots his arrow up into the air and eventually after a long search finds his arrow in the mouth of a frog who is sitting in a bog – his frog princess! He does not really want to accept his fate but knows that he must take this frog home as his wife. What amazing imagery. How often does the inner feminine feel like a gross frog stuck in the mud? Of course, a bog is also an in-between place between water and earth, sometimes referred to as a crossing place, and so a magical and mysterious place.

The Tsar 'tests' his sons' wives and each and every time the Frog Princess fulfils the three 'feminine' tasks given her, to perfection. This

---

[22] <http://www.artrusse.ca/fairytales/frog-princess.htm> at 19 December 2016

she does this during the night while the prince is sleeping. She goes onto the veranda, throws off her frog skin and becomes the princess she really is. The veranda, where the Frog Princess achieved her tasks for the Tsar, is again an in-between place, between the home and the outer world like the bog between earth and water. I imagine that the veranda is high off the ground, on an upper story outside the bedchamber, perhaps. This in-between place would be the Alam Al Mithal, the mysterious realm where all inner work happens.

In the first test, the Tsar demands the wives to make him a shirt – fit for a tsar, of course. Embroidery is considered an almost sacred art in Russia according to Nirtan. The embroidery is made of symbols to protect the body from evil influences, as indeed is the shirt made by the Frog Princess. Her shirt is really the only one fit for a tsar. The second test is to make a special bread for the Tsar. The other wives are now jealous and want to discover the secret and so spy on her. The Princess realises this and plays a trick on them by pouring the dough directly into the stove. This is mysterious as you can't do that with a Russian stove. Nawab suggested that it might be a reference towards the Middle East, where there are stoves dug in a hole in the ground and the dough is poured into the side of this hole, while the fire is burnt at the bottom of the pit. It could well be a reworking of an original Middle Eastern tale. Good bread is one that does not smell of smoke as it does when in direct contact with fire.

The symbol of the stove and its importance in these fairy tales reminds me of the symbol of the heart in Sufism. The heart is the organ that produces true intuition and the knowledge of God and the divine mysteries. Of course this 'heart' is not our physical organ, although there is a reflection in the subtle organ of the heart chakra. For Sufis the heart is one of the centres of mystic physiology. The knower's heart could be said to be the organ by which God knows Himself and reveals Himself to Himself. The power of the heart perceives divine realities and is like a mirror in which the form of the Divine Being is reflected. We talk about polishing the mirror of the heart. When I asked my teacher how we can purify the heart, he said that it was Love which purifies the heart, and I think this means feeling and knowing Love.

Finally, the Frog Princess, Vassilisa, the daughter of a tsar, is asked to show herself at a great banquet, but how can Prince Ivan take his frog wife to the ball? But the princess again has a plan and tells him to go to the ball alone. She will arrive after him, to a great clap of thunder – so once again it is sound which heralds the manifestation of the Divine feminine. A loud knock and a clap of thunder make the palace shake, as the princess arrives in a gilded carriage drawn by six horses.

She is so very beautiful - wearing an azure gown studded with stars and a shining caplet on her head. Prince Ivan leads her to the great oak table for the banquet. Here is a magical description of a sacred sacramental meal – Vassilisa sips some wine pouring the rest into her left sleeve, and nibbles at some swan meat dropping the bones into her right sleeve. Her sisters-in-law see what she is doing and copy her actions, again without any understanding of the mysterious ritual she is performing. After the eating and drinking, it is time for dancing, and this time Princess Vassilisa leads Prince Ivan onto the dance floor. Now she waves her left sleeve and the sacred wine transforms into a beautiful lake which formed in the hall. The lake of magical feminine powers. Then she waved her right sleeve and the bones, which represent the indestructible masculine life principle, manifest as white swans floating on the lake. The swans representing the solar power, gliding on the lake demonstrate the union of masculine and feminine principles. This is the sacred marriage - a complete transfiguration (a change of form or appearance into a more beautiful or spiritual state).

Again, the princess has performed wonders and is recognised as the queen that she truly is – in both the inner and outer realms. However, to do this she had to leave her frog skin behind, and the prince, finding it lying on the veranda, throws it into the stove and burns it. He wants his beautiful princess, as she was at the ball, for ever. This burning of the frog skin is so irrevocable. If one sees Ivan and the princess as aspects of the same person, then we could see the act as the application of the individual will overriding the natural unfolding of the psyche. The motive of not waiting long enough is repeated in a number of different tales, but it is also an expression of the very real wish to make the Divine Union permanent. We are not content to have moments of revelation subsequently covered by limitation. To achieve the real permanent state of union (in the white palace), however, a lot of hard work is required. Ivan is rebuked for such a rash act but this is also a common theme. The seeker is constantly warned about the dangers and difficulties of the path, a journey that no one but a fool would undertake not only for the difficulties, but also because it travels in the opposite direction to the usual worldly journey. (Nawab). My own feeling is that Vassilisa may not have been able to rid herself of her frog skin and it may have needed this drastic act by her prince. It could also mean that the feminine principle needs the masculine principle of logos (that includes action and will) to continue to evolve. Also, in alchemical processes, we see that being subjected to fire is necessary for the next stage to emerge – painful as this can be.

I felt myself very exposed and horrified by Ivan's act of burning the frog skin. How could he do such a thing? It was important for me to understand how much this meant to me - I had also hidden behind my frog skin for so long: it was a way of disappearing into myself and getting on with the inner issues of life. It seems to me that many women grow quietly behind their frog skin. As soon as the princess finds out that her husband, Prince Ivan, has burnt her frog skin in the stove, she would have felt devastated and exposed. Her response was to immediately turn into a cuckoo, and fly away. But she does give the prince the hint that she is to be found with Kashchey the Deathless, far, far away. When faced with such a life-threatening exposure, all that was left for Vassilisa was flight. Now Prince Ivan must go on a long journey in search of his Soul.

When Ivan finally meets his guide, a wise old man, we have direct speech, so rarely used in this story. He says: 'Ah, Ivan, the Prince, why have you burnt the frog skin? It was not you who put it on and it should not be you to take it off.' It feels that there is incredible wisdom hidden in these few words. Yes, we would like to speed up our own 'waking process' and remove the veils, but we also would like to do this with our loved ones. It is said that there are 77 thousand veils between us and Allah, but that there are none between Him and ourselves.

Life has to progress in its own time and forcing something against the course of this natural flow could well have negative consequences. Murshid says that we should not wake people up against their will, and we should raise their consciousness slowly according to their natural development. Murshid also speaks of certain laws of nature, and that we should not judge what is right and what is not right according to our limited understanding. As the old teacher in the story says; If you have not put this ugly skin on, then you should not force its destruction.

This part of the story reminds me of a lovely woman I knew many years ago. She had been a schoolteacher, was beautiful, sensitive, caring and deeply spiritual and so she married her 'prince'. He was wealthy and successful and she became a trophy wife – a perfect wife, in a perfect marriage and perfect mother – a wonderful cook and entertainer at her husband's dinner parties. She completely put her real self aside even to the point of faking any pleasure she might have had in the intimacy of her sex life. Thus, when I met her she was unfulfilled, bored and desperately unhappy. She was unable to 'come clean' with her husband for many reasons, one of which was that she thought that he now needed her the way she had made herself be for him, and thought he probably couldn't cope with the person she really was. Perhaps she could not have coped with that either. I don't think that she believed her husband was up to the task, nor could she bring herself to admit that she had been so dishonest with him for all those years. Perhaps her husband had burned her frog skin after he first 'saw' her in her complete womanhood, as he wanted her to be like that all the time.

So, she too turned into a cuckoo, and thus was imprisoned in the white stone palace of her husband's expectations. He wanted to show her off as his possession without love or care for her soul. This is Kashchey, the Deathless. In acting a part that is not real, but serves only the patriarchy, women do a disservice, not only to themselves, but also to other women and to the men they partner. We all fall into this trap to some extent. It is difficult for a woman to be authentic in outer life especially if she is working in the business world, or in an industry that is male dominated. We can become animus-driven and lose our connection with our soul. We see this manifested in women who treat other women as rivals for the favours of the patriarchy (whether male attention or corporate promotion) and commit acts of cruelty to other women, on the pretext of serving the best interests of the company or organization.

I like the idea of secret women's business which our Indigenous people follow in their beliefs and rituals. Both men and women have their own traditional inner work to do in special sacred places and this is respected and held sacrosanct. I remember being taken to a beautiful place in Litchfield National Park, near Darwin, which was a sacred place for aboriginal women. There was a deep round pool hidden in green tropical vegetation with a waterfall cascading into it. Only women were allowed to swim in that pool and there was a cave behind the pool, which had to do with preparing for birth, I think. It was said that if men swam in that pool they would die. Only women understood the 'business' of that sacred place.

In our story, the bog is permeated by water. In our Sufi breathing practice we recognise the principle of water always finding its way to the ocean, flowing around obstacles in its way, always flowing towards oneness. The Frog Princess's submission to her tests and overcoming of all obstacles in a graceful, knowing way, shows us how the feminine principle manifests its wisdom and grace.

Of course, the Beloved is one of the great symbols of God and the Soul for Sufis. We only have to read the poetry of Rumi and Ibn Arabi to see this. The Soul, or Beloved, is feminine and must be found and integrated by the hero, which is the masculine active principal within us. But in the *Frog Princess*, this was not to be. Now that the frog skin has been thrown into the stove and burned, the princess is no longer able to take any active part in the story. She is captive and it is up to Prince Ivan to find and release her from this place.

After a long series of tasks and challenges the prince, after meeting an old teacher and guide, makes friends with the animals (instincts or traits) and the elements. He finally meets the Baba Yaga who teaches him to conquer Kashchey the Deathless, who perhaps among other things, represents avarice. He sits on the riches that he has accumulated and does not share them with anybody. He wants to make us believe that he is deathless and unconquerable and is ruler of the whole world.

This sounds so much like the ego, but it, or he, can only be conquered by the one who conquers himself.

We now find ourselves at my favourite part of the story. Prince Ivan follows his ball (fate) as it rolls along the shore (another in-between place!) until he comes to a little hut standing on a chicken leg at the edge of the forest. This is the abode of the Baba Yaga, the witch of Slavic fairy tales. The symbol of the little hut at the edge of the forest functions in the same way as the veranda – it is an in-between realm. Sometimes the hut is found on the seashore rather than the edge of the forest, but it means the same thing. The hut is standing on a chicken leg and turning round and round. There are no windows or doors. The spindly chicken leg makes me think of a Qutub or 'pillar' that is at the centre of the mystical realm. Also, when doing Zikar the participants turn around this inner centre or 'pole', like the whirling dervish turning around his own centre. It is the pole of the internal microcosm and the centre of the world. It is here that the visionary can meet his personal Holy Spirit, who in communicating to him the order to undertake his pilgrimage, has announced him or herself as a companion and celestial guide. Communication with the 'Alam al-mithal' is possible only at the 'centre of the world.'[23]

The journey is towards a cosmic centre and the mystic life becomes more intense as we turn around the central pillar or Qutub.

We are told that the Baba Yaga's hut contains a stove on which the Baba Yaga lies. Again, the stove symbolises the great Heart and centre of all, and I find it most astonishing that it seems to be the 'altar' on which lies the Baba Yaga with her nose pressed up against the ceiling. In other words, there is no room on top of the stove for anything else except the Baba Yaga. So for me, the Baba Yaga represents the great Teacher, or Guide of Souls, for those who know how to face her and request her help. It is interesting to note that in our first encounter with the hero in the *Little Humpbacked Horse* story, Ivan is also lying on top of a stove. The house of the Baba Yaga is constantly turning but Prince

---

[23] Henri Corbin, *Alone with the Alone, Creative Imagination in the Sufism of Ibn 'Arabi*, pp.277-288.

Ivan has been taught enough to know what to do in this situation. He says his incantation, 'Turn your back to the forest and your face to me'. In other words, face me so I can enter the deep forest or mysterious realm. When the prince enters the house of the Baba Yaga she questions him immediately but he rebukes her and asks for food, drink and a hot bath. This, intentionally or not, is an echo of an old Sufi teaching (referred to by Hazrat Nizamuddin Auliya, and therefore older than him) about the duties of hospitality, that the dervish or Sufi seeker must first offer salaams, then food, then conversation. It also shows how we can expect to be helped by the Teacher when we recognise his/her role in our quest. Of course, Baba Yaga knew everything that was happening and explains how difficult and dangerous it would be to get the Princess away from Kashchey the Deathless. Prince Ivan stayed the night and was clearly guided in that deep and mysterious realm, perhaps in meditation or trance.

Afterwards, the Baba Yaga teaches the Prince how to find Kashchey! She tells him that to kill Kashchey, the prince must realise that Kashchey's 'death' is right at the point of a needle, the needle is in an egg, the egg in a duck, the duck in the hare and the hare is sitting on a stone chest which is in a lofty oak and Kashchey guards the oak, as he would the apple of his eye. This is mysterious and seriously long and difficult work – to the point literally, the place where his disjunction with his soul originated.

This reminds me of Sufi training where we are asked to look at the feeling or experience we are working with, and then go into the memory behind the memory, deeper and deeper until we arrive at the core issue, the first time we are able to return to the source of this issue in memory.

In finally snapping the point of the needle – an outwardly impossible task, the small self no longer has a hold and the soul is free. Ivan goes to the White Palace to find his Beloved. This White Palace is one of those magical places, which is known to Shamans and Mystics – they know how to find it. She runs out to meet him and kisses him on the lips. He has achieved his great Opus.

Let us reconsider, as an example, the story of the trophy wife that I mentioned earlier. The husband would attempt to redeem his inner beloved, his beautiful wife. To do so, he would have to go back from his current situation, where his wife is 'acting' the part of the perfect wife that she feels that he wants. He would have to look at his expectations, attitudes and experiences with his Beloved, to face his ego and his inadequacies, insecurities, his anger and perhaps blame, right back to his first moment of love for her. From when he first 'saw' her without her frog skin, in her full glory. He also 'burned her frog skin', so to speak, and she was left to perform and act the part he wanted of her. For women, it is a different journey, but we also lose touch with our soul, and it is the hero in us, who has to liberate 'Her' so that we can be set free. This is done by being seen in our full glory, by the masculine part of our selves, by being mirrored just as Petru mirrors the Goddess Venus / Freya in his encounter with her. He sees her beauty!

Again, in the story of the trophy wife, there was a man in our therapy group who saw her just as she was behind her frog skin and could reflect this beautiful soul quality that he saw in her, back to her so that she could 'see' this reflection and understand that part of herself. As women, we sometimes find this reflection in strange places, and at strange times. Men also find a model of their Beloved in an outer woman.

Ibn Arabi writes most beautifully about the daughter of his teacher, whom he eventually married. She was beautiful, learned, and pious and her presence uplifted everyone who came in contact with her. She was the embodiment of the Divine Sophia for him.

She was his Beloved and he saw her without her frog skin. This is such a powerful vision and it would be almost impossible to see the real woman behind this archetype. When we fall in love, we do actually project the archetype of the Beloved, onto the one we love. This could be called infatuation and, often when we withdraw our projections from our sweetheart and see our Beloved as they really are, we either fall out of love, or we learn to love and have an authentic and loving relationship with our Beloved.

When Ibn Arabi explains an allusion to the young girl Nizam as, in his own words, an allusion to *'a sublime and divine and sacrosanct Wisdom (Sophia), which manifested itself visibly to the author of these poems with such sweetness as to provoke in him joy and happiness, emotion and delight, we perceive how a being apprehended directly by the Imagination is transfigured into a symbol thanks to the Divine light, that is a light which reveals its dimension of transcendence. From the very first the figure of the young girl was apprehended by the Imagination on a visionary plane in which it was manifested as an 'apparitional Figure of Sophia aeterna.'*[24] It is a very real and authentic experience of the archetypal *Sophia Aeterna*. It is an experience of the Divine Light and Wisdom.

So the Soul or Beloved is re-cognised and reflected to the one who carries this image in his heart forever. For the girl who is perceived as such, being *seen* actually frees her own soul and allows her to meet with her Beloved. The Soul reflects everything around it, but is unaffected by it and remains pure. We need to keep the mirror of our soul clear and we do this by our practices, especially the sacred practice of Zikar, which is about remembering the Divine One and totally forgetting our small self, or ego, to achieve Unity.

This is the true meaning of the search for the Soul or Beloved. It is complex, difficult and requires guidance along the way; first from outer teachers like the old man, and then from powerful inner teachers, such as the Baba Yaga. It is the outer teacher who guides and teaches the seeker how to reach and interact with the inner guide. This is a story which is very powerful and instructive.

---

[24] Ibid, p.139.

Cinderella and the Sacred Hearth

Having worked for so long on the *Frog Princess* story and learning so much from it, I now wondered if there was a central female hero in any fairy tale written from a wholly feminine perspective. So I asked Nawab if he could recommend one for me. This he did - sending me the story of Cenerentola. This is one of those tales collected chiefly in Crete and Venice by Giambattista Basile, Conte di Torone who died in 1637[25]. This fairy tale is an original version of the very old and much loved Cinderella story, which still has so much appeal I think because of its deeper mystical meaning. It tells a fascinating story of the sacred quest from the point of view of the feminine. Zezolla, the heroine, is the only person in this story who is named.

Zezolla is the daughter of a prince and much loved by him. She has recently lost her mother and now desperately longs to reconnect with that loving, essential Wisdom which her mother must have embodied. Zezolla, therefore, encourages her father to marry her nurse and governess, in the hope that this will fulfill her longing.

At the wedding celebration, Zezolla receives a message, perhaps an intuition, from a dove that lands on her sill, or wall. Once again, the sill, or wall, represents that in-between place we have discussed before. It is significant and gives a hint of coming trouble for her as a result of her father's new marriage. In fact, it is very wrong for a prince to marry someone who is not at the same level of evolution as himself. Remember, that we are talking about archetypes here. On an inner archetypal level, a prince should marry a princess and to do otherwise causes untold difficulties and hindrances in the journey of both partners. The dove tells Zezolla that if she ever needs anything, she should send the request to the Dove of the Fairies on the island of Sardinia and she will instantly have her wish.

---

[25] Giambattista Basile, 'Cenerentola" in *Stories from Pentamerone* < *http://www.gutenberg.org/files/2198/2198-h/2198-h.htm#chap06*> at 4 January 2017.

Zezolla clearly has a connection with the Dove of the Fairies in Sardinia – a very old island where there are still traces of the ancient veneration of the Goddess. The female followers were called Fairies and there are still fairy grottos and relics to be found in Sardinia. The outer female secular world, as represented by her stepmother and stepsisters, does not understand Zezolla, although they try to do so at first. It is very difficult for 'normal' non-mystical or non-spiritual people to understand the inner world, and they try to make up for this with outer things, like beautiful clothes, food or trinkets. This does not satisfy Zezolla and she is very quickly relegated to the lowly hearth, where she is even given a new name of Cenerentola. We also are given a new name when we are baptized as a Christian, or initiated on the Sufi path. For Sufis, the name is given to us by our teacher and reflects an aspect of ourselves, which we hope to realise. I wonder if the name Cenerentola reflects her position in the central hearth / heart of her home and community.

What can we learn from Zezolla's 'fall' from the royal chambers to the hearth? When we first encounter the Frog Princess in the previous story, she has just 'caught' the prince's arrow in her 'frog' mouth as she sat in a bog – a place between earth and water. We learn that the Frog Princess was bewitched by her father (a tsar), because he was jealous of her feminine wisdom which has been viewed with enmity by the fearful patriarchy. We do not know more than that but we do have a narrative on how the Princess Zezolla came to be in the hearth amongst the cinders, a place between earth and fire. It was her longing for the 'Mother' she has lost: the creative feminine, the sublime and essential depth of Wisdom, the feminine realm of Sophia. This was surely not easily found in the patriarchy of that day by the emerging feminine in an adolescent girl. Zezolla tries to find it in her stepmother who, to her credit, really does attempt to give Zezolla the love and teaching that she needs. But all this happens in the outer secular realm that is subservient to the patriarchy; there is no connection with that deeper heart place for which Zezolla longs. She rejects the life of a noble woman in the patriarchy and the patriarchy likewise rejects her.

I think this could reflect the original 'fall' of the Feminine, even of the divine Sophia. The women of that world, her stepmother and stepsisters reject her. So, she is left to follow her own spiritual path in her heart. The mystical feminine is disguised by a frog skin in the *Frog Princess* story, or veiled and hidden in the hearth among the cinders in this story - both quietly working on themselves in a deeply inner way. They have not forgotten who they are and their real spiritual essence, and they know, or at least intuit, their purpose in life. Zezolla accepts her guide and teacher is the Dove of the Fairies in Sardinia and she clearly understands the tradition that she was born into. In the *Golden Chisel* story, the hero also knew and understood his tradition, and so was able to do the inner work alone, and evolve spiritually without an outer teacher. This is a rare phenomenon, but recognised amongst Sufis.

So, for Zezolla to be stripped of her name, her real identity, and given a new name befitting her new humble 'lowly' status in life seems to be a mean and demeaning act from the point of view of the patriarchy. From this point of the story, we will now refer to Zezolla as Cenerentola, until she is recognised as the wise and spiritual woman that she truly is. In truth, a mystical person has to learn to 'be in this world but not of it' as the Sufis say. What I find fascinating here is the realisation that the hearth was the realm of the once supreme Goddess, Hestia, in times before the patriarchy and the worship of Zeus dominated. Hestia's domain is the realm of Sophia and it encompasses the mystical aspects of the heart and hearth, as being our own centre, the centre of the home, the community and the state. This realm is about peace, the rejection of war and conflict, with an absence of ego. It is the dominion of Love and Harmony, a place where the heart is King.

Now the Prince (Cenerentola's father) must go to Sardinia on affairs of state, so he asks his daughters what gifts they would like brought back for them. The stepdaughters want all sorts of things that girls would want like - dresses, hair ornaments, trinkets and toys. Then the prince asked his own daughter 'as if in mockery', 'What would you have, Child?' She answers, 'Nothing, Father, but that you commend me to the Dove of the Fairies and bid her send me something; and if you forget my request, may you be unable to stir backwards or forwards; so remember what I tell you, for it will fare with you accordingly.' Her request is extraordinary, in that she tells her father clearly what she wants, what he must do, and what to say exactly, as well as the consequences should he forget. Metaphorically, this will happen if he ignores his feminine spiritual side, his real daughter. The real Cenerentola is no shrinking violet, but a wise and strong woman, who is working to complete herself and who knows she needs a teacher and practices to do this.

The prince goes about his business in Sardinia, but he does indeed forget Cenerentola and her request. On boarding the ship to take him home, he finds that the ship is stuck fast just as Cenerentola foretold. When he realises what he has done, he goes immediately to the Grotto of the Fairies, commending his daughter to them and asking for them to send her something, precisely as Cenerentola asked. The request is like a ritual prayer to the Dove of the Fairies. As a result, a beautiful maiden steps forth from the Grotto, thanks his daughter for her remembrances, sends her love and tells the Prince that his daughter should be merry and of good heart out of love for her. This message is all about Love and the heart. Then the beautiful fairy gives him a date tree, a hoe, a little gold bucket and a silk napkin, for Cenerentola, adding that the bucket is to water the plant with. Cenerentola is overjoyed with her gift, and immediately plants the date tree in a pretty pot, hoes the earth around it, waters it and wipes the leaves morning and evening with the silken napkin. She now has a beautiful practice of devotion to do every morning and evening. This part of her journey is complete. Cenerentola has connected with her teacher, the Dove of the Fairies, and has been given practices, similar indeed to those practices still given to this day by spiritual groups and Sufis.

She does these practices with delight and love and she grows very quickly in the inner arts. like the 'Art of Personality' which Hazrat Inayat Khan talks about in his teachings. The growth of the date tree and her inner growth mirror each other, so that it comes to a point where she can make a wish and it will manifest. Her first wish is to be able to come and go from the house at will, without being noticed by her stepmother or stepsisters. She is able to go about her business unknown and unseen, just like the Frog Princess.

Then there was to be a great feast where the young King was to attend. These celebrations were probably held on the summer and winter solstices at a time of transition in the heavens when the Celts believe that the realm of Fairy is felt to be close to that of mankind. They call this the 'Thin Place', which is the in-between space in time where anything can happen

On three occasions, after Cenerentola's sisters have left for the ball, she runs quickly to her little date tree and repeats her incantation and makes her wish. Each time she has become stronger and more powerful in her practice. The first time she sees herself as a Queen, the second time, young damsels appear and prepare her for the ball, so that she is decked out 'as glorious as the sun', and the third time, she instantly finds herself 'splendidly arrayed and seated in a coach of gold' with many servants around her, so that she looked just like a Queen. Each time her stepmother and sisters do not recognize Cenerentola, but she is noticed by the young King who becomes ever more fascinated, curious and attracted to her. He feels he has to find out more about her and where she lives. So each time, as Cenerentola leaves the feast, the King sends his servant (representing his ego) to follow her.

The first time when Cenerentola sees that she is being followed by the young King's servant, she throws down some gold coins to distract him and quietly returns home to her usual place in the hearth among the cinders, leaving the servant to scrabble on the ground gathering up the gold coins. Next time the servant follows Cenerentola on her way home, but now she throws pearls and jewels (aspects of the feminine) which she uses to distract him, so that she can slip away yet again. The final and third time, as Cenerentola leaves the ball-room, the King's servant keeps close to her coach. He is no longer able to be distracted, but runs swiftly by her side. This shows that the King and his servant (his ego) are also gaining in mastery. As the coach now sets off at such a pace, the servant is not able to keep up on foot. Cenerentola runs away quickly and loses one of her pretty slippers. The servant dejectedly picks up the slipper and takes it to the King, telling him everything that had happened.

The King on seeing the slipper remarks that if the 'basement' is so beautiful, then the rest of the 'building' must be truly beautiful. He has to find out where his beautiful 'Queen' is to be found.

He makes a proclamation to summon all the maidens in the country, high born and low, beautiful and ugly, to a banquet, so that he can try the slipper on all those assembled. Of course, the slipper does not fit any of those maidens assembled. In this story it does not describe the slipper as being of glass, as in the Cinderella story, and many think glass is a mistranslation. But the slipper is really a metaphor for a standpoint – a place where the maiden touches the earth. It could even be said to be the in-between place between Cenerentola and the earth. This would be totally unique to Cenerentola, and so no one else could claim it.

As the slipper did not fit any of the assembled maidens, her father had to admit that his daughter had been left behind. His excuse being that 'she is always on the hearth and furthermore is a graceless simpleton who is unworthy to sit at the King's table.' How terribly shocking this is, but it is really another version of the frog skin. The divine Sophia, in this case Cenerentola, has had to be in hiding so to speak, to protect herself.

The fully evolved feminine *Sophia* or *Hestia* still needs to find her male counterpart, her King. Each has to find the other so that they can rule together in harmony and in peace, but it must be said that without Sophia, the King cannot rule. She is at the centre of the heart / hearth, the home, community and state. Her qualities are Sufi qualities and in living our practice and our realisations we live the Sufi life. To achieve Unity and experience what this really is, leads further and deeper into the Mystery. It is not a goal or something to achieve, it is a process of Being and of constant realisation.

Resolution and Understanding

My personal journey began with the horrifying theft of my little five year old girl's heart, and its replacement with a hailstone by the wicked witch. I had wondered if something had happened to me when I was five years old that might have frozen my warm and happy child's heart. Before I was born, my parents fled Vienna (in early 1939) after Hitler's Anschluss, a flight that I think my mother never quite recovered from. They found a new home in a small community of refugees in Derry, Northern Ireland. My birth in 1943 heralded a new beginning for these disparate people in a place so far from the culture of pre-war Vienna. Then I remembered! When I was five, my mother took me on a journey through post war Europe to visit her family in Vienna. My mother was not Jewish, but had converted to marry my father. My father was the only one of his family except for his mother, to survive the Holocaust, but I was not consciously aware of any of this for many years to come. So, already the shadow of the Shoah must have been felt in the depths of my outwardly happy life.

On that journey to Vienna I remember being frightened and cold, waiting for trains to arrive at empty platforms, in the darkness - trains which never seemed to come. I was terrified of using the toilet on the train by myself. It was so loud and noisy out in the corridor, the toilet door was heavy and I thought I should never get out again if I ever entered. In the toilet I could see the track flashing by below and thought I would surely fall in. I suppose my mother must have shown this to me at some stage but then probably refused to leave our luggage in the carriage to accompany me. I was left to face the monster toilet on my own. I could not, and so of course I wet myself out there in the rocking corridor. I eventually arrived in Vienna to meet all my aunties feeling very uncomfortable, miserable and alone - I was too ashamed to tell anybody. My mother was so entranced at being with her sisters again that I was ignored, or at least that is how I felt.

Then, later, I remembered seeing the terrible destruction of the bombing in Vienna. The building where my parents had lived, on what was once the beautiful and elegant Mariahilferstrasse, was a heap of rubble. I felt my mother's distress. She did not even know which building her home had been. There was nothing left of that beautiful elegant life and home she had known. I remember her weeping bitterly! Did my mother's distress and my experiences in Europe in 1948 seep into my being and turn my heart into a hailstone? Was my once warm and happy heart so very overwhelmed? And my adored father was not with me to love and hold me. I so missed him.

So, it is then that in my odyssey through these five fairy tales, I marvelled at what I had discovered -the vestiges of real spiritual truths within the narratives. The symbols were consistent through all the tales, with the exception perhaps of the more modern story of the *Little Humpbacked Horse*. Although they came from such a diverse range of countries and cultures, the thread of spiritual knowledge in the stories held together. There is an underlying Truth that suggests their mystical origin: that they were once used as teaching tales, much as Sufi stories which are used to this very day.

In addition, I wanted to explore aspects of feminine spirituality – I was annoyed that so often the hero in fairy tales I had read was male. In Sufi poetry, the Beloved is so often female, so how was I as a woman to have a loving relationship with the Beloved? Was she my soul? How does the feminine relate to the Soul when she is Soul herself? There are so many kinds of Love with only one word in English for this. I had to discover the various aspects of Love and what it was that had been frozen in me.

When I first heard the story of Golden Chisel at a retreat many years ago, it opened up a whole new world for me. The 'Truth' I was searching for seemed to lie even in this very ancient Chinese tale. I realized that, I too have been creating my own 'Ideal of God' and that this has been constantly evolving. The 'God out there', of my childhood Sunday school was now obsolete for me.

After my interest in *Golden Chisel*, Nawab simply sent me a story when he felt I needed one. These fairy tales were a means of guidance for me. I learned from them in ways I did not realise, especially regarding the importance of both the stories and my guidance through them. A wonderful 'field' is created when a Teacher is connected to the deep imaginal realm of the heart. There is no ego present and so the 'villagers' in Golden Chisel and students, hearing the teacher, understand the message, each according to their own level of evolution. The more 'realised' people there are in a group, the stronger the 'field'. This kind of transmission cannot be learned from books; it must come directly from the living heart; from the sacred 'field'.

When our inner guide is damaged, as was the little stone ram in Golden Chisel, this transmission cannot occur, as I experienced myself. At one time I was totally disconnected from the inner flow of the 'Water of Life', even in my daily practice. It was a terrible feeling. For two years I struggled with my reactive feelings - hurt, resentment and frustration at the situation I found myself in. I was frozen in a space and felt abandoned and 'let down' by my teacher, who (rightly) refused to get involved. In the end, my antagonist and I, in our common frustration, were able to meet and be open with one another. Although completely different in our temperament and background, we were able to find more common ground than we would have imagined. It was through this goodwill that we were able to re-forge the 'fore-foot' of our personal ram with compassion and love – the gold with which the new forepaw was forged. We had both suffered through this, but now understood one another and were able to become loving friends. The water flowed again for both of us and I am eternally glad that we had achieved this beautiful outcome.

We had both resented our teacher for not 'helping' or facilitating us in resolving our differences, but this is not the place of the teacher. The teacher is not a therapist, or a friend, or a life coach. Kabir Helminski tells the story of an old Sufi Shaikh who refused to allow himself to take the role of Shaikh in his group saying, 'If I am your Shaikh, there will be no one to show you how to treat a teacher. Choose someone from among yourselves, and then see the kind of support and respect that I give to him or her. That will be best for you.'[26]

We have to learn how to treat the teacher; with the utmost respect, and love – every hint or suggestion made should be examined and followed. Many students do not even pick up on the 'hint of the Shaikh'! A teacher will never give advice either, although they may well make suggestions sometimes. My own teacher would sometimes say, after a lengthy pause "Well, Nuria, have you considered -----?" That works. I know of one student who would argue for hours, given the chance, and would not accept the hint or suggestion of the teacher, and so she has not progressed at all over many years. Her ego will not allow her 'let go' of her own ideas and understanding of truth. As the old Shaikh said, we have to learn to be a mureed (student) first. In the words of Hazrat Inayat Khan: 'The relation that exists between Murshid and mureed is so subtle and so delicate that only a few persons can understand it. It is not a relationship between a professor and a student. It is not a relation between an engineer and apprentice. The one who does not know it, for him it is nothing; the one who knows it, for him it is everything'. The teacher cannot confer illumination. When the oil is ready, he can provide the spark. So, this complex and subtle relationship develops over the years. We must not see our Shaikh as a human being, in the sense of an ordinary imperfect person with their flaws and foibles, but as an 'embodiment of the Master, the Spirit of Guidance.' Eventually when we have internalised our teacher to such an extent, then we have annihilated our ego in the state of 'Fana Fi Shaikh'.

It must be understood that false teachers and prophets do exist and we must be very careful in choosing our teacher. Generally, when a person presents him or herself as a teacher, dresses the part and gives a good performance, they are not necessarily authentic teachers. The real teacher is extra-ordinarily ordinary and hidden: s/he has to be found. When I first saw my own teacher he was dressed very casually and doing his ironing in the corridor of a retreat centre. I was not impressed.

---

[26] Kabir Helminisky, *The Knowing Heart. A Sufi Path of Transformation*, Shambhala, Boston, 2000, p.123.

There is an amusing Sufi story which demonstrates this fascination with phenomena and hoped for 'magic' in our leaders. A wise old Shaikh was sitting in the village square with his mureeds around him when a pigeon dropped out of the sky dead in from of him. He picked up the poor bird which was totally lifeless, held it tenderly in his hands, breathed a long Huuuu—and the bird came back to life and flew off into the sky. This act did not go unnoticed and before long there were many people interested in the Shaikh. His followers grew until he did not have so much time for his original mureeds. Then one day, after Zikar, the Shaikh lifted his buttock and emitted a loud fart. The people were astounded that this holy man could do such a thing. Very soon the people withdrew from the group until it was nearly the size it had been originally. Those remaining were disappointed but the Shaikh remarked, 'You see, there are those who come because of a pigeon, and leave because of a fart.'

Many expect to be spoon-fed when they sit in a group, but the teacher cannot confer illumination. It is long and difficult work. Sometimes even the Tsar or King is not genuine, as is seen in the story of the *Little-Humpbacked Horse*.

Rasul is a Teacher or Messenger who has brought and transmitted the message and Hazrat Inayat Khan is that Rasul for those of us who follow the Universal Sufism of Hazrat Inayat Khan. He passed from us on 5 February 1927. When we are open and the spark has ignited in us, then the fire of Love illuminates our heart. The teacher can be closer to us after death, than when he was alive. Hazrat Inayat Khan said, 'Those who come after me will have the possibility of being closer to me than those who know me in the flesh.' His work in bringing a form of Universal Sufism to the West was unique and difficult, but he brought his teachings whose central message is Love, Harmony and Beauty, to the world and welcomed all and was open to everyone. So, we eventually also reach the stage of Fana Fi Rasul, where our ego is melted into that of our teacher and there only exists the One.

The *Fairy of the Dawn* is an unusual tale; there are clear stages and depths in the spiritual quest. In the first stage, the guide or teacher is the archetypal wise woman or witch as embodied in the hero's nurse, who had also been his father's nurse. She is already denigrated as a witch, but guides the hero to find his steed, his magical horse who helps him fight the fierce dragon guarding the gateway over the abyss to the inner realm of '*Alam al-mithal*'. I find it interesting that this witch also helps the brothers, so she does not discriminate – much like the angels.

In the first two tales of *Golden Chisel* and the *Little Humpbacked Horse* there seems to be no external teacher, but in each an inner guide is won or crafted. The stone ram of Golden Chisel, the little humpbacked horse of Ivan, and the brown horse of Petru each take the role of a *Psychopomp*, or steed, which carries and guides the hero from one realm to the next. In the story of *The Fairy of the Dawn*, it is the nurse and guide who teaches the hero, Petru, how to find his magical brown horse, which then guides and carries him to the other realms as a true *Psychopomp*. So in these five stories, there appear three flying steeds to carry and guide our heroes.

In each story there is a journey to be made through the inner realms, to places which we begin to recognize. There are woods where we encounter magical creatures like the Firebird, and the Tsar Maid in the *Little Humpbacked Horse* and in the copper, silver and gold woods in *Fairy of the Dawn*, where the hero overcomes the Welwas and gains more magical horses to guide him. When we go deeper into ourselves, as the heroes' journey deeper into their centre, they come into the land of the Goddesses, the great Feminine Essence. In the *Little Humpbacked Horse* story, it is the ocean and the moon, In *Golden Chisel* it is the Yellow River, and in the *Fairy of the Dawn* it is the realm of the three Goddesses. Here the heroes encounter the great inner teachers like the Baba Yaga and the Goddess Venus / Freya, who are very similar in many ways. They teach the heroes how and where to find their goal, be it the release of the Princess Vassilisa or to gain the Water of Life to heal the Emperor, Empire and the Goddess Venus / Freya. The Feminine has been relegated to a very negative aspect and this is the wounding to be found and healed in each of these stories.

In *Fairy of the Dawn*, our hero is told to trust no one on his return home. In fact, his brothers, when he meets them, try to trick him out of the sacred water and take all credit for themselves. In the *Little*

Humpbacked Horse, Ivan's brothers similarly try to trick him so that they can steal his horses. We can learn from this that, even though we achieve the highest realms and levels of mystical knowledge, our egos can still betray us and steal our inner connection. We have to be constantly vigilant.

Once there, the various difficult and dangerous challenges of life are to be negotiated. We must not allow ourselves to be distracted, otherwise the demons have to be fought again and again. We must endure fire and ice to arrive at the next level. Next, we find ourselves in the realm of each of the Goddesses, who it seems to me are relegated to their own realms and are no longer revered or even noticed in our world any more.

I find this very sad and disappointing, but I have certainly encountered this attitude in my career in my working life. The feminine in many of its aspects must be hidden. Only in my practice of psychology could my feminine side be used openly, in empathy or 'feeling with' another. This is healing, as demonstrated in Petru's encounter with Venus / Freya. But our hero, and we ourselves, must recognise and be guided by our inner teacher in whatever form. We must learn to treat each Goddess with the greatest of respect so that she can help us in our major opus. When in her white castle the Fairy of the Dawn guards the sacred and healing water of life. To confront her openly would be dangerous: when we are in the presence of great spiritual power, it can be so overwhelming; we lose all sense of ourselves and cannot function at all. This happened to me once when in the presence of a great teacher. I still do not quite remember anything of what I did or said for that whole afternoon. I just could not function consciously. So we must learn to pacify this greatest of all Fairies by playing the flute of Krishna and making the sacred sound Hu to put her and her court to 'sleep', so that we can achieve our aim to take the water.

When we chant Zikar and turn around our own centre, we remember the Divine One Allah. Nothing else is there, either beautiful or horrible to distract. There is only One. Then, we gain the Water of Life. We must not allow ourselves to be so overwhelmed that we cannot function. Thus, only then can we can take the Water of Life, while kissing the Great Fairy of the Dawn, and crowning her with the golden wreath we have woven from our spiritual life. In this tale as in the story of the *Little Humpbacked Horse*, we become aware of betrayal and trickery by our nearest and dearest. These are profound lessons. Who can we trust? Only our inner guide and teacher. This is another of our great realisations.

In my dream, mentioned earlier, I found myself face to face with the source of life and water, the verdant place which is also the home of the teacher or guide. The creature from the deep was Lover and Guide, in a quite different way to the Friend who was right there behind me. The creature gave love and warmth and touch. It was a numinous heartfelt feeling.

The Frog Princess story has the hero first using his intuition (shooting an arrow) to find his Soul, his wife. She is his Frog Princess, but he has a long and hard journey to discover who she really was and how to rid her of her frog skin. I could really relate to this story right from the beginning, because of the recognition that I had also hidden behind a sort of frog skin for many years and that it was only by being forced to 'come out' from behind the frog skin that I was able to move on with my life. I was always at the back or in the middle of a group and would never ever have ventured to be out front and leading. As one of my bosses said once, 'she leads from behind' it was very insightful of him. One year I was a participant at our International Summer School in Holland, fully expecting to be part of the audience and enjoy the experience and the teachings. Imagine my horror when Pir-o-Murshid Hidayat Inayat-Khan, our Leader, asked me to read one of the Sacred Teachings the next afternoon, in front of the whole assembled Sufi school. I could, of course, not refuse!

One of the senior leaders, soon to become my mentor, took me outside and had me practice projecting my voice towards our Heart and Wings symbol high on the wall of the Temple. I have a soft, quiet voice and so had great difficulty with this. By the next day I was in a state of nervous collapse and as I stood doing practices in the small chapel next to the hall, I wondered where I would get the inner strength and support needed to perform this task. Certainly not from Pir-o-Murshid

Hidayat, or Murshid Nawab, who would be in the front row. Then I felt that our Murshid and Rasul, Hazrat Inayat Khan, was there right behind me. I understood that I should let go of my fear, my ego and small self, and let him, my inner teacher speak through me. This I was able to do. However, when up on the stage and asked to move perhaps a few inches towards the raised microphone, my feet were glued to the floor. I could not move. My knees knocked and my legs shook. Luckily, I was wearing a long yellow robe and so I hope no one noticed the quivers. Afterwards – and again I have no memory of giving the teaching - Pir-o-Murshid Hidayat came up to me with tears in his eyes, gave me a huge hug and told me I sounded just like his mother when she gave similar teachings. I had been able to throw off my frog skin and show an authentic part of myself. I could be someone that I did not yet know, and I needed to learn this at a very deep level. Things were never the same again after that, and I can now happily put my small self aside and let Hazrat Inayat Khan 'come through' in a loving way. It was not a performance, as my ego was not involved – it had gone to sleep.

In the *Frog Princess* story, Princess Vassilisa flies away to the realm of Kashchey the Deathless, when her frog skin was burned. Perhaps, had I not conquered my fear, and put my ego to sleep, I too would have 'flown away' to that dark realm where Kashchey rules, rules, to put on a performance of how I thought I should act, rather than coming from the Heart. It is pretending to be what we are not which belongs to the world of Kashchey.

The Baba Yaga really had an impact on me. I could feel and imagine her magical, mysterious 'house' on its spindly leg, facing the deep dark forest. In other stories she actually flies on a broomstick, much like the flying steeds which carry the heroes. That the prince was not afraid and knew exactly what to say to her and do to make the house turn towards him thus giving him access to the Baba Yaga, deeply impressed me. He had learned mastery while on his journey through life with his earlier 'Wise Old Man'. He meets the Baba Yaga with such courage, he even scolds her for not greeting him properly. I was astounded that he could do this. This puts Baba Yaga in the realm of being a powerful teacher, who will only help the seeker who has evolved enough to trust that her role is to help him fulfil his quest, if he understands and follows her advice implicitly. She knows before being told, exactly what has happened to the princess, where she is, and how to rescue her. The prince needs great mastery and feminine wisdom for this task – it is very tricky indeed. In the intricate process guided by Baba Yaga, our hero, the prince, has to bring all his previous knowledge and experience to bear.

This last series of tasks is long and complex. All the creatures he has previously helped, now come to his aid; they could be understood as representing traits, or aspects of ourselves, which we discover and use on our journey. The traits, or instincts, are not necessarily positive from our usual point of view, so we notice that the prince actually wants to 'kill' them when they first appear to him earlier in the story. We understand that we must get to know and recognise all the parts of ourselves, so that we can recognise them in others and understand how to deal with them. The bear represents great strength and fortitude which is needed to uproot the great oat tree that holds the cask in its crown. The inner structure has to be uprooted before we can move on. Our whole understanding of our world, our attitude, background, beliefs and culture have to be destroyed to make way for transformation. Then the cask falls out of the tree and is smashed to pieces, so we understand that there is indeed something locked away in our inner cask, which contains the seeds of the next stage. It releases a hare which jumps out of the chest and runs as fast as it can go. The hare could represent nimbleness of mind outwitting dull brute force, but the hare is also a companion of witches and of Freya, the great Goddess of Love. But immediately another hare races out of the chest, catches the first hare and tears it to pieces.

When we discover a trait within ourselves, such as being quick witted, we have to develop this and understand it – really know it, but then it becomes your enemy and so has to be defeated, by the very trait it has become. It takes a thief to catch a thief. So, if we become quick-witted, we could in fact become very tricky, indeed the hare is the creature of the trickster. So, this aspect has to be overcome by itself. We know and understand it and so use that nimbleness to 'catch' it when we are tempted to use it. Of course, by recognizing these traits in ourselves and saving them, so to speak, we learn to recognise them in others, so that they can be combated. Every trait has its uses – in the right time, and the right place.

Next a duck manifests out of the pieces of the hare and flies up into the sky. The duck can be seem as deceit, or chatter, and could easily follow the mastery of quick-wittedness. Deceit follows the trickster, and this too has to be recognised, and even used. Every trait in us has its uses but then we learn to master it. Now a drake flies after the duck, striking it to release the cosmic egg – the hidden origin and mystery of Being - which falls into the sea. Prince Ivan weeps bitter tears and is in despair – how can he find this precious egg? Just as Ivan in the story of the *Little Humpbacked Horse*, waits for the Tsar of the deep to find the Tsar maid's signet ring. There is a time in many of these stories, where the hero feels this way, at a most difficult stage in the quest. It seems to be part of the process, so we should not lose hope when we too fall into a depression. We also need patience, as there is a distortion of time when we are in the depths of the inner realm. It seems very, very long. But suddenly a pike swims up out of the depths with the egg in its mouth. We do not know how this has happened. The pike, like the feisty perch in the *Little Humpbacked Horse*, is a fighting fish – aggressive and cannibalistic. So, again, there is a quality that is necessary on the quest. Sometimes it is anger and aggression that we need to fight our adversaries, but we must be in control of this anger and use it wisely. It is now the prince who breaks the egg and finds the needle whose point he must break. The most difficult and subtle task. It is like finding the tiniest dot, which is at the centre of the circle, which is everything. How do we do this? That point contains the whole universe – with singlemindedness, focus and concentration, we can break that point, so that we know that we are part of the One. When this happens we are free and Kashchey (the world of materialism and the ego) is dead to us.

If we examine the quandary of the husband in the story of the trophy wife, we might get some idea of what would have to occur for him to redeem his wife. He would have to examine and expose every aspect of his desire for his inner beautiful 'Princess Vassilisa', as he saw her at the feast, as she was when he first fell in love with her some twenty years ago. He would have to acknowledge his ego and pride, which wanted to show her off to the world. His expectations that she would always be what he wanted her to be, in the bedroom, kitchen and as a mother and mate. With each act he would have driven her further and further away from him by treating her as an object and the vessel for the expectations of his small self. That the prince was able to achieve this, says much about his love, courage and humility - to first uproot the giant oak tree representing the whole structure that his attitudes and assumptions were based on. The goal being the seemingly impossible task of breaking the point of the needle – the point where he burned her frog skin. This act had to be overturned. Having done this, he finds her running towards him from the white castle where she had been held. She –the beloved, who is his soul, is freed.

In the *Cenerentola* story we see the process and journey from the feminine mystical perspective. Here the teacher and guide is the Dove of the Fairies and we get some beautiful insights into the practices and being of Cenerentola, as a Queen in her own right, much like the Tsar Maid who becomes a female Tsar. I was much buoyed by the knowledge that the more we do our practices, the stronger we will get, so that we can achieve anything we wish for. I was further enchanted by the total belief system of Hestia / Sophia and how much it was in tune with Sufism. If we understand that the Heart is the centre of our home, our community and our State, and that its governor must be a devotee of that Goddess, then we can feel how this can create the Love, Harmony and Peace, and Beauty necessary for a spiritual Life. How we can make this happen in our world is a big issue, but it must begin with ourselves, how we are in our own Being, so that others can see that it is the only way to be happy and at peace.

In remembering the tale which so frightened me as a child, I wondered what was its outcome? How did the little princess get her heart back in the original fairy tale? At a New Year's party some years ago, someone recognized the story and was able to give me the name of the book and its author. It was not, in fact, an ancient fairy tale, but one written and published in the 1940s. It was 'The Little Pearl Heart' in the Kathleen Fidler *Omnibus*. I found a copy and discovered why I had forgotten it. Even as a child I must have sensed there was something deeply wrong with the whole premise as far as I was concerned! The hero was a young boy, who, having a long series of rather tedious adventures replaces her stolen heart with a pearl. The princess, cold, hard and passive with her hailstone heart, seemed to be unable to do this for herself: she needed the male hero to do it for her. I must have found this unsatisfying as a child.

The narrative of Cenerentola's process was thus such a relief and so healing for me, mainly because Zezolla the heroine was the only one whose inner journey is told. She did not need a hero to undertake the quest for her. I could totally relate to this especially as a Sufi. Historically, there seemed to be a basis to her story, and in it we understand the complete process of soul from young girl without a mother, to the Being of the Goddess Sophia. In a sense, it is so easy to relate to and I loved the exposition of the practices that she was given by the Dove of the Fairy. They are so much like our Sufi practices, and the outcome is also the same. The story was so accessible once I had recognised the key.

My Story - Woven In

During the past five years I was on a quest to discover who and what my father's family were, and thus in some ways finding who I was. These family members were never spoken of, to the point that I did not even realise that I knew nothing about them. It was just the way it was, and I never questioned it. However, I must have somehow taken in a lot by osmosis, so that the shadow of the Shoah became my own shadow. My search for my ancestors on my paternal grandmother and grandfather's side led me to finally know who I was and where I came from – a family of philosophers, rabbis, historians, industrialists, merchants, butchers, and traders. They all perished in the Shoah (twelve close relatives) except for my grandmother and my aunt, and in the process I found my father's second cousin, who got out of Vienna by Kindertransport as a young girl, and who now lives in New York, aged 90. I watched an interview with her where she told of her experiences and of working with children who had been released from concentration camps after the war. My protective barrier started to crack – tears came and I could not fight them off. I was faced with the reality of what had happened to my family and the desperate cruelty that humans are capable of.

Shortly after this, I was sent a link to a 'young' friend of my parents who I knew quite well when I was a teenager. She had been liberated from Belsen when she was perhaps 15 years old. She had barely survived but took up art as a form of therapy. She painted what she had experienced as a child in the Lodz Ghetto, Auschwitz, the death march and Belsen, and with each picture there was a poem. (*The Last Goodbye, Holocaust Paintings and Poems*, by Edith Hofmann). I downloaded this book and had a complete meltdown. I cannot describe the images in picture and poem, but the one that affected me most was a picture of skeletal sets of twins behind barbed wire – they were being experimented on. My two sons are identical twins. I still weep when I think of this! So my heart, which was frozen, finally broke open, as Nawab once told me it needed to. 'Your heart has to break – open, Nuria' he said. This was the only way I could melt my hailstone heart and regain my own warm and happy heart. It was a breakthrough and totally unexpected. Things have been so different since then, although this was only a short time ago! These events happened in parallel and in such a synchronistic way that I can only believe that my journey had a purpose and was divinely guided.

In reflecting on the major themes within these tales, I found that they were also fundamental Sufi teachings. Finding those deep and in-between places is a common theme in fairy tales; from the centre of the dried pond of the village in *Golden Chisel*, through to the bog and the veranda in the *Frog Princess*, and the window sill in Cenerentola. We can all find this space within us and there are, of course practices, that help take you there. From doing these practices we achieve realisations, which enliven us and realign us with the divine being, and provide a base, like the hearth, from which to work. These realisations inform the practice and are actually never ending. This is life changing.

The other great symbol that is common in these fairy tales, is that of the heart, represented by the Russian stove which is linked to the spiritual guide. The hearth also represents the heart, the fire of the heart and the divine love, which is the energy and fuel for our life's work. Murshid Hidayat Inayat-Khan has repeatedly said that Sufism is the mystical base or core of all religions, and there is certainly evidence of this in the old mystery Goddess religions of ancient times. People were taught through the oral practice of storytelling and some stories still contain vestiges of these old truths, wisdom and practice. Sufism is the religion of the heart, if it is a religion at all.

I was reminded that my own process has been through these fairy tales, given to me by my teacher. The tales themselves evolved, as I have told here, but there was no conscious thought as to their choice. Nawab offered stories and I chose those that appealed to me at the time. I did not actually reject too many. Intuition is indeed a wonderful thing; when the student is ready the teachings will appear. That they have held together and told such a beautiful story of the feminine – of the soul and our inner journey and evolution, shows that they have a true, mystical grounding. I am so grateful to my teachers Pir-o-Murshid Inayat-Khan, and Murshid Nawab, as well as our Sufi community, for sustaining and supporting me over the years.

I hope you enjoy the stories I have worked with, and that they will provide you too with many insights and learnings. Any insights or understandings you may have are valid and true for you, and it is important to honour your own journey. Each journey is different and yet the same.

Remember that your way is the Path of the Heart, and listen to the sometimes strange creatures and beings who are your guides and teachers along the way. These wonderful stories can be revisited time and time again, with perhaps different insights and understandings. The stories are archetypal and so contain hidden mystical dimensions for us to discover; they go back to the dawn of mankind just as Venus / Freya told Petru. They are part of us and we are part of them.

CENERENTOLA OR CINDERELLA

enerentola is an original version of the Cinderella tale, which goes back to the early 17th century and is one of a collection of tales that were gathered from Crete and Venice. This story has elements of Sufi story telling in its narrative.

It is certainly a story about the evolution of the feminine, although the introduction of the tale indicates that it is also about malice and envy in girls and women, and how they get their comeuppance. Unusually, in this tale the main characters are all female, whereas the males are archetypal or in a role, for example, the Prince, or the King. Zezolla is the main character and she is actually the only one who is named. She is the heroine whose task it is to evolve herself as a complete woman and Queen.

In the setting of the story, there is a Prince, who is a widower, who has an only daughter, Princess Zezolla - '*so dear to him that he saw with no other eyes than hers*'. So, this girl has no mother, the Prince no wife; there is no mature feminine aspect in this household. The Prince, who sees the world through the eyes of his daughter, is limited in his own inner feminine. The Prince '*kept a governess for her, who taught her chainwork, knitting, and point lace, and who showered her with such affection as no words can tell.*' However, the Princess was very lonely and longed for her mother. It shows that although the governess seemed to give her everything she could, there was still something lacking. So often we all long for the mother that we perhaps experienced in infancy – all giving, all loving, meeting our every need and desire; the 'good mother'. There is also a spiritual aspect to this longing. It is a longing for the Divine, the One Being who provides all the love and provenance we need. It is this longing for the deep spiritual aspects of Sophia / Wisdom that we are all looking for. The path of wisdom comes from this real inner feminine spiritual aspect (Sophia).

The Princess is so obsessed with the desire for Mother that she eventually convinces her governess to make an attempt to woo her father, the Prince. The governess now instructs Zezolla to do as she says, so that the Princess will have everything she wants from her as a mother. It is clear from the story that her mother has not been dead very long, as the mourning period was not yet over. At first the Prince does not take his daughter's suggestion for him to marry her governess seriously, but, as time goes by, she wears him down, so that he finally marries the governess and holds a great feast at the wedding.

It seems to me to be deeply wrong, at a psychic and spiritual level, for the Prince to marry the nurse. Jung talks about the importance of 'marrying' your equal psychologically and spiritually; our inner Beloved should be at the same level of evolution as we are. As Pir O Murshid Hidayat Inayat-Khan has said: there is a **hierarchy** of the soul, but a democracy of the heart. In other words, at a soul level, a prince should marry a princess and vice versa.

It is interesting that at the feast there is already an intimation of things to come. While the young people were dancing, Zezolla was standing at the window of her house. Why was she not also enjoying the party? Why was she not dancing with the other young people there? After all, this was what she had wanted. Whilst she was standing at the window, a dove came flying and perched upon a wall, and said to her, *'Whenever you need anything send the request to the Dove of the Fairies in the island of Sardinia, and you will instantly have your wish.'* It seems to me that the dove is like an intuition or inner voice, which tells her that she can ask for whatever she needs from 'the Dove of the Fairies'. A dove is a spiritual messenger and it is interesting that there is a small dove carved into the canopy over our Murshid's tomb. Most importantly, the dove is sacred to all Great Mothers and Queens of Heaven. Doves depict femininity and maternity. There is a difference between the dove which visits Zezolla with its message and the Dove (as a proper noun) who is clearly a person and leader of the Fairies.

The Island of Sardinia is a very interesting place for the Dove of the Fairies to reside. Sardinia is much older geologically than Italy itself and has a very old and mysterious history / mythology. Its peoples could well have been Phoenicians or Carthaginians, but much has been written suggesting that it might well be the Atlantis, as written about by Plato. It would seem that ancient Goddess religions have had a strong hold in Sardinia. It is clear also that the Princess already has a connection with and knowledge of Sardinian Fairy culture, through her parents. The Phoenicians certainly visited Sardinia in their trade – obsidian and silver were mined there and traded to all parts of the Mediterranean, especially Egypt. Astarte was the chief Goddess worshipped by the Phoenicians. She was connected with fertility, sexuality, and war and one of her symbols was the dove. So this Dove of the Fairies seems to me to be the remains of a Sophiac Goddess religion, or cult, gone underground, only to be found by the seeker who is pure of heart and the true mystic. There are vestiges of the Sophiac Goddess cult still found in Sardinia today. When Zezolla had her intuition regarding help from the Dove of the Fairies, she obviously knew about the role of Sophia – it was certainly in her field of experience. It is intriguing that Sardinia also has impressive standing stones, which are oriented east-west, that is to the winter and summer solstices, like the megalithic stone circles in Britain and Ireland, but which have not been found anywhere else in the rest of Europe.

So for five or six days, the story goes, '*the new stepmother overwhelmed Zezolla with caresses, seating her at the best place at table, giving her the choicest morsels to eat, and clothing her in the richest apparel.*' But before long the new stepmother '*began to bring forward six daughters of her own, for she had never before told anyone that she was a widow with a bunch of girls.*' I have been wondering at the significance of six girls, why six? Six is the number of harmony and equilibrium, the most productive of all numbers but it could also simply mean twice times three, which means very many daughters. The stepmother could well be the archetypal real mother, with her many daughters representing the archetypal daughter. We could say that all girls our own age are our step-sisters. The stepmother praised her daughters so much to her husband and talked them up in such a way that *'at last the stepdaughters had all his favour, and the thought of his own child went entirely from his heart. It fared so ill with the poor girl that she was finally brought down from the royal chamber to the kitchen, from the canopy of state to the hearth, from the splendid apparel of silks and gold to dishcloths.'*

The hearth becomes the new realm for Zezolla, but the hearth was in ancient times the shrine of Hestia, the first born of the Olympian gods and goddesses and the chief of the goddesses in the early days, but practically unknown later when Zeus became the chief god and the patriarchy became dominant. Every household's hearth was in fact Hestia's shrine and the implications of this are fundamental to the understanding of this story. Hestia was the daughter of the Titan God, Cronus, so she is the first of a new race of Gods on Olympus. The symbolism of the hearth should not be overlooked; it becomes the realm of Cenerentola. The central hearth also had a ritualistic focus for government and was served by the most powerful state officials. Hestia is the virgin goddess of the hearth, and also of architecture and the right ordering of domesticity, the family and the state. It is said that both Apollo and Poseidon vied for her hand in marriage, but for her to choose one over the other would have meant war, so she chose to remain a virgin and serve her brother, Zeus, in his household hearth. Peace became one of Hestia's major attributes. Her name means the Essence, the true nature of things. We see that Zezolla's descent to the hearth and becoming Cenerentola really means that she is now, quietly and unobtrusively in the service of the feminine, of Sophia / Hestia and the inner life and mysteries

It was Hestia's traits, not her actions that most defined her, Hestia was gentle, mild, forgiving, peaceful, serene, dignified, calm, secure, stable, welcoming and, above all else, well-centred, the guardian of inmost things. She was non-judgmental and forgiving, her "unconditional love" and calm acceptance inspired the love and trust of others in return. Dependable and caring, Hestia was always there for others and helped them to manage their lives, which were certainly more exciting than her own.

The circle symbolized Hestia as the 'complete' goddess, the goddess who was whole, 'one complete within herself'. Hestia was seen as, not only psychologically 'centred', but also as representing the centre, the centre of the home and family, the city, and even the world itself.

As the Goddess of Architecture, Hestia intended that homes should be built from the centre out, with the centre being a hearth that contained her sacred flame.

In her longing for 'mother', Zezolla in a sense chose to move from the life of a princess, to a place of the heart and hearth, of the feminine qualities of the Goddess Hestia, and so to serve the great Goddess. It was a fall within.

Not only was her condition changed, but even her name, for, instead of Zezolla, she was now called Cenerentola'. Poor Zezolla was brought down from the royal chambers and royal life, to the hearth and the cinders, so that she even lost her name. She was no longer called Zezolla, but Cenerentola. The significance of this name change should not be overlooked. In Sufism when we are initiated on the path we are given a Sufi name by our teacher and guide, usually one of the 99 Beautiful Names, or aspects of Allah. It is much the same in other religions - in Christianity we are given a Christian name at baptism, and choose the name of Christian saint at confirmation. A new name indicates an initiation into a new way of being and a new life. What a huge change for the Princess. The Prince was a man who loved his daughter and respected her, but who was perhaps easily led, distracted, or manipulated in his feelings. His own feminine feeling side was not developed and so he relied on the women in his life to take care of these things. He had lost his inner connection to Sophia, the Divine Feminine, Sophia / Hestia, his inner wisdom, his soul. Men can often leave the emotional side of life to their womenfolk, rather than connect directly. It could be that the Prince had got so caught up, or involved in the hard outer material side of the feminine (from his new wife and step-daughters), that he easily forgot his real daughter, or at least put her out of his mind, as perhaps recognising her existence was not comfortable for him. The Princess Zezolla has now taken on her most important aspect in her evolution of the true inner feminine / Sophia. The beautiful, peaceful and wise aspects, which are inner and unseen.

She now 'lives' in that inner world or realm, at the centre or heart of the household and the world.

The story continues: *'It happened that the Prince had occasion to go to Sardinia upon affairs of state, and calling the six stepdaughters, asked them one by one, what they would like him to bring them on his return.'* Interesting that he is going to that very ancient land where the Goddess Hestia was once powerful, and also interesting that he is going on affairs of state, given that officials of state in ancient times were the follows and devotees of Hestia. The girls wanted girlie things – dresses, head-ornaments, makeup, toys and trinkets. *'Then the Prince asked his own daughter, as if in mockery, 'what would you have, Child?' 'Nothing, Father,' she replied, 'but that you commend me to the Dove of the Fairies, and bid her send me something; and if you forget my request, may you be unable to stir backwards or forwards; so remember what I tell you, for it will fare with you accordingly.'*

This is extraordinary really. First of all, the Prince asks his daughter 'as if in mockery'. Does this mean that he is afraid to show his only daughter kindness and courtesy in front of his new wife and step-daughters? Perhaps his attitude had changed so much that he no longer saw her as his beloved daughter, and had so repressed his knowledge of her. Again we see that Zezolla wants to establish her connection to the Dove of the Fairies in Sardinia.

The Dove of the Fairies

That her father is going there on state business surely means that there has been a familial connection with the place and that the Princess is well aware of this and connected to it. What is also interesting is that Zezolla knows or intuits that her father will forget her request and so lets him know that his forgetfulness will have certain negative consequences. Zezolla has a knowledge and understanding of the group and culture of the Dove of the Fairies and the required procedures in that relationship. All spiritual groups have this kind of understanding in their process. This also shows that Zezolla is a strong and wise woman and certainly no shrinking violet. The more modern image of 'Cinderella' as languishing amongst the ashes of the hearth is completely misplaced.

'Then the Prince went his way and did his business in Sardinia and procured all the things that his stepdaughters had asked for, but poor Zezolla was quite out of his thoughts. Going on board a ship to set sail to return, he found that the ship could not get out of the harbour, there it stuck fast just as if held by a sea-lamprey.' So by ignoring his daughter (soul) or forgetting her completely, his whole psyche was stuck and unable to move in the ocean of the unconscious Unity. This happens when the true feminine or soul is ignored. We get stuck and cannot move out into the vastness of the inner ocean. The Prince was now completely involved in the material outer world with his new wife and stepdaughters and his inner spiritual connection with the feminine was forgotten.

'The captain of the ship who was in despair and tired out, laid himself down to sleep, and in his dream he saw a fairy, who said to him, 'Know you the reason why you cannot work the ship out of port?' It is because the Prince who is on board with you has broken his promise to his daughter, remembering everyone except his own child.' We could see the captain as being the ego who controls our 'vessel' and we are often given information through dreams or intuition. *'Then the captain awoke and told his dream to the Prince, who in shame and confusion at the breach of his promise, went to the Grotto of the Fairies, and, commending his daughter to them, asked them to send her something.'* This Grotto of the Fairies was most likely the spiritual centre of a feminine 'fairy' mystical spiritual group. As already said before, Sardinia was known to have such centres and groups from its distant past. Note also that in the story, the

significance of the Grotto and the Fairy is recognised by their being accorded the status of proper nouns. There is a megalithic complex of stone tombs in Sardinia shaded by groves of trees, called 'The House of the Fairies' in the old language. The Prince knew where to go to find the Grotto of the Fairies, and this again suggests that he once knew and had a connection with this place, and the Fairies.

'And behold, there stepped forth from the grotto a beautiful maiden, who told him that she thanked his daughter for her kind remembrances, sent her love and bade him tell her to be merry and of good heart out of love to her. And thereupon she gave him a date-tree, a hoe, and a little bucket all of gold, and a silken napkin, adding that the one was to hoe with and the other to water the plant.'

The message from the Fairy for Zezolla was full of love and came from the heart, while the date tree, like the tree of life, symbolises nature, the earth, and the whole manifestation. Zezolla was to care for this tree as her spiritual practice; to water it from her little gold bucket, and to hoe the earth, so that it can breathe and to get rid of the weeds; to be mindful of nature and serve the Goddess in this way. Sufism is about Love, Harmony, and Beauty and these are reflected in the practice and message given to Zezolla. An early teacher once told me that if you can't love God then love nature. Hazrat Inayat Khan wrote a beautiful book of nature meditations, which are really profound, and it is lovely to walk slowly while breathing in and out to the rhythm of one of these sayings. For instance, 'Let the sun of Thy glory shine in my heart.' Or 'I see Thy beloved beauty in all colours and forms.' When I look up at my special tree, I often wonder that this huge old tree came from a small seed and used only the earth, rain, air and sunlight as its nutrients. Zezolla's tree being a date tree also provides sweet fruit and nourishment. One of the Sufi Movement's activities is called Zirat, which represents a mystical awakening, experienced through working upon oneself, freeing the mind from unwanted thoughts and regrets which, like weeds, present a hindrance on the path of inner culture. The word Zirat means agriculture, referring in this context to the symbolic work of the farmer digging out old roots to prepare the soil for the new crop, and watching over the various stages in the cultivation of the precious seed.

So this gift from the Fairies is most symbolic. The date by itself symbolises fertility, whereas the tree symbolises the whole of manifestation and the dynamic life, as opposed to the static material life that the Prince was now involved in. The tree also symbolises the feminine principle of nourishing, sheltering, protecting, - the supporting aspect of the Great Mother. Clearly the Grotto of the Fairies was a place of 'worship' of a Great Goddess, such as Hestia, and it had developed this spirituality of the feminine. The golden bucket for watering the date tree has a depth of meaning. Gold represents the light of the sun, divine power, and the splendour of enlightenment and also of God representing the uncreated light or Noor – the highest value to be attained. The water to be used to nourish this sacred plant symbolises the source of all potentialities in existence. It is unmanifested like Noor and is the liquid counterpart of Light. It also relates to the Great Mother and the *Prima Matria* or Great Womb. It is interesting that waters are equated with the continual flux of the manifest world, with unconsciousness, and forgetfulness. Water dissolves, and purifies - washes away and regenerates. The hoe would be used to loosen the soil around the tree, so that it can breathe and also to take out the weeds which could grow around the tree and choke it.

'*The Prince, marvelling at this present, took leave of the fairy, and returned to his own country. And when he had given his stepdaughters all the things they had desired, he at last gave his own daughter the gift which the Fairy had sent her. Then Zezolla, out of her wits with joy, took the date-tree and planted it in a pretty flower-pot, hoed the earth around it, watered it, and wiped its leaves morning and evening with the silken napkin.*'

So Zezolla now has a daily spiritual practice to do and she does this diligently, with care and love. We need to do our own practices joyously and with mindfulness. I like the way Zezolla even wipes the leaves of the tree, and that she planted it into a pretty flower-pot. There is such love and tenderness in that act. Love, Harmony and Beauty are the core of Sufism, so our practice should be contained in something beautiful. Thus we are more able to see the beauty of the world around us. When we look for beauty we find it. Zikar means remembrance (of God) and so Zezolla remembers the Divine Being in her morning and evening practice with the rising and setting of the sun.

My husband, Azad, used this analogy of the divine in nature in his homily at our retreat with Murshid Nawab (March 2015). *'Murshid Inayat wrote: 'The idea of God is inborn in man. The God-Ideal is the flower of the human race and this flower blooms in the realization of God.' I recently planted a packet of Zinnia seeds and a lot of seedlings sprung up as a consequence of this. They required a lot of care, due to aphid attacks, but as with all seedlings it was wonderfully rewarding to see them grow and progress. Initially, when the first flower bloomed it was a disappointment – I had never grown these flowers before and had expected better. The flower just looked like a single petaled daisy, but then, within a few days, emerging from the centre there came another layer of petals followed by another layer and then another layer all emerging from the centre itself which contained its own beauty as this was comprised of a crown of five tiny golden stamen flowers. So, from the relatively simple act of growing some seeds we can learn a deep and wonderful lesson! Murshid writes: 'Is not man the seed of God? Is it then not his life's purpose to bring forth divine blossoms?' I was in two minds whether to use this story in this story, but my first message from the Bowl of Saki one Sunday read as follows: 'sincerity is like a bud in the heart of man that blossoms with the maturing of the soul'. When you consider that a tiny little seed contains everything that is required to produce, or grow, the flower, it is simply breathtaking.*

I would like to add that Azad cared for his Zinnias much like Cenerentola cared for her little date tree. He wiped the leaves and checked on them every morning before doing his practices. Indeed, I would say they became part of his practice in a very beautiful way.

For Cenerentola to transform herself into the noble, beautiful princess she really is, requires her to 'undress' and then clothe herself in the aspects of the date tree that she has so lovingly cared for. To be noble, beautiful and loving and to embody this means she would indeed be unrecognised as such by her family, who only see her as the lowly Cenerentola that they have made her into. It is much like the Frog Princess in the previous story; taking off her frog skin to complete the inner tasks. Zezolla clearly learns to do this and practices it at will. I imagine that she watches and learns about the 'world' when she is not on the hearth.

'In a few days the tree had grown as tall as a woman, and out of it came a Fairy, who said to Zezolla, "What do you wish for?" And Zezolla replied that she wished sometimes to leave the house without her sisters' knowledge.' When we are totally prepared for our practices and we do them with focus and concentration, in the way Zezolla has done them, our inner tree grows very quickly, so that it can indeed grow to the size of a woman – just the right 'size' for her level of evolution, and out of it came a Fairy and asked Zezolla what she wanted. That a fairy should manifest out of the tree is not surprising; this could be seen as a manifestation of soul. Once, many years ago, when I was very unhappy on being abandoned by my 'beloved' and it seemed that my life had come to a standstill and there would never be any love in it, I had a similar experience, perhaps a vision. I was sitting at my desk at work when I saw a beautiful peach coloured rose in front of me and slightly to the left. It opened and out of its centre came a beautiful, shy, delicate 'fairy' like spiritual Being. I knew that this fairy was a part of myself and that I had to nourish and look after her. I felt so happy and at peace and my inner Fairy grew and evolved over the years. The 'spiritual practice' that Zezolla was given can be seen in the light of the practices that we, as Sufis do; in our external Zikar we say 'This is not my body, this is the temple of God'. We learn to realise that our body is the temple of God and so we need to prepare and purify ourselves for this. In alchemy, the crucible is the container in which the process of transformation happens, the process of turning base metal into gold. This is a spiritual process and the container like the flower pot is our self and should be made pure, clear, and beautiful.

Then Zezolla has to nourish the tree and water it twice a day, just as we should do our practices twice a daily. When we dissolve and flow into contemplation after our morning breathing practice, it is then that we can be hoeing and weeding. We should look at our actions of the day, just passed, when we do our Wazifa contemplating on the Divine aspects such as kindness, forgiveness, patience and gratitude. At the same time we are weeding out negative aspects - perhaps reactivity without understanding another person. Anger, frustration, vanity, self-indulgence, and self-absorption could all be seen as weeds which must be controlled or mastered. Hazrat Inayat Khan's book *The Art of Personality*[27] is a wonderful text for helping us have mastery of ourselves and thus become a beautiful human being.

I really like the image of Zezolla wiping the leaves of the date-tree with the silk cloth that she was given, and it makes me think that this is also part of a sacred ritual, perhaps to polish the leaves so the plant can breathe, or perhaps to make the leave or fronds beautiful and shiny or reflective.

Jung explains that our personality develops with the ego and it is worn like clothes or an overcoat to cover who we really are. Our inner work is to cast off our false persona and become our true self. Hazrat Inayat Khan has written profoundly and beautifully on this in his teachings on 'The Art of Personality', where we are taught how to do this. Hazrat Inayat Khan teaches:

'- *man is created to show humanity in character. It is this which makes him a person. There are many difficult things in life, but the most difficult of all is to learn and know and to practice the art of personality.*'

'*Nature, people say, is created by God and art by man; but in reality in the making of personality it is God who completes His divine art. It is not what Christ has taught that makes his devotees love him; they dispute over those things in vain; it is what he himself was. It is that which is loved and admired by his devotees. When Jesus Christ said to the fishermen, 'Follow me, and I will make you fishers of men', what did it mean? It meant, 'I will teach you the art of personality which will become as a net in this life's sea.' For every heart, whatever be its grade of evolution, will be attracted by the beauty of the art of personality.*'

'*The art of personality is not a qualification. It is the purpose for which man was created, and it leads man to that purpose in the fulfilment of which is his entire satisfaction. By this art man does not only satisfy himself, but he pleases God.*'

'*Gratefulness in the character is like fragrance in the flower. A person, however learned and qualified in his life's work, in whom gratefulness is absent, is devoid of that beauty of character which makes personality fragrant. If we answer every little deed of kindness with appreciation, we*

---

[27] Hazrat Inayat Khan, *The Art of Personality*, The Sufi Message Volume 3, Motilal Banarsidass Publishers, Delhi, 1989. p.214.

develop in our nature the spirit of gratefulness; and by learning this we rise to that state where we begin to realize God's goodness toward us, and for this we can never be grateful enough to His divine compassion.'

Gentleness is one of the main qualities of Hestia and is also one of the principal aspects taught in the *Art of Personality* as we can see.

'Gentleness is the principal thing in the art of personality; one can see how gentleness works as the principal thing in every art. In painting, in drawing, in line and colour it is gentleness which appeals most to the soul.'

'It is mainly gentleness which is the basis of all refinement. But where does it come from? It comes from consideration, and it is practiced by self-control. There is a saying in Hindustani: 'The weaker the person, the more ready to be angry.' The reason is that he has no control over his nerves; it is often lack of control over oneself which is the cause of lack of gentleness.'

'No doubt one learns gentleness by consideration. One must learn to think before saying or doing. Besides one must not forget the idea of beauty. One must know that it is not enough simply to say or do, but that it is necessary to say or do everything beautifully. It is the development of the nations and races which is expressed in gentleness. Also, it is the advancement of the soul's evolution which expresses itself in gentleness. Nations and races, as well as individuals, will show backwardness in their evolution if they show lack of gentleness.'[28]

When the emerging fairy asks Zezolla for her wish, Zezolla did not wish for material things. She only wanted to leave the house without her sisters' knowledge. The Fairy answered, *'Whenever you desire this, come to the flower-pot and say:*

My little date-tree, my golden tree,
With a golden hoe I have hoed thee,
With a golden can I have watered thee,
With a silken cloth I have wiped thee dry,
Now strip thee and dress me speedily.
And when you wish to undress, change the last words and say,
Strip me and dress thee.

---

[28] Ibid, p.218.

This seems to be a ritual chant or prayer in that Zezolla remembers and acknowledges her care for the date-tree as a reflection of her care for her inner realm. In this way she can be presented to the world as she would wish to be seen. This means that it is her inner development and insight into herself, by doing her practice, which relates to how the date-tree has developed, and this in turn relates to how she can be presented in the outer world. I imagine that she will have had many trips and adventures into the world and the court before the next stage in the story. She is perhaps practicing how to be this new self which is emerging, and which she is keeping secret from her sisters and her family. Secrecy is very important in our inner work. We are often told not to teach, preach or evangelise to others unless they ask us. Murshid says that we, like Zezolla, should practice being Sufis in our everyday life, and only tell others when they ask why, or how, we are who we are. There would be a way that Zezolla could transform herself so as to be unrecognised by others, such as a fundamental change in her attitude and bearing. She would not be Cenerentola languishing in the ashes of the hearth. I find it interesting that on her return she reverses the whole process and the date-tree again takes on the inner aspects she has been working on, and in the outer realm she is her usual self.

The story goes on: *'When the time for the feast was come, and the stepmother's daughters appeared, dressed out so fine, all ribbons and flowers, and slippers and shoes, sweet smells and bells, and roses and posies, Zezolla ran quickly to the flower-pot, and no sooner had she repeated the words, as the Fairy had told her, then she saw herself arrayed like a queen, seated upon a palfrey, and attended by twelve smart pages, all in their best clothes. Then she went to the ball, and made the sisters envious of this unknown beauty.'*

It does not say that she was actually arrayed like a queen, but that Cenerentola saw herself not as Cenerentola, but as a Queen. This reflects an inner queenly attitude and way of being which would not be recognised by anyone in her family. She is arrayed like a queen. She rides a palfrey – a most expensive and highly bred horse used by royalty and the nobility, especially in ceremonial occasions. That there are twelve smart pages could represent the complete cycle, the spiritual and temporal order. Twelve is an important number – there are twelve signs of the zodiac, twelve months of the year of which there are six male and six female, twelve hours of each day and night, twelve days of return to chaos at the winter solstice, and the twelve days of Christmas. The pages thus represent the whole cosmic order, which serves her and which she serves.

The introduction to the story says that the whole story is about envy amongst girls, and here again it says that she made her step-sisters envious. I think this misses the point deliberately. These stories were made as secret teachings and so are disguised, but in our own depths we understand, without sometimes realising it, the truth contained in the story. That it is really about our spiritual evolution, and that envy can be something which holds us back in our evolution.

At the feast *'Even the young King himself was there, and as soon as he saw her he stood magic-bound with amazement, and ordered a trusty servant to find out who was that beautiful maiden, where she lived.'* So the young King, who is Zezolla's archetypal counterpart, recognises her and needs to find her. *'The servant followed in her footsteps; but when Zezolla noticed the trick she threw on the ground a handful of crown-pieces which she had made the date-tree give her for this purpose.'*

We know that Zezolla has been prepared and has a strategy. She knows exactly what she is doing. *'Then the servant lighted his lantern, and was so busy picking up all the crown-pieces that he forgot to follow the palfrey; and Zezolla came home quite safely.'* If we see the servant as part of ourselves, perhaps as our ego, this shows us that we can easily get distracted by other things that we consider valuable or important at the time. When we are on the quest for the Beloved, we need to be focussed. Life itself can be so alluring and distracting sometimes! When Zezolla got home she changed her clothes, as the Fairy had told her, before her wicked sisters arrived. To vex her and make her envious, they tell her of all the fine things they had seen. So Zezolla becomes Cenerentola again and 'takes in' everything her stepsisters have to say to her. I would imagine that she would have been quite interested in how her sisters perceived the whole situation. As women, many of us are in competition with one another and like to boast or put forward our own idea of the world and our place in it. Everyone has their own understanding of the world and often these are quite different from one another. It is through the eyes and ears of the ego that we see and interpret our world, so each of us would understand a situation quite differently. The step-sisters have been to the ball and described what they saw and felt from their own perspective. In our spiritual practice and evolution we come to see the world beyond the illusion of our ego and attitudes.

'*But the King was very angry with the servant, and warned him not to miss finding out next time who this beautiful maiden was, and where she dwelt.*' It is interesting to note that the king knows that there will be another opportunity, indeed these great feasts could well have been celebrating the summer and winter solstices. In the quest for the Beloved there is always another opportunity when we fail, until our Beloved is found, although I also think that sometimes opportunities are limited and we should be careful not to miss them.

'*Soon there was another feast, and again the sisters all went to it, leaving poor Zezolla at home on the kitchen hearth. Then she ran quickly to the date-tree, and repeated the spell, and instantly there appeared a number of damsels, one with a looking-glass, another with a bottle of rose-water, another with the curling-irons, another with combs, another with pins, another with dresses, and another with capes and collars. And they decked her out as glorious as the sun, and put her in a coach drawn by six white horses, and attended by footmen and pages in livery.*'

Whereas the first time Zezolla asked the Fairy to transform her, Zezolla saw herself arrayed like a queen, but this time she is actually prepared and presented as a queen. We are given much detail in her preparation and presentation. There are personal servants to help her dress and prepare for the ball; it is like the outer self is being made to reflect the inner, which has been formed by constant daily practice in caring for the 'tree'. The phrase 'they decked her out as glorious as the sun' is telling. The sun is central to the 'religion' of the Fairies, just as it was to those people who built the great Stone Henges, which were aligned to the summer and winter solstices. In Sardinia there seems to be a connection with these Henges to a Matriarchal culture of the Fairies, as there was in the time of the worship of the great Goddesses. The feasts themselves could well be the major celebrations related to the summer and winter solstices. The sun is generally connected with the masculine, and the moon with the feminine. In this story there is only mention made of the sun and of the feminine. The symbol of the looking glass, or mirror, and the rose water seem to be important. As Sufis, our practice is to constantly clean and polish the mirror of the heart, so that our soul self can be reflected there. The rose symbolises perfection and completion - the mystery and heart centre of life. Rosewater would thus be the fragrance of the perfection and completion that Zezolla is attaining.

'No sooner did she appear in the ball-room than the hearts of the sisters were filled with amazement, and the King was overcome with love.'

The presence of such a Being would indeed amaze all who saw and experienced her. The King was overcome with love for her as his counterpart. She was *his* Queen and she would complete him; it was through her that he would rule. He recognised this, but of course there was still a mystery. He did not know who she was.

'When Zezolla went home the servant followed her again, but so that she would not be caught she threw down a handful of pearls and jewels, and the good fellow, seeing that they were not things to lose, stayed to pick them up.'

This time Zezolla throws down pearls and jewels to distract the servant. Pearls are lunar and symbolise the life-giving power of the great mother, the feminine principle of the ocean; whereas jewels generally symbolise the heart, light and heat. These are the most precious feminine qualities she is casting before the King's servant to distract him and so protect herself. The feminine principle so often allures the male ego away from the true mystery which is Unity, but Zezolla was able to use the servant's distraction to disappear again.

'Meanwhile the servant had returned slowly to the King, who cried out when he saw him, 'By the souls of my ancestors, if you do not find out who she is, you shall have such a thrashing as was never before heard of, and as many kicks as you have hairs in your beard.'' When the servant (perhaps our small self) gets distracted, the King or Higher Self gets very angry and threatens dire and painful physical punishment. It is interesting that the King swears by the souls of his ancestors, which means that his spiritual lineage is extremely important to him. All the great Beings and Teachers before the King, are part of him. In Sufism we talk of

'Fana' which mean annihilation of the small self or ego into that of the Teacher, Rasul and finally into Allah or God. The servant's or ego's distraction shows that the King does not yet have mastery of himself and so has not annihilated it into his forbearer Teachers. Kicks and a thrashing would mean that we could physically sustain injuries perhaps from 'accidents' if our ego gets distracted from the path.

The next (and third feast) was held. With the sisters safely out of the house, Zezolla again goes to the date-tree, and *'once again repeated the spell. In an instant she found herself splendidly arrayed and seated in a coach of gold, with ever so many servants around her, so that she looked just like a queen.'* This time the transformation happened in an instant, so we see that each time Zezolla is becoming stronger in her inner power. This is about our own evolution and growth through practice and inner work.

'Again the sisters were beside themselves with envy; but this time when she left the ball-room, the King's servant kept close to the coach. Zezolla, seeing that the man was ever running by her side, cried, 'Coachman, drive on quickly,' and in a trice the coach set off at such a rattling pace that she lost one of her slippers, the prettiest thing that ever was seen.' This is the point where the speed of the transition from one realm to the other, was so fast that she lost her pretty slipper. What does this really mean? Sometimes, when there is a very quick transition like this, some part of the realm we are coming from, is still 'seen' in the realm we have moved to. For example, I well remember wakening from a dream very quickly and literally seeing a middle aged woman sitting in bed next to me reading. She was completely unaware of me and, what was very strange was that she was not part of any dream that I could remember. I stared at her for quite a while until she faded away. So vestiges of my dream realm could still be seen on awakening when I transitioned quickly. Perhaps that part of the king (his ego) could see Zezolla's slipper well after she disappeared in her coach.

Regarding the slipper itself, in ancient times, slaves and servants did not wear or have shoes, nor would their feet fit into shoes. By habitually going barefoot, their feet would be very calloused and broad – certainly not a dainty little foot that would fit into a slipper. The slipper would have to belong to a member of the 'nobility'. Shoes show us the kind of stand we have on the earth and also who we are. In past life regression hypnosis, as we transition into a 'past' life, we are asked to look at our feet, so that we can see who we are, or were, in that past lifetime. At one time I remember seeing the curved pointy-toed shoes of a court jester! So a shoe or slipper can tell much about us.

'The servant being unable to catch the coach, which flew like a bird, picked up the slipper, and carrying it to the King told him all that happened. Whereupon the King, taking it in his hand, said, 'If the basement, indeed, is so beautiful, what must the building be. You who until now were the prison of a white foot are now the fetter of an unhappy heart!'

This time the servant was not distracted and was able to give the slipper to the King and explain all that had happened. The King was full of wonderment at the beauty of the slipper and thought how 'if the basement is so beautiful, what must the building be.'

The slipper is the boundary, or place between ourselves and the earth, and reflects the 'standpoint' we have in the world. It is Zezolla's standing (the way she can balance the inner and outer realms) which entrances him, and his heart is now completely captured. He must find out who and where she is. In ancient times, buildings were built around the central hearth, which is why Hestia is also the Goddess of architecture, so this could be a reference to the fact that if the slipper or basement / hearth of the building is so beautiful, then the rest of it would be especially beautiful.

'Then he made a proclamation that all the women in the country should come to a banquet, for which the most splendid provision was made of pies and pastries, and stews and ragouts, macaroni and sweetmeats – enough to feed a whole army. And when all the women were assembled, noble and ignoble, rich and poor, beautiful and ugly, the King tried the slipper on each one of the guests to see whom it should fit to a hair, and thus be able to discover by the help of the slipper the maiden of whom he was in search, but not one foot could he find to fit it. So he examined them closely whether indeed everyone was there; and the Prince confessed that he had left one daughter behind, 'but,' said he, 'she is always on the hearth, and is such a

graceless simpleton that she is unworthy to sit and eat at your table.' But the King said, 'Let her be the very first on the list, for so I will.'

First of all the King ensures that all the maidens in the realm will come to try on the shoe by providing good and ample food for all, so that he could check the fit of the shoe perfectly, to a hair. In other words, it would not do if the shoe was either too loose or too tight. Of course the slipper did not fit anyone there. But when the slipper did not fit any of the assembled maidens, Zezolla's father, the Prince, had to admit to the King that his daughter was left behind. I find his description of her really interesting. He did not know his daughter anymore, but only saw her through the eyes of the patriarchy. How could his perception of her be so different from her 'reality'? 'She is always on the hearth,' he says.

The hearth is the interior spiritual centre – the heart centre of the home and of the feminine dominion. It is about fire in its feminine-earth aspect. The hearth is the place where Cenerentola is always to be found and it is interesting that the myth of Hestia, the Greek Goddess of the hearth, has many parallels to that of Cenerentola. I think it is the worship of Hestia, driven underground, which may well be the basis of this story.

One of Hestia's early temples was on Crete, where perhaps this story came from. Hestia's main duty was to keep the domestic hearth fire going and, since the hearth is immovable, Hestia was unable to take part in any processions or rituals. So, perhaps her father, the Prince, did not think of his daughter because she was part of the hearth and unable to leave it. Hestia was known for her kindness and gentleness. Most interesting is that she rejected marriage with Poseidon and Apollo, and swore herself to perpetual virginity, so rejecting Aphrodite's values which would have been the values of her step mother and her sisters. This is important if we are to make a comparison of Hestia with Cenerentola. Hestia is rarely portrayed but in classical art she is occasionally depicted as a woman, simply and modestly cloaked in a head veil. How like Cenerentola that sounds. Her very simplicity would have made her seem unworldly and thus like a 'simpleton'. No wonder it did not even occur to her father to bring her to the King.

Her father also says that Zezolla is a graceless simpleton who is unworthy to sit at the King's table. By graceless, perhaps he means without the airs and graces that his stepdaughters and most other young girls would be employing. I would imagine that Zezolla would be quietly going about the practices of the Dove of the Fairies and developing a deep inner personality, which could be seen as simple or naïve. Most spiritual and evolved beings do seem to be very simple and unsophisticated and would not usually be found at a King's table.

But the King understands and wills it that Zezolla should be the first on the list for the next day. So the next day Zezolla arrived accompanied by her 'wicked' sisters. *'When the King saw her he had his suspicions, but said nothing'*. So even though Zezolla is not presenting herself as a queen, as she was at the previous feasts, there was still something in her, or about her, that the King recognised and was drawn to. After the feast came the trial of the slipper, *'which, as soon as ever it approached Zezolla's foot, it darted on to it of its own accord like iron flies to the magnet.'* Magically, the slipper finds its way back onto Zezolla's foot where it belonged. There could be no doubt that she was indeed the mysterious maiden the King was searching for.

'Seeing this, the King ran to her and took her in his arms, and seating her under the royal canopy, he set the crown upon her head, whereupon all made their obeisance and homage to her as their queen.' The canopy signifies royalty and sovereign power, but also relates to the Sacred Tree of Enlightenment, which puts me in mind of Zezolla's little date-tree. The crown, of course, also signifies sovereignty, and the highest attainment. It is clear that all who were there understood that the Queen had been found and made their homage and obeisance to her.

In this story, Zezolla is the only one who is given a name and a real identity, and it is her coronation which completes the story. It is unusual that there is no sacred marriage or *conjunctio* here. It is solely about the completion of feminine spiritual evolution.

'When the wicked sisters saw this they were full of venom and rage, and, not having patience to look upon the object of their hatred, they slipped quietly away on tip-toe and went home to their mother, confessing, in spite of themselves, that----'He is a madman who resists the Stars.'

The final comment comes from the wicked step-sisters. They, like others who do not understand the inner mystical life, hate and fear it. But they also know that one cannot resist destiny or the unfolding of the soul into Unity with the Divine. The King and Queen are united to rule. They have mastery over both manifested and unmanifested life – the seen and unseen Beings. Zezolla's evolution shows us that there is a destiny which rules our lives, and that we are all drawn to this and live by it, whether we realise it or not.

THE FROG PRINCESS

would like to thank Murshid Nawab for giving me this story to work with, both as a Sufi story and a story about the evolution of the feminine. I also thank Nirtan for her wonderful insights into the Russian female psyche, and into the meaning of the story itself as one of her favourite stories. As in true Jungian analysis, all the various characters in the story are part of one Being and the story itself is the unfolding of the self through the spiritual journey. It also demonstrates the aspect of the feminine principle which must evolve within all Beings to be the partner and soul mate of the masculine principle.

This story, as in many other Russian stories, begins with a Tsar who has three sons. The tsar or king often represents the heart in Sufi teaching tales, and the fact that there are three sons simply means a multiplicity, as three is the first number to which 'all' has been appropriated. In Russia the tsar was all powerful and actually owned not only the serfs, but the nobles as well. The word 'tsar' comes from the word 'Caesar' and the tsar really was seen as a 'God King'. The Tsar in this story wants his sons to be married, so that he can have grandchildren. The sons are in agreement and ask for their father's blessings, but seek his advice on how to find a suitable wife.

The Tsar answers, *'My sons, take your bows, go out into the open field and shoot an arrow. Wherever it falls, there you will find your wife.'*

The eldest son's arrow fell into a nobleman's courtyard, where it was picked up by the nobleman's daughter. The second son's arrow fell into a merchant's courtyard, and it was picked up by the merchant's daughter.

But the third arrow shot by the youngest, Prince Ivan, rose so high and flew so far that he did not know where to look for it.

The arrow represents the piercing masculine principle, and an arrow shot from a bow represents the consequences of actions which cannot be recalled or revoked. In a way, the arrow lands where the Prince's spirit takes him.

So, when the eldest son's arrow fell into a nobleman's courtyard, this really meant that this was the result of that man's actions and inner leanings. His 'consort' or anima (inner feminine) was to be the daughter of a nobleman. Although she can be seen as a suitable bride, the true inner beloved of an eldest prince, the son and heir of the Tsar, should really be a Princess.

When the second son's arrow falls into a merchant's courtyard, this Prince's inner beloved is the daughter of a merchant. This is the highest he can achieve, as this is the level of his own anima or soul, his level of spiritual evolution. Like his elder brother, he has not yet evolved to attain a Princess, as he should have.

Both sons find their wives, or inner anima figures, in the realm of the human, or of outer consciousness. Both of these wives show their lack of spiritual discernment in their unrefined behaviour.

The youngest brother in fairy stories is always the hero and in this case he is named - as is often the case – as Prince Ivan. Ivan perhaps represents the human being; the noun itself is masculine in Russian, but applies to all human beings. He has shot his arrow so high and far that he has to go looking for it.

When the young Prince Ivan shoots his arrow up into the air, he is in search of higher goals, or spiritual ideals. He represents the human being on a spiritual journey in search of his soul.

He started to walk and at last came to a marsh. In the marsh he saw a frog with his arrow in its mouth. Prince Ivan has aimed very high and far and it is interesting that he walks in search of his arrow. To walk is to travel on one's own two feet, connected to the ground. Two indicates duality, and the opposites, which have to be united or integrated, such as male and female, masculine and feminine, the solar and the lunar. His arrow is found in a marsh – a place where there is earth and water, an in-between place where no humans reside. It is an otherworldly place. These places are also called crossing places, where the human and the mystical realms intersect. The frog is a lunar symbol and is a rain-bringer and in Russian is feminine in gender. Interestingly, it also symbolises eroticism. The moist skin of the frog denotes life and resurrection, as opposed to the dryness of death. The frog really represents his soul or inner Beloved. So, although Prince Ivan does not recognise the meaning of the frog having caught his arrow, or indeed that the frog is his Princess, it has landed in the right place. Once the seeker starts to look inside, he finds his soul all covered up with ugly veils like that of a frogskin and sitting in the marsh. Sometimes when we are stuck in a frustrating situation and cannot see our way out of it, we think about it as being stuck in a bog or marsh. It is a pretty devastating experience. The mouth can be seen as the entrance to the underworld – a place of transition.

Ivan asks the frog to give him the arrow, but the frog replied, *'Then take me for your wife. But you must, for it is the Tsar's will.'* The frog knows that she is right for the prince and that it is the will of the Tsar that they should marry.

At first the prince tries to avoid it, but eventually he has to accept his fate and carries the frog home. Sometimes when we first discover our own anima, or animus in the case of a female, they are in a very primitive form. We all have a contra-gender side to our nature – women have an animus side, which is the masculine, and men have their anima, or feminine soul side. Women tend to be more animus-driven these days, as they have to function and work in the more male dominated outer working world. So, women are also on a quest for their soul, but their journey is quite different from that of their male counterparts. In my first dream, where I discovered my animus (masculine) side, he was in the ocean – more fish-like than human, and I had to fish him out and shower the salt water from him. He was so weak he could not stand up. So, I think that Prince Ivan has really found his anima in the depth of his unconscious and, perhaps, in a very 'primitive' frog-like form. Through his inner work, the beauty of his soul will evolve through this frog feminine side of himself. Also, it is interesting that a frog, as an amphibian, can inhabit both earth and waters, the realm of material consciousness and the unconscious. So, finding the frog princess represents finding his inner awareness and being.

The Tsar then arranged for the three marriages to take place: his eldest son to the nobleman's daughter, his second son to the merchant's daughter, and the unhappy Prince Ivan to the frog. After the weddings, the Tsar summoned his sons again, and told them; *'I want to see which of your wives is the finest needlewoman. Each one is to make me a shirt by tomorrow.'*

The sons bowed to their father and went to tell their wives. But when Prince Ivan arrived home he sat down looking very miserable. The frog was jumping around the floor, and it asked him, what was wrong and if he was in trouble. Notice that the frog is talked about as an 'it' and is not yet even recognised as feminine, although 'it' is the wife of Prince Ivan. As far as the story and Prince Ivan are concerned, it is just a frog and yet frog in the Russian language is always feminine. How often is it, that real women are treated like this in the outer world – as this unbeautiful, moist, diffuse type of essence, which the masculine (including the masculine in animus-driven women) does not yet understand or relate to? However, Prince Ivan is able to tell 'it' his troubles, *'My father has ordered you to make him a shirt by tomorrow.'*

Here we realise that this is a story, not only about the integration of the feminine, into the masculine psyche, but also a story for the feminine herself. These tasks which the Tsar gives his sons' 'wives', are tasks for all women to work on, within their own psyche. Women have to live in a masculine patriarchal world, while at the same time unfolding their own psyches. The feminine is the soul itself, so for women these tasks are often hidden – intuition and sensitivity are part of this soul quality, which in spiritual life is encouraged and developed, in the outer life it is covered over – as with a frogskin.

The frog answers *'Do not worry, Prince Ivan, you just go to bed. You will feel better after a good sleep.'* In other words, the task or work is to be done when asleep and in that other realm of the deep unconscious. When Prince Ivan goes to bed, the frog jumped out onto the veranda, threw off its skin and turned into the wise Princess Vassilisa, a maiden so beautiful that words could never describe her. She clapped her hands and cried, '*My faithful attendants gather round and listen to me. Sew for me by tomorrow morning a shirt like the one my own father used to wear.*'

The frog jumped out onto the veranda, so first of all it has to go to a place outside the apartments where they live, and yet not right outside in the gardens. The veranda is an 'edge' place, sometimes referred to as a 'thin place' – an in-between place neither inner nor outer, perhaps one could say that it is in the first and closest level to consciousness.

Then the frog throws off her skin and transforms into what she really is – a beautiful princess. She asks her attendants to make a shirt like her father used to wear. So, we know that her father was a Tsar, and that, being the daughter of a Tsar, she knows exactly what kind of shirt to make. Our soul understands and knows how to create wonders.

We wonder why she is covered with a frogskin, but the skin is a covering of who we really are – we all develop a skin, or persona, and some would say that in the development of this persona, we are losing our original essence. In effect, the clothes we wear can be seen as symbolic of our persona, so when the Tsar asks for a shirt to be made, he really wants to know or to test if the wives (the feminine soul side of his sons) know what is correct and proper for a tsar to wear. There is also a task for the feminine to complete – to make this special garment for the Tsar to wear. The Tsar, who represents the 'heart', needs to wear a special shirt or garment to show his true position.

To wear a skin is also to take on the power or manna of the animal and this puts the wearer in touch with that animal and its instinctual knowledge. Princess Vassilisa would learn how a frog exists in water, which is the realm of the Great Mother, and the Unconscious, as well as on land or the marsh. This is the realm of the Intuitive and of instinct.

When the Prince woke up next morning the frog was jumping about the floor again, but a shirt wrapped in linen was already lying on the table. He was overjoyed. He picked up the shirt and took it to his father.

Notice that the frog is always jumping about – it is not passive but always alive and engaged like the soul. Notice also that Prince Ivan takes what the frog has made, but there is no appreciation or thanks given, nor indeed surprise expressed. It is taken for granted, which is how we deal with this inner part of ourselves. It is the same when we have an insight or good idea – we just accept this and hopefully trust our intuition. Prince Ivan accepts and also trusts his 'frog' soul.

When Prince Ivan arrived to see the Tsar, the Tsar was receiving the gifts from his two elder sons. The eldest son spread out the shirt his wife had made. As the Tsar accepted it, he said, '*This is a shirt for everyday wear.*'

When the second son spread out his shirt, the Tsar said, '*I could only go to the bath in that.*'

Then Prince Ivan unfolded his shirt; it was embroidered with gold and silver threads in intricate patterns. The Tsar took one look at it and declared, '*Now that is a shirt! I can wear it on important occasions.*'

The nobly born wife of the eldest son had made a shirt which befitted her own level of evolution – an everyday shirt for a Tsar. She did not have the skill, knowledge or imagination to make something worthy of a Tsar.

The merchant's daughter who was the wife of the second son did not even manage an everyday shirt, but could only make something the Tsar would wear to his bath, not even one to be seen by his family or friends.

But when the Tsar saw the most beautiful shirt made by Prince Ivan's wife, he knew this was something specially made for a tsar and to be used in important occasions, where he was wearing the mantle of a tsar – in the role of God King. Only a princess would be able to make such a shirt, as only she would know intimately what a tsar requires. The gold thread in the shirt symbolises the sun and the quality of sacredness, and the silver thread symbolises the moon and virginity, so that the moon with the sun represents the Queen with the King, a balance of the masculine and feminine. The intricate pattern on the shirt shows the harmony and integration of the two – the King and Queen, interwoven and as one. The soul understands and creates beauty in everything she does. Embroidery was often made with symbols protecting the person from evil influence but in this case it was made to enhance and promote the person of the Tsar.

Now the older two brothers realise they were too quick to laugh at Ivan's wife, but they then decide that she is a witch. Isn't it interesting that when a female does something very special, creative, mysterious or clever, then she is immediately labelled a witch! The feminine cannot be seen as wise and creative in the patriarchy. Perhaps this is why she has to wear a frog skin.

Now the Tsar sent for his sons again and told them, *'Each of your wives is to bake a loaf of bread for me by tomorrow. I wish to find out which is the best cook.'*

When Prince Ivan arrived home after seeing his father, he looked so miserable that the frog asked him what the matter was.

'You have to bake a loaf of bread for the Tsar by tomorrow.' Ivan answered.

Once again the frog tells Ivan to go to bed and that he will feel better after a good sleep. There is always a truth in this - to go to bed and have a good sleep, but it is interesting to notice that Prince Ivan trusts the frog and does what his is advised. The answer often comes to us from the realm of the deep unconscious, from dreams or visions, and many problems have been solved in this way. It is a direct knowledge which we have access to when our soul part is present and active.

The elder sons' wives had first made fun of Prince Ivan's frog wife, but now they had changed their minds, and wondered about the frog's wisdom. They therefore sent an old kitchen woman to spy out how the frog was going to bake the bread. This story is about the feminine and, as in other such stories (Amor and Psyche), jealousy or envy rears its head among the women. The frog, being wise, realises their scheme. After kneading the dough, it makes a hole in the top of the brick oven and pours the dough through the hole. The frog has tricked the other women and so guards its secret. To pour the dough straight into the brick oven means that the outcome of their work – the dough - was put on the fire uncontained and unprotected by a tin. It is also no small feat to make a hole in the top of the brick cover.

The whole process is a metaphor for our own inner processing – if we do not contain our experience when we pour it out into the fire of the world, it gets burned and destroyed. There is a way of working with the dough, which we learn from and by doing our spiritual practice.

This part of the story, of the pouring of the dough into the stove, is very mysterious. 'In reality, it cannot be done with a Russian oven, which is a huge construction that takes a quarter of the space of the Russian hut. The Russian oven is made like a Swedish stove oven, with many vents that go in circles inside this huge monster of brick and mortar to keep the heat inside the house, rather than sending it straight out into the forest. There are various opening vents on the sides of the stove, but you would not be able to pour anything inside, or scrape anything out of them. The stove seems to me to be like a huge heart. Nawab suggested that the pouring of the dough might be a reference towards the Middle East, where there are stoves dug in the ground and the dough is poured onto the side of this hole, while the fire is burnt at the bottom of the pit.

The oven is said to be brick, so I wonder if the fact that it is made from the earth, is relevant. The old woman told the wives what she had seen, and they set to work to do the same literally and without any understanding.

What does it mean for the women to bake bread for the Tsar? Bread is an important symbol, which means life; the food of the body and the soul; the visible and manifest life. It is also a symbol of union, having many grains in one substance, in other words the multiplicity within Unity.

Bread in Russia (as in many other countries) has a religious and symbolic importance that goes beyond just its basic role in daily life. The word bread (khleb) was used in Russian for 'wealth', 'health' and 'hospitality'. Bread played a central role in peasant rituals; bird-shaped breads were baked in spring to symbolise the return of the migratory flocks. In the peasant wedding, a special loaf was baked to symbolise the newly-weds' fertility. At peasant funerals it was customary to make a ladder out of the dough and put it in the grave beside the corpse to help the soul's ascent, for bread was the sacred link between this world and the next.'[29]

The frog princess had the dough kneaded and I think that all women symbolically know how to do this (it is the raw material after all). It is

---

[29] Orlando Figes, *Natasha's Dance: A Cultural history of Russia*, Penguin Books, London, 2002, p.165.

in the baking of the dough that the frog then leads them astray. After all, we have to cook or process the material we are given to work with. I wonder what the old kitchen maid thought about pouring the dough directly into the oven. She certainly was not a 'wise old woman', so they chose the wrong person to spy for them, but, then again, they were not wise in their interpretation of what they thought was happening. They took it literally, which happens when teachings are passed on by third hand, via someone who does not appreciate or realise the significance of what is taking place. Imagine someone watching me doing my Sufi practice and then telling someone else how it is done. They would not understand the inner truth and wisdom of the practice.

After I had finished working with this story, I had a very profound dream. In the dream, I experienced an aboriginal ritual, which was chanted in their mystical language of the Dreamtime. I could feel myself as part of the creation, of nature – it cannot be described. Then, later, and to my surprise one of our group was doing the same chant – she had seemingly written it down phonetically and she was attempting the same ritual, but without any understanding of what she was doing or even what the outcome should, or could be. Her copy of the singing was very good but it was not 'real' – there was no numinosity.

After Prince Ivan went to bed, the frog jumped out onto the veranda again, turned into the wise Princess Vassilisa and clapped her hands, as she said, *'My faithful attendants gather round and listen to me. Bake for me by the morning, soft white bread like the bread I ate at my father's table.'*

Once again, the bread is the same as the bread the Princess ate at her father's table, so she knows what is fitting for a tsar. It is white and soft; white is the colour always worn at a sacrament, and symbolises transcendent perfection, purity, holiness, light and illumination, but most importantly spiritual authority. It is refined, as befits a Tsar.

When the prince woke up the next morning the loaf of bread was already lying on the table. Once again the inner work is done when we are 'asleep' or meditating in the night time when we are not taken up with worldly affairs. This is when we are open to the depth of our being and where the soul / frog can do her work. The bread was decorated with various intricate designs, and its crust was the shape of a city with walls and gates. The Prince was delighted, wrapped the bread in clean linen, and took it to his father.

The intricate designs on the load of bread are similar to the intricate designs on the shirt and are significant of links and connections, patterns, as in sacred geometry. They have a meaning. The city on top of the loaf, with its walls and gates, could signify protection – a place which is guarded or defended, and is the sheltering and enclosing aspect of the feminine.

When Prince Ivan arrived the Tsar was already receiving the loaves brought by his two elder sons. But their wives had poured the dough into the ovens, just as the old woman had told them to do, and all they had to show for their labour were two burnt cinders. The Tsar took both the loaves and sent them to the servants' quarters. Sometimes people copy what others do, without having the wisdom to know what they are really doing. In sacred and secret ceremonies or rituals, an outsider watching would neither see what is really happening nor understand, as there is a grade of attainment or (spiritual evolution) needed to work at the various levels. So, in mimicking such a ritual or ceremony, the result is a burnt offering, and the outcome of the process can be dangerous or uncomfortable, like the burnt bread. It was lucky that they themselves were only wounded in their pride or ego.

When Prince Ivan handed his father his loaf the Tsar said, *'Now this is such good bread, it should be eaten only on great occasions.'*

The loaf, like the shirt, was only for special occasions, as befits a tsar in the high role of his office. It is Divine.

The Tsar had arranged a banquet for the following day, and he ordered his sons to attend with their wives. The thought of his frog wife attending a banquet made Prince Ivan feel far from cheerful, and he returned home with his head hanging. As usual the frog was jumping about the floor. When it saw him it asked? *'Prince Ivan, what are you looking so miserable for? Has your father said something unpleasant to you?'*

Prince Ivan replied, *'How can I help looking miserable, frog? My father has ordered me to bring you to a banquet; and how can I show you to people?'*

This time, the feminine is asked to show herself and act in an appropriate way. She has passed all her tests so far, but this is a tricky one. Through the inner work, the beauty of the soul has started to throw out some light by creating wonders like the marvellous bread and the magnificent shirt while still remaining invisible. Now she is being asked to make herself visible, to show herself to the world. How can the frog show herself as the princess she is? What is being asked of it? To be seen as beautiful, noble and wise, as well as refined in her being.

Again the frog answers, *'Do not grieve, Prince Ivan. Go off to the banquet by yourself, and I will follow later. When you hear a knock and a clap of thunder, do not be afraid. If anyone asks you what it means, just say: 'that is my little frog who is coming riding in a little box.''*

So Prince Ivan went off to the banquet alone. His elder brothers arrived with their wives dressed in their finery, wearing their jewellery, their faces painted and powdered. They laughed at Prince Ivan and asked, 'Why did you not bring your wife with you? You could have carried her in a handkerchief. Where did you find such a beauty? You must have searched all through the marshes for her.' Women can be so very cruel and bitchy, to and about, other women. This is one of the lessons that women have to learn not to do. *As one of the copper rules states: judge not another by your own law.* And one of the silver rules: *use tact on all occasions*, and the golden rule: *when you possess something, think of the one who does not possess it.*

It is also interesting that women are harsher judges of other women than men are. In current times, despite all the progress of feminism, this is still sadly the case, as women compete for the attention and favours (which may not be only sexual favours, but also include promotion and approval from the patriarchy).

The Tsar, his sons, their wives, and all the guests sat down at the oaken tables, which were spread with embroidered tablecloths. But before they started to feast, there was a loud knock and a clap of thunder, so powerful that the palace shook. The guests were alarmed and jumped out of their seats. But Prince Ivan said, *'Do not be afraid. It is only my little frog coming. She is riding in a little box.'* Once again, I find it reassuring that prince Ivan really trusts his frog wife, even though he does not really know who or what 'it' is. He trusts his intuition, which he has already followed successfully in earlier parts of the story. It is important to trust our intuition, even when it seems ridiculous. Once we have followed our intuition in this way and found that it works, we can have perfect confidence in this intuition, which can come from our unconscious, in meditation, or in our dreams.

It is also interesting that a loud sound – a knock and a clap of thunder - heralds the Princess's entrance into the human world. Sound does indeed herald the deep unconscious and this sound can be so loud that it can shake the ground we are standing on – our inner groundedness.

The little box symbolises the feminine principle of containment; enclosure or the womb. This is important for the feminine principle, which is diffuse and receptive, and so needs to be contained and held. It is still small at this stage.

A gilded carriage drawn by six white horses drew up at the Tsar's front door, and the wise Princess Vassilisa stepped out. She was wearing an azure gown studded with stars; on her head was a shining chaplet; she was so beautiful that the guests just sat and stared. She took Prince Ivan by the hand and he led her to the oaken table. That the table is of oak is important. Oak is a masculine symbol of strength and protection, but it also represents the sky and Fertility Gods and is associated with thunder and the Thunder Gods. Given that thunder precedes the arrival of the Princess, this is significant. In Greek mythology the oak is the emblem of conjugal devotion and happiness.

Princess Vassilisa's carriage is gilded or covered with gold, which represents solar energy, and it is drawn by six white horses. Six is the number of harmony and equilibrium and of the union of opposites or polarity male and female – it is the perfect and most productive number – $1 + 2 + 3 = 6$. It also symbolises creation as in the six days of creation. The white horses also seem to represent the solar power, as a symbol of light and life, as well as wisdom and the mind.

There is so much detail in this scene, that it is important to analyse this properly. Princess Vassilisa wears a gown of azure blue, which is the colour of the Great Mother, Queen of Heaven, (and Mary, who is also referred to as the Queen of Heaven). Indeed, the name Vassilisa means

Queen. Stars are attributes of all Queens of Heaven. She wears a shining chaplet or crown often made of flowers. It is interesting to note that in the veneration of Mary, in the Russian and Greek Orthodox Church and the Catholic Church, she is often depicted in icons with her head pressed against the head of the baby Jesus. In the Catholic Church, Mary, as the Queen of Heaven, is depicted with a halo of stars, and dressed in a white gown, with a blue mantle.

Prince Ivan finally sees his soul without the ugly cover; he sees his beloved in her full glory, as the perfection of beauty. It is like a first realisation of the inner world, or even like falling in love.

The guests began to make merry, but the wise Vassilisa only takes one sip from her glass, and pours the rest into her left sleeve. She is treating the meal as a sacred sacrament by only taking a sip from her glass. The left side is the side of the feminine or inner, so she takes in and transforms the sacred wine into her own self – integrating spirit into her feminine essence.

There is much to be said about being embodied and the immanence of the Divine: it is something that the feminine understands. We are so often looking towards a transcendent God 'out there', rather than feeling and being the embodiment of an imminent God.

Next Vassilisa nibbles at her plate of swan meat, and then drops the bones into her right sleeve. In Christian mythology the swan represents purity and grace and can also represent the Virgin Mary, whereas elsewhere the swan is seen as solar, the dawn of the day and the bird of life. It can also be seen as a sacrament like the body of Christ, but with a feminine essence. Literally, to be embodied in Grace. The bones that she has dropped into her sleeve could represent the indestructible life principle, but it can also indicate resurrection. The right side symbolises the outer life or the manifest. Note that roast swan with saffron was on the menu at the wedding feast of Tsar Alexei in 1670.

The two elder brothers' wives notice what she is doing and, once again, they follow her example, but without understanding what she is really about. How often do we also do this – follow the example of someone whom we admire – someone more evolved than we are on the spiritual path, and blindly copy what they do, without having understood and integrated the experiences. This integration can take years of inner 'work'.

After eating and drinking, there was then time for dancing. The wise Vassilisa took Prince Ivan's hand and they danced together, and she danced so beautifully, and so marvellously, that all the guests were amazed. I was fascinated that it was the wise Vassilisa who took the lead in this dance, which again shows that this is a story of and for the feminine. It is the feminine which has to take the lead in the inner journey – she is the soul or 'The Inner Beloved' of man. Beethoven addressed his beloved as, 'My Immortal Beloved'. As women, we also have to take the lead without sometimes seeming to. It is subtle. Sometimes women need to lead from behind.

Then while she was dancing the dance of life, she waved her left sleeve and suddenly a lake was formed in the hall. This lake is the dwelling place of magical feminine powers as in the story of the lady of the lake. A very old folk myth tells of a sacred city that was hidden underneath a lake. The earliest oral versions of the legend went back to the days of Mongol rule and could well contain the remnants of a Sufi teaching tale relating to the inner journey to wholeness and unity. Many 'old believers' of early Christian Russian Orthodox beliefs, fled to the lakes and forests after persecution by the newer Orthodoxy, which merged with the Greek Church and came under the auspices of the Tsar, who used the Church to administer to the people. The lake and the forest then became symbols of a very sacred place, a natural church where they worshipped. These were communities with no hierarchy – it was a communal life with lay teachers. Many pagan rituals were merged with the practice of this community.

When Princess Vassilisa waved her right sleeve, white swans floated on the lake. So Vassilisa has manifested, or perhaps resurrected, this purity and grace of the Divine feminine principle. It is of course the swan, or goose, that laid the golden egg from which the Self is born.

The Tsar and his guests were filled with astonishment. The elder brothers' wives also danced and when they danced they waved one sleeve, just as the wise Vassilisa had done, but they only sprinkled the guests with wine. This is what happens when we have not integrated the spiritual teachings, and simply emulate the ritual practices without having 'cooked' the inner nourishment. It comes out unabsorbed and is destructive, or at the very least messy. When they waved the other sleeve – that is, the outer manifestation of the 'teachings', only the bones flew out, and one bone hit the Tsar in the eye. He was so angry that he drove the wives out of the palace. This time the ritual was destructive, having actually hit the Tsar in the eye. The eye is a very important organ here. We are not told which eye, so this indicates simply the symbol of the sun god's life giving power. The eye's power is incarnated in the God-King – in this case the Tsar. There is an eye of the soul by which Truth is seen. So for the Tsar to be hit in the eye is indeed a destructive and devious thing to do even if it was done unconsciously. The evolved soul, as represented by the Princess Vassilisa is creative and has access to the inner realms of love, harmony and beauty, whereas those who simply try to copy her, achieve destruction and dissolution.

The story so far has been within the realm of the Tsar; in other words it has taken place in the outer life, the secular life which we all live. The first part of our life is taken up with establishing ourselves in the world, then in midlife we begin the next part of our journey.

Meanwhile Prince Ivan quietly slipped out of the hall and hurried home. He found his wife's frogskin lying on the veranda and threw it into the stove, where it burnt in the fire.

Without knowing why, this seemed to me to be a horrifying and destructive act. However, fire is creative and purifying as well as destructive. Having seen his Beloved, his soul without her ugly cover, Prince Ivan wants to rid his Beloved of her frogskin and be always in union with her. To do this he burned the frogskin, her outer garment and disguise.

When Princess Vassilisa returned home she saw that the frog skin was gone. She sat down on the bench and said to her husband sorrowfully, *'Ah Prince Ivan, what have you done? If you had waited only another three days I would have been yours for ever. But now I must say goodbye. You can look for me in the thirtieth kingdom beyond three times nine lands. There you will find me with Kashchey the Deathless.'*

The Princess does not understand why Prince Ivan has done this terrible deed and says that she only had another three days to go till she was free. But the number three is the first number of multiplicity, and is also symbolic of wholeness and the soul. Three days is a long time in reality, so she is talking in symbolic language. I have a feeling that there would never have been a perfect time for the Frog Princess to burn her frogskin, and that she would never have been ready, so it is for the male principle, or the active principle, to take the lead to reveal her true nature. In this way, the fairy tale recognises that we have to act in the world as it is, as we are, and that it is through the quest itself that our true nature becomes revealed and refined.

This is the next stage in the Frog Princess's journey of completeness. She must leave and say goodbye. In the process of feminine spirituality, there is always a time when the feminine must withdraw into herself, away from the world and continue with her evolution – the process of completing herself. However, for the masculine, the hero has to find his Beloved Soul and win her back. This is the hero's journey. He has been the instrument of burning her outer frogskin, and this pushes both her and him into the next stage of evolution. It is now time for the masculine to take its step. Prince Ivan has not yet done the work on himself; he has not conquered his nafs or small self. He needs to start on his own spiritual journey.

Prince Ivan and Vassilisa can be seen as two aspects of being. Their two journeys are mirror images of the inner journey of the masculine and feminine principles.

The Princess Vassilisa gives Prince Ivan plenty of hints for his journey, all of the hints contain the number of completeness – three. In Slavic mythology the moon god is triple-headed. Princess Vassilisa says she will be in the thirtieth kingdom beyond three times nine lands – a realm very, very far away in the depths of the feminine principle. Thirty is three times ten, and ten is symbolically the number of the cosmos – the paradigm of creation. The decad contains all numbers and, therefore, all things and possibilities. It is interesting to note that ten is the perfect number and a return to unity. Thus, this realm is central and fundamental to life, and is both ever-present, as well as so very far away. The three times nine lands, beyond which the thirtieth kingdom is to be found, are further multiples of three. The nine is composed of the powerful 3 x 3 triple triad, meaning completion, fulfilment and attainment – the beginning and the end, the alpha and the omega.

So, the Princess is to be found with Kashchey the Deathless. In other myths Kashchey is an evil, ugly, bony old wizard, who principally menaced young women. It is said that Kashchey cannot be killed by conventional means targeting his body. His soul is said to be hidden separate from his body, inside a needle, which is in an egg, which is in a duck, which is in a hare, which is in an iron chest (sometimes the chest is crystal and/or gold), which is buried under a green oak tree, which is on the island of Buyan in the ocean. As long as his soul is safe, he cannot die. If the chest is dug up and opened, the hare will bolt away. If the hare is killed, the duck will emerge and try to fly off. Anyone possessing the egg has Kashchey in their power. Kashchey will then begin to weaken, become sick and immediately lose the use of his magic.

Kashchey the Deathless may actually be the Prince's egoic self; he represents avarice. He sits on the riches, which he accumulates, and does not share them with anybody. On the other hand, he could also represent the patriarchy, as I have come to believe. Kashchey wants us to believe that he is deathless and unconquerable, the ruler of the whole world. But he can be conquered by the one who conquers himself.

At this point in the story, the Princess turns into a grey cuckoo and flies out of the window. Grey is the colour of wisdom, but can also be about the death of the body and the immortality of the soul. A cuckoo also usually heralds spring, so it seems to indicate both death and rebirth. In other versions of the story, Princess Vassilisa turns into a swan, rather than a cuckoo, and it is really more fitting that she would turn into a beautiful noble swan, given her connection with the swan in the story. The cuckoo is not well regarded in Russian folklore. Nirtan says that 'the cuckoo tells you the number of years you are going to live. When you go into the forest, you count the number of cuckoo calls and guess how long your life is going to be.'

The Prince weeps bitterly as his wife, Princess Vassilisa, flies away, but then bowing to all four points of the compass he goes off into the world to seek his soul wife. What does it mean to bow in the four directions? In the Lakota tradition, the Great Spirit comes into manifestation through seven directions – Grandfather (the heavens above), Grandmother (the earth below), to the west we seek wisdom, to the north we walk a path of seeking health, of balancing mind, body and spirit. The east represents kindness and generosity to ourselves and others, and to the south is purification. Grandfather and Grandmother represent the ways of masculine and feminine energy – always in balance with each other and always equally important. The seventh direction is that which you will find when you live all six. That is your centre, your path, your path to the spirit world.[30]

In European mythology, north is related to coldness and darkness – the land of the dead, with south representing the noonday sun, fire, warmth, and the masculine principle. These are the opposites. West is autumn and the dying sun, and is associated with dying. The Isles of the West is where the Celtic warriors go when they die. East is the rising sun, dawn, spring and hope. It is the direction of worship for all the solar gods, so again east and west are opposites of birth and death.

Prince Ivan, by bowing to all four directions, is honouring all aspects of the great journey he is about to start. He walks for so long that he wears out his boots; his clothes are torn, and the rain soaks through his cap. This is indeed a very long time and a long, long journey.

One day he happens to meet a very old man, who says, '*Hello, young man! What are you seeking and where are you going?*'

The Prince told the old man how he had lost his wife, and was now seeking her. Notice that when Ivan finally finds his teacher (in the old man), we have direct speech, so rare in this short story.

The old man said, '*Ah, Prince Ivan, what made you burn the frogskin? You did not have to wear it or take it off.*'

It feels like incredible wisdom is hidden in these few words. Yes, we would like to speed up our 'waking process' and remove the veils, but life has to take its turn and forcing something against the course of natural flow might bring negative consequences. Murshid Nawab

---

[30] Pansy Hawk Wing, 'In Relation', in Hilary Hart, *The Unknown She: Eight Faces of an Emerging Consciousness,* The Golden Sufi Center, California, 2003, pp. 71-72.

(my teacher) says that we should not wake people up against their will and we should raise their consciousness slowly, according to their natural development. The old man's response also speaks of certain laws of nature, we should not judge what is right and what is not right, according to our limited understanding. If we have not put this ugly skin on, then we should not force the one that wears it to take it off. Patience, or letting things develop in their own course, and trusting that things will develop when it is the right time, is perhaps another great test of life. This is a point to ponder – it is really often much simpler to keep the covering over the soul – the inner journey is dangerous and difficult. The skin had to be burned, so that the feminine (the soul) could be released from her spell – her imprisonment. The feminine in us is often, if not always, imprisoned, in the world of the ego and patriarchy, where the soul is hidden deeply in the many levels beyond Kashchey's body. It is the task of the feminine to free herself from this imprisonment, and it is the masculine which must assist in this by actively following the quest consciously.

However, the old man goes on to say: '*The wise Vassilisa was born cleverer and wiser than her father, and he was so angry that he ordered her to be a frog for three years. What is done cannot be undone. Take this ball; wherever it rolls, you boldly follow after it.*'

So, the turning of the wise Vassilisa into a frog was in the nature of a punishment for her being cleverer and wiser than her father, who was also a king. Her father's action is about not honouring the wisdom of the feminine principle – in fact, fearing it and so trying to banish it from his thought. This has been the fate of many wise women, indeed the feminine in our culture. The task of women is, therefore, to rise above this 'punishment', to be freed from it and, in becoming free, to become who we really are. This is our life's task. How do women live as women in a patriarchy which does not recognise their wisdom and value? Perhaps this rejection by the patriarchy comes because the feminine is the feeling, intuitive and emotional side of nature; it comes from Eros rather than Apollo. Remember also that we are talking about the feminine aspect in man.

The old man gives Prince Ivan a ball to follow wherever it rolls.

The ball symbolises either the sun, or the moon – the power of solar or lunar gods moving the celestial bodies across the skies. So for Prince Ivan to follow the ball, is to follow his fate, wherever it takes him. The wise old man is, as we have seen, both a spiritual teacher and guide. He understands the quarrel between Princess Vassilisa and her father, as well as her exile in the realm of Kashchey. This can be seen as the eternal combat of the soul versus the ego, both of which are part of one Being and are thus connected. While the ego rules, the soul is in exile in the marshes; when the ego is conquered, the soul rules supreme.

The Prince thanks the old man and follows the ball across open country, where he comes across a bear and takes aim intending to kill it. But the bear speaks to him in a human voice, *'Do not kill me, Prince Ivan. Someday I shall be of service to you.'* The Prince takes pity on the bear and goes on his way without shooting it. The bear signifies initiation, new life in the form of a resurrection, and so it has an association with rites of passage. Prince Ivan is starting on a new journey, and the bear is a symbol for this first stage. The bear is described in masculine form in this story, and I believe that the first chakra can also be seen as masculine. The bear, and all the animals Prince Ivan encounters, speak with a human voice. He is told not to kill animals at this stage of inner initiation. This shows us that we must honour our inner 'animals' (traits), rather than kill them off, as soon as they make their appearance.

As he walks, Prince Ivan sees a drake flying above him. He again takes aim to shoot, but the drake also speaks to him in a human voice, *'Do not kill me, Prince Ivan. I shall be of service to you.'* So again, he has pity on a wild creature, and goes on his way without shooting the drake. In many other stories a duck frequently appears, but in this story the creature is said to be a drake, meaning specifically male. The duck is a mediator between sky and water, so the drake in this case could be symbolic of the yang, or Jalal energy, of the air. Air is a masculine noun in Russian, and these stages of initiation could well be related to the elements. The bear being masculine, could be related to the power of the Earth (although Earth is a feminine noun, the power is masculine).

The same happens with the hare, which comes running past, and again Ivan lets a wild creature go on its way. Note that all the creatures know who the Prince is and address him by name. They also know that they will be of service to him at some stage in the future. Now the hare is a lunar animal and is a yin / Jamal attribute of all moon deities, and so represents birth and resurrection, as well as intuition. It is said in the story that the hare came running past, and, indeed, the hare is associated with speed and, therefore, perhaps lightening. Fire itself as an element (it is a masculine noun) is the next stage or level of evolution. In the Sufi element breathing practice the lowest element is Earth, then Water, Fire, Air and Ether which is the highest and finest element.

Next Prince Ivan comes to the blue sea and sees a pike lying on the sand on the shore. It was barely able to breathe and it says to him, *'Prince Ivan, have pity on me; throw me back into the blue sea'*. So he throws the pike into the sea. To have reached the blue sea is very important, as Prince Ivan has come to the realm of the great mother, the source of all life and containing all possibilities in manifestation. It is unfathomable, like life itself, and can be considered to be the deep unconscious, so finding a sea creature lying on the shore really means that a part of his own unconscious has been thrown up onto the earth, which is not its own element. So, Prince Ivan must again throw the pike back into the sea and not let it die. When Russian stories mention sea, it is most probably large freshwater bodies, like big lakes. Pike is feminine in Russian and is, thus, a wise freshwater fish, king of the fish, in fact. The pike, together with water, is a feminine symbol, but the pike itself can symbolise the wisdom of the waters.

In this story, the water is the highest element, as it symbolises the whole depth of the unconscious, the ocean, or sea, of which we are all drops in the unity of consciousness.

Prince Ivan has had to learn compassion for the animals and, in doing so, for the instinctual parts of himself. His reaction to kill, or repress, parts of himself must be sublimated, as these creatures will later aid him on his journey, as we shall see. Indeed, when we are disciplined and evolved enough to acknowledge our uprising instincts, honour them and let them go, rather than repressing them, we have gained in self-mastery. We could also see these creatures as traits, which come from the natural world. We could say that we do have to know when, and why, we chose to access some traits or aspects of ourselves, that could otherwise been seen as negative. The traits are neither good nor bad in themselves; they simply are. Harm comes from exercising them blindly, without discrimination. Prince Ivan, in sparing the lives of the bear, the pike and the hare, is then able to access their qualities in a knowing way, without bringing harm. The power and ferocity of a bear could be frightening, but one day useful. Similarly, the speed and trickiness of a hare, while frowned upon, may also come in handy, while the aggressiveness of a pike, especially when we are in the depths of the sea, can be the difference between life and death. All traits are part of the One and should not be ignored. As Murshid Hidayat has often said, 'Being spiritual does not mean we have to be a doormat.' Hidayat himself was very feisty, direct and assertive and it stood him in good stead in his long life.

The first two animals / elements that Prince Ivan encounters are masculine: the bear with earth, and the drake with air. The next one is feminine: the hare with lightening or fire, and the last, and highest one, is both masculine and feminine, being the pike with water. This is a progression towards the higher and more oceanic wisdom of the feminine or the soul. This is second stage of the journey, where Prince Ivan has overcome his instinctual reactions and mastered the small self. This usually happens in mid-life on one's journey.

The next stage then relates to the highest element which is ether and is not of the outer world at all. Prince Ivan follows the ball as it rolls along the shore and at last it rolls into a forest. There the Prince sees a little hut standing on a chicken leg, and twisting round and round. So Ivan says to the hut, 'Little hut, little hut, stand just as you were built, with your back to the forest, your front to me'. This is so like an incantation.

This little hut is the home of the Baba Yaga – the witch of Slavic fairy tales. I feel that this myth originates in the matriarchal times, perhaps just as the patriarchy and Christianity were becoming prevalent, or dominant, in eastern Europe. The great forests of the Komi region are still the meeting point between Christianity and the old shamanic paganism of the Asiatic tribes. Christianity was thus a veneer over the ancient pagan culture concealed beneath the Russian one. The influence of Asia was manifest in Russian language, customs, in melodies and harmonies and in all their fairy tales. The motifs and metaphors were thought to come from Persia (Byzantium) and from Mongolia (via the descendants of Genghis Khan). Both Persians and ancient Russians have idealised the tree as part of a sacred cult, so this hut standing on chicken legs, represents the sacred tree and is symbolic of the dwelling place of the sacred.

The Baba Yaga is the wise old woman, or shaman, who taught the people of the forests. The figure of Baba Yaga and her chicken-legged house might also be a relic of the conflict between Christianity, growing from the royal court and the cities, to the traditions of the pre-Christian 'pagan' people living in the vast forests of northern Russia. This divide has existed in Russia right up to the 19th century. Although the peasants would have been devout Christians, the old myths and superstitions remained in the folk memory. 'Turn your back to the forest and your face to me' thus means, I am entering the forest, the realm of old, mysterious beliefs.

The little hut turned with its front towards him, and its back to the forest, demonstrating that with the right attitude and incantation, having journeyed thus far, the realm of the mysterious is accessible to the seeker.

I find it interesting that Prince Ivan knew exactly what to say and do when confronted with the chicken-legged house! It sounds like an incantation – part of a rite or ritual. He had clearly done the inner work, so that he could proceed safely into the realm of the Baba Yaga. The little hut did indeed turn with its front towards him, and its back to the forest. He went inside, and saw the old witch, the Baba Yaga, lying on top of the stove, her chin resting on the shelf at the top of the stove, and her nose pressed up against the ceiling. Baba Yaga is said to be a guardian spirit of the fountain of the Waters of Life and of Death. She rules over the elements and is the Arch-Crone, the Goddess of Wisdom and Death, the Bone Mother, a wild and untamable nature spirit bringing wisdom and the death of ego (and, through death, rebirth). The image of her lying on the stove face up to the ceiling seems to indicate that she is at the centre of warmth and safety (the hearth). The stove, or 'Kachelofen', is the tiled stove used in eastern Europe and Russia for warming the whole house, and also for cooking.

Lying on top of the stove could also suggest that she is in a meditative position – off the ground, as is the house, and just under the ceiling – an in-between place, perhaps of spiritual practice. The house is like a tree-house, as we will see later in the story, and is connected with the ancient mythology of the oak.

However, it is said that the Baba Yaga appears to have no power over the blessed and the pure of heart, who are protected by the power of love, virtue or a mother's blessing, and she reveals her all-knowing, all-seeing and all-revealing side to those who dare to ask.

The Baba Yaga's House

There are stories where the Baba Yaga helps people with their quests, and stories in which she kidnaps children and threatens to eat them, so seeking out her aid is usually portrayed as a dangerous act, requiring proper preparation and purity of spirit, as well as basic politeness.

'Why have you called on me, young fellow?' the old witch asked him. *'Are you seeking your fortune, or are you running away from it?'* This is actually a profound question which we should all perhaps ask ourselves before we embark on the next stage of our journey. It is also a question that Baba Yaga often asks in a ritualised way.

Prince Ivan has no fear and asks for what he needs. What he needs is the sort of thing one would ask of a mother, *'You old scold, the prince answered, before you start asking questions, you should give me food and drink and a hot bath.'* There are laws of civility in dealing with these sacred energies. They expect companionship (taking bread with them), a sharing of energy that becomes forever a part of whoever partakes. But before bread can be broken, one must first know how to ask for it, for such food is not freely given to strangers. Note that bread was seen as a sacred link between this world and the next; it was connected with the folklore of the stove, where the spirits of the dead were said to live.

So the old witch Baba Yaga gave him a hot bath, gave him food and drink, and put him to bed, much like a good mother would. Then, and only then, did the prince tell her he was seeking his wife, the wise Princess Vassilisa.

'I know, I know,' the old witch said. *'Your wife is with Kashchey the Deathless now. It will be difficult to get her away from him; Kashchey is not easy to deal with. His death is right at the point of a needle, the needle is in an egg, the egg is in the duck, the duck is in the hare, the hare is sitting in a stone chest which is in the crown of a lofty oak, and Kashchey the Deathless guards that oak as he would the apple of his eye.'*

So of course the Baba Yaga knows what is happening – she is all knowing and all seeing – a wise old woman teacher. She tells Prince Ivan what he needs to know about where Kashchey the Deathless resides and how to deal with him.

Prince Ivan spent the night in the old witch's hut, and next morning she told him how to get to the spot where the lofty oak was growing.

The Prince found the spot, and saw the oak standing, rustling its leaves; in its crown was a stone chest, so high that it was very difficult to get at. Spending the night in Baba Yaga's hut would indicate a time spent in the 'underworld' as in the night world of deep meditation. He was being taught practices and ways of finding the great oak tree, and learning how to use what he has previously learned and experienced with the animals.

Let us look at the very complex symbolism of this scene. First of all, who is Kashchey the Deathless? As we have said before, Kashchey represents our own egoic self, the small self which is greedy; which wants the richness and power of the world and does not want to share it with anyone. It is the egoic self which captures the soul. This small self is very much part of the patriarchy, which took over the role of the feminine in our culture so long ago. It appears that in Siberia and the Slavic cultures, the matriarchy survived longer than it did in other parts of Europe, so that the Baba Yaga is a remnant of the times where the wise old women teachers and shamans guided the ways of the villages and the people of the forests.

The Komi region in the north, just west of the Ural Mountains was a meeting point between Christianity and the old shamanistic paganism of the Asiatic tribes. 'It was a 'wonderland' where 'The people's action is accompanied by secret magic rituals.'[31] There were tales of shamans who flew off on their horse-sticks to the spirit world. This would certainly explain the stories of the Baba Yaga witch-like figure flying off on her 'broomstick'. The Komi believe in a 'living soul' which shadows people throughout their lives, and prayed to the spirits of the water and the wind, and spoke to fire as to another person. This people are said to be descendants of Mongols from the time of Genghis Khan, and the Turkic peoples of northern and central Asia as well as Slavic Russia.

Kashchey is that patriarchal ego which steals away the real powerful and magical being of the feminine. He holds the souls of wise women such as the Princess. This is still happening of course. And it is indeed difficult to get away from him. The egotistic small self, also of course

---

[31] Figes, *Natasha's Dance*, p.358.

thinks that it is separate and unconquerable – ruler of the whole world and of ourselves. It can only be conquered by the one who conquers his or her self. Even though the patriarchy is on the surface dominant in Russia and Eastern Europe, behind the facade, the society remains matriarchal: Most work is done by the women, they rule the family life; they hold their families together and support their men and children.

The lofty oak tree is symbolic of the world centre (axis mundi), which is really the whole of manifestation and the synthesis of heaven, earth, and water. The tree also symbolises the feminine principle, the nourishing, sheltering, protecting, supporting aspect of the Great Mother. In a way, the house on chicken legs with the Baba Yaga lying on top of the stove is a reflection or representation of life in this tree.

'Throughout the major cultures of Europe the oak tree has been held in high esteem. To the Greeks, Romans, Celts, Slavs and Teutonic tribes the oak was foremost amongst venerated trees, and in each case associated with the supreme God in their pantheon, oak being sacred to Zeus, Jupiter, Dagda, Perun and Thor, respectively. Each of these gods also had dominion over rain, thunder and lightning, and it is surely no coincidence that oak trees appear to be more prone to lightning strikes than other trees, whether because of their wood's low electrical resistance, or the fact that they were frequently the largest, tallest living things in the landscape.

The trees were known as the scenes of pilgrimages, ritual ambulation, and the recital of prayers, as well as places of healing. With its branches reaching up into the sky, and roots deep into the earth, the oak can be seen to dwell in three worlds – a link between heaven, the earth, and the underworld, uniting above and below. The tree itself could be an allegory to our own structure of the world, and to our inner chakra system - the tree of life. The crown of the great oak is the highest place to be – it is like being in the heavens.[32]

And here is found the stone chest. The stone chest is static and is the opposite of dynamic life – it is an aberration and does not belong in the tree at all. The axis mundi, or tree of life is in the midst of everything, joining the three worlds and making communication between them

---

[32] Figes, *Natasha's Dance*, p.358.

possible, and it also gives access to solar power as it rises to the sunlight. This is what Kashchey wants and guards jealously. In Roman mythology the oak is primarily the tree of the Sky God, Zeus or Jupiter, and in Celtic mythology the oak also symbolises the masculine power of the Druids, which is paired with the feminine mistletoe. In the oak of this story, there is no feminine and this is the point and issue here. The feminine has been relegated to the deep forests with the Baba Yaga.

The stone chest could be seen as an omphalosi, a point of communication between God and man; and also a point where man can regain paradise, or find enlightenment. This stone chest is hollow – it holds something important and sacred. It holds esoteric treasures of hidden knowledge. It holds the life of the phoenix.

The crown chakra is of course the highest point of our inner tree system, and it takes time and practice to open this chakra point. We need a teacher to show us how to get to that opening.

Earlier in the story, Prince Ivan spared the bear, and this is the first animal which came to help the Prince. The bear runs up and tears the oak up by its roots. This bear is hugely powerful and can upset / uproot the whole realm and structure of our outer life, of our ego – how we see life and the manifestation of life. Everything is uprooted in the process. There is always destruction before transformation, a death before rebirth. This is a dangerous space to be in – without proper preparation and teaching, we would possibly not survive the uprooting of our inner world tree. It is the masculine bear as part of the earth element which can bring this necessary upheaval about. The egoic structure sees us as being separate, rather than part of the whole universe. To suddenly see that we are no longer separate is a huge upheaval – we know that we are the 'drop in the ocean', or part of the mind of God.

Next the heart has to be broken, broken open that is, before we can have access to its wisdom. This is painful! The chest is like the heart, which contains a treasure which is to be attained.

The chest falls and is smashed to pieces. So the rigidity of stone and the heart of the seeker is smashed to allow life, growth and death. Often, when something is rigid, rather than flexible or flowing, it is easily smashed.

Now a hare leaps out of the chest and flees at top speed. Life, light and fire in the form of a hare were encased in the stone chest. A second hare chases after it, overtakes it, and tears it to pieces. A hare, representing the feminine qualities, is very fast and it is only another hare that can catch it and tear this 'creature' or inner trait to pieces. At each level of our inner structure something important has to be destroyed. Only like can destroy, or create like, so it is the hare which Prince Ivan, the seeker, has understood and released earlier in the story, which now can destroy the hare which was held in the stone chest of his heart. In destroying the original hare which was held in the stone case, a transformation can happen. First the tree was uprooted, now the captive hare must be torn to pieces. The whole structure of the ego must be annihilated, but not the ego itself. In the chakra system, alternate chakras are masculine and feminine, as the Kundalini rises from the base of the spine. In this analogy the masculine bear, which uprooted the tree, and the feminine hare contained in the chest, were destroyed by the liberated hare. When we reach this level of mastery this all happens in a flash of intuition, without thought, which is why this part of the story is over so very quickly.

A duck then manifests out of the pieces of the hare, and flies right up into the sky. The duck is the mediator between water and sky, so we have gone from the feminine fire symbol of hare to a female duck who carries an egg – a mediator between sea and sky. The transformed hare, now a duck carries the egg within it.

However, as the Prince watched, a drake flew at the duck; and as the drake struck her she let fall the egg, and the egg dropped into the azure sea. Note that a duck egg is also blue. The duck and drake together depict the union of lovers, but in this case, as we see, the drake had to strike the duck to release the egg. The egg is the cosmic egg – the life principle and potentiality of everything – the germ of creation. It is the hidden origin and mystery of being. So this egg is the life force within us which is released; this gives us the energy and power to continue the process.

The cosmic tree is sometimes depicted as growing from the cosmic egg. Sometimes the egg is depicted as floating on the waters of chaos. In this case, the egg is dropped back into the ocean of the unconscious.

When Prince Ivan saw this, he shed bitter tears - how could he ever find that egg in the vast sea? This is the stage where we find ourselves disheartened, just as Prince Ivan was. How can we ever find the egg in the vastness of the deep unconscious, which is the 'Collective Unconscious'; the realm of the Gods and the Archetypes.

But suddenly a pike swam up to the shore with the egg in its mouth. When we spend time in contemplation, or meditation, we find ourselves floating in the ocean of the inner realm – often we find insight and discovery. The old wise pike is that part of us which inhabits the watery realm, grants our wishes and brings us the treasure – the cosmic egg.

So, the great wise fish of the ocean finds the egg and brings it to the prince. Once we have our spiritual practices and understanding at that level of the deep unconscious, there is a part of us that can then find the egg easily. These are related to levels of evolution, or depth of practice, as well as the opening of the chakras.

This time it is the prince who breaks the egg, takes out the needle, and sets to work to snap its point. At each stage the perception of a 'normal' level of understanding of the world has to be overturned. First the tree is uprooted by the bear, then the stone chest crashes to the ground and breaks open, the hare runs out and is torn to pieces by the other companion hare and transforms into a duck, which flies up into the sky. The drake strikes the duck to release the egg, which falls into the ocean and this egg is found by the wise old pike, and broken by the Prince. The cosmic egg contains the needle, or point, which in turn must be broken. Sometimes we can get to the level of finding the cosmic egg, the source of all life and creation, but we can go no further. To break the point of the needle is the most difficult and almost impossible task of all – but what does this mean? The point of a needle is the smallest point that can be imagined – the smallest dot is a small circle from which a bigger one grows. There was once much speculation about the number of angels which could dance on the head of a pin, or how many universes were manifest on the head of a pin. These were deep philosophical questions about reality – about the hidden and the manifest. In the story it says that Prince Ivan set to work to snap its point – I imagine that the ultimate task does indeed take a lot of inner work, as this is about the ultimate control of the ego, but not the destruction of it. It is about one-pointedness – total concentration and presence on the work. There is a lovely mystical description of God, as a circle whose centre is everywhere and whose circumference is nowhere. David Tacey believes that God is radically present with us and closer even than our own breath, a presence that is nearer to us than is comfortable to admit. The conventional image of God that so many people have, has to be destroyed so that the deeper reality of God can be experienced.[33] This is the point that has to be broken.

The inner work is about being conscious of the nafs, or small self, to the point where it can be transcended. A bridge has been made between the Self and the ego. The point where there is only the One. At this stage the small self does not have a hold on us anymore and the soul is free. Kashchey is dead!

Then the prince goes to Kashchey's white stone palace to find his princess soul. It is interesting to note that the Prince, or the masculine principle, still has to go to Kashchey's white stone palace to unite with his Beloved. Stone is the basic material which signifies the imperishability of Supreme Reality. Ultimately, it is indestructible and returns to the Source. The white palace is the dwelling place of perfection, simplicity, light, sun, purity, chastity. Very early Russian churches were built of white stone, where the peasant's houses and those of the nobility were of wood, so the white stone palace was symbolic of the pure dwelling place of the sacred. In this respect the scene reminds me of the Grail legend, where Parsifal arrives at the Grail castle. There he knocks on the door and gains admittance. But before he is allowed to drink from the Holy Grail he must answer the riddle of the Grail 'Whom does the Grail serve?' The Grail is the source of all – the cup that is never empty, it also represents the soul.

When the Prince arrives in this sacred space, the wise Princess

---

[33] David Tacey, *The Spirituality Revolution: The Emergence of Contemporary Spirituality*, HarperCollins, Australia, 2003.

Vassilisa runs out to meet him, and kisses him on his lips. She of course was always aware of what was happening to him and so ran out to meet him and gives him that kiss on the lips, denoting a true meeting of lover and beloved, a meeting and joining of opposites. Robert Johnston contends that the masculine principle must find the grail castle, but the soul, the female principle already lives in the castle. [34]

Once the masculine and feminine unite in this way, the One, that we are part of and which is part of us, can return home, which is everywhere and nowhere.

So Prince Ivan and Princess Vassilisa return home, and they live happily to a ripe old age.

After this great opus, or journey within, we return to the world and live happily ever after, as the stories say. We are in the world but not of it.

Sometime after I had finished this exposition, I was still wondering what this journey really means for the feminine herself. What is the spiritual process for women in finding their Soul?

Then I had a very profound dream which I think explains the next step. In the dream I was with a man who had been the love of my life in a way. I think I had projected all my inner Beloved onto him, and indeed he had very much made me a complete woman, after I had lost myself in a heart- breaking divorce. He had shown me love and made me feel loved and lovable. So there I was in the dream and I knew this was the last time I would ever see him.

He said, *'I loved you!'* I felt surprised – I was never sure that he really had loved me.

He also said *'You lied!'* I answered, *'I lied to myself – I believed it too'.* Then we hugged and he was gone.

Then there appeared a young girl of about six or seven years old. She was beautiful, but not in a conventional way. She was also very wise and very mystical – she was mine, but she really lived with another couple that I could not quite see. I realise that in giving up and letting go of

---

[34] Robert A Johnston, *He: Understanding Masculine Psychology*, Harper & Row, New York 2002.

my image of 'my lover', I was able to see and get to know my soul. I also realise now, that she looked a lot like me when I was that age.

So, perhaps for women once we have had this meeting with our soul mate, there is another stage of evolution, where we, as complete Beings, recognise our soul – know that she has always been here with us, as we are part of Her. It is this journey of understanding, of the realisation of Soul and our relationship with her, which this fairy tale so clearly shows us.

Regarding the soul, Hazrat Inayat Khan has said that:

'The condition of the soul may be likened to a mirror. It reflects the object which is before it, but that object is not engraved in the mirror; it only occupies it during the time it veils it. In the same way, the soul is veiled by experiences; in other words, our experiences may delude the soul, may cover it or bury it, but they cannot penetrate it. Also, what is called individuality is only a temporary state, and as soon as the soul has awakened it no longer attaches much importance to individuality, which is something made up of garbs borrowed from the different planes. It is like a doll made of rags. When we understand this we give all importance to the soul, the soul which is real, which comes from the real, and which seeks after the real.

The final question is: what can be the purpose of the creation of man? Is anything gained by it? Yes, the realisation attained by the experience of life. And it is a divine realisation when the experience has led the soul to that height where it is no longer only an individual soul, but where it is conscious of all planes of existence, not only of the source but of all the planes of limitation. And when all the inspiration and power latent in man are within his reach, then that realization is called perfection.'[35]

---

[35] Hazrat Inayat Khan, *Sufi Teachings, The Sufi Message Volume 8*, Motilal Banarsidass Publishers, Delhi, 1994. p.162.

THE FAIRY OF THE DAWN

his story begins with the usual 'Once upon a time' which immediately puts it in the realm of myth, but it also has one of those cryptic comments which makes it real and indicates that the story did happen – in some mythological realm, (perhaps outside of time and space).

The setting or cast of this story begins with an Emperor, who is very great and mighty, and whose realm is so large that no one knew where it began and where it ended. This tells us that the Emperor's realm is more inner than outer – the realm of consciousness whose boundaries we do not know. He is a sort of father figure, a bit like a childhood concept of God. However, in Sufi stories the king or emperor often represents the heart. In the story everyone knew that the emperor's right eye laughed, while his left eye wept. So, outwardly he was seen as laughing, but on the inner, the left side, he wept. Nobody knew why this was so and although one or two (note not many) brave men had asked the emperor, he only laughed at the question.

This motif of the King, who has one eye that laughs and one that weeps, is more famously known from Prophet Mohammed's flight to heaven, where he saw Adam looking to one side and smiling, and looking to the other side and weeping. I think that this might be something to do with our inner or God's reaction to the good and evil of mankind.

This Emperor had three sons – like morning stars in the sky – which is another hint that this tale is 'otherworldly'. The first, the eldest son, Florea, was tall and broad shouldered, the second, Costan, was small of stature, slightly built but had strong arms and a stronger wrist. The third, and youngest son, Petru, was tall and thin, more like a girl than a boy, spoke little but laughed and sang all day long. That he sang and laughed all day would mean that he is balanced (left and right side of the brain, if you like), but also balanced in feelings and connected to soul and the feminine. As Pir-o-Murshid Hidayat says – the soul is happy, and music is the way to the soul. Jungians would say that the soul is feminine and the spirit masculine. Petru was seldom serious but had a way of stroking his hair over his forehead when he was thinking, which made him look old and wise enough to sit on his father's council. So I would say that Petru our hero has a well-integrated feminine side, and that he has a degree of wisdom when he wants to 'go there'.

Petru wants to know the secret of why his father's one eye weeps and the other laughs. He asks his brothers to ask their father but they are afraid, so he asks the Emperor himself. 'May you go blind!' exclaimed the Emperor in wrath 'what business is it of yours?' and boxed Petru's ears soundly.

Petru tells his brothers what had befallen him, but he had noticed that his father's left eye seemed to weep less and his right eye to laugh more, since he had asked his question. He decided to try again, after all what did two boxes on the ears matter. He did not mind the pain / discomfort if it helped his father.

So he put his question a second time and had the same answer, but now the left eye only wept now and again, and the right eye looked ten years younger. Petru knew that this was true and he wanted to continue to ask the question till both his father's eyes laughed together. This he did, so that the emperor's eyes were now both laughing and so he told Petru his secret! His right eye laughs when he looks at his three sons and sees how strong and handsome they all are, the other eye weeps, because he fears that after he dies the sons will not be able to keep the empire together and to protect it from its enemies. *'If you can bring me water from the spring of the Fairy of the Dawn, to bathe my eyes, then they will laugh for evermore, for I shall know that my sons are brave enough to overcome any foe.'* So here is the quest which was given only after Petru passed an initial test of accepting the boxed ears to make the

Emperors eyes laugh. That it is the left eye of the emperor that weeps is very significant. The left is the sinister, dark side. 'Sinestre' means left in French, but it is also the feminine, receptive, inner side of us, the intuitive side. This is a quest for the feminine.

I have been wondering about the meaning of these symbols of the laughing eye and the weeping eye. The God of our childhood certainly presents as a good God – in fact the English word for God comes from the German word gut, which means good. This is the first issue we come across because if God is all good, then how come he lets all the bad things happen in the world – how come there is evil in the world. If evil is a lack of good and God is everywhere how come, there is evil? So when God or our higher self, or heart, sees all that is bad in the world then perhaps his left eye weeps? We have free choice after all – a choice to follow our conscience or inner voice, or give in to our ego and follow our small self. Greed, a quest for power, a desire to look good, and many such things are ego and these are the things that we have to see in ourselves in order to combat them, and become the best possible human being that we can be. When we see these negative parts of ourselves our 'higher Self' weeps. This really is our quest. The first step is our realisation of this, so when the Emperor sees that his son is pondering these things and looking inward, he is happy and weeps no longer, because he knows his son will follow the quest. His other sons were not able to get that far, so although the older two sons take up the quest it was really given to Petru, because he was able to understand his father. The Emperor wants to leave his kingdom in safe and strong hands.

There are always three sons in these fairy tales and it is always the youngest that takes up the task properly. In this story the youngest has already proved himself equal to the task that he has been given, but it is first discussed with his older brothers. First, the oldest one leaves on the quest riding the best horse in the stables. Perhaps three symbolises the many or multiplicity of people in the world. Only one is really called out of the many. Not everyone is a mystic or even wants to be one.

The first brother Florea rides for three days and nights – a long time indeed; like a spirit his horse flew over mountains and valleys and finally came to the borders of the empire. The story here gives us a clue that this journey is like spirit. Here was a deep, deep trench that girdled it the whole way round and there was only a single bridge by which the trench could be crossed. This bridge can be seen as a crossing between the conscious world of the Emperor to the unconscious unknown inner realm. Florea headed for the bridge and there he pulled up to look around him once more, to take leave of his native land. I think that this was his first mistake – he stopped and looked back! Once we are on the path we should never stop and look back. It is a bit like the story of Lot's wife, who looked back and turned into a pillar of salt.

When he turned back to the bridge there was a dragon, a huge and horrible monster with three heads and three horrible faces, all with their mouths wide open – one jaw reaching to heaven and the other to earth.

Florea did not wait to give battle but spurred his horse and fled he knew not where. The dragon heaved a sigh and vanished without leaving a trace behind him. Dragons, as monsters like this, are said to be 'masters of the ground' against which heroes, as conquerors and creators must fight for mastery of the land; they are guardians of treasures and of the portals of esoteric knowledge. Florea was afraid and did not even take the dragon on, so the dragon was not happy about this, which is why I think he sighed and disappeared. When we first go into silence / meditation, it is very difficult and uncomfortable, and for some people even frightening, so frightening that they never try again. It can feel like death or that they are dying.

After the year and a day, Costan left the land to go on the same journey. This time the dragon was even more fearful and the three heads more terrible than before. Costan took off and rode away even faster than his brother. This often happens when we don't fight or overcome a particular issue – it comes back even more horrendous than before.

Petru was now alone and so one day he told his father that he must go after his brothers. His father gave his blessing. Note that Petru told his father, while his brothers did not. Petru has a connection to his Emperor / heart.

This time, when Petru came to the bridge, the dragon was even more dreadful than the one Florea and Costan had seen, for this one had seven heads instead of only three. Three is the first number which indicates multiplicity – overcoming duality, but seven is the number of the cosmos and completeness. With the three of the heavens and the soul, and the four of the earth, seven is the first number, which contains both spiritual and temporal. It is perfection – and it is also the number of the Great Mother. The numbers are very significant in these stories or myths. Also, remember that there is no feminine in this story so far.

Petru only stops for a moment when he sees the dragon, but then 'finds his voice' and yells at the dragon to get out of his way. The dragon did not move, so Petru draws his sword and charges the dragon. In an instant, he is surrounded by fire all around him as the seven heads spew flame. It is the struggle with the dragon, which symbolises the difficulties that must be overcome in gaining the treasures of inner knowledge, and overcoming the dragon really means attaining self-mastery. The dragon can be seen as the ego, or small-self in reality. Yelling / commanding the dragon with the mind does not work – quite the opposite. We can't will our inner dragons or tricks of the mind to disappear and allow us into the realm of silence and meditation. Neither does fighting it, even if it is with the sword of discrimination. The horse neighed and reared at the horrible sight and Petru could not use his sword, so he dismounted and holding the bridle, and grasping his sword he still could not overcome the dragon.

Petru holds the bridle in his left hand (inner control) and the sword in his right hand (action). He cannot see because of the fire and the smoke – the dragon is solar (fire), so our first obstacle is fiery and energetic, but also transforming. He decides that he has to go back and get a better horse. The horse here symbolises the intellect, wisdom, mind, reason and nobility, so Petru did not have the stability of a sufficiently developed wisdom / mind (or practice) so that he could use the sword of discrimination to overcome his ego.

When he returns his nurse, old Birscha was waiting for him eagerly. She told him she had known he would have to come back, as he had not set about the matter properly; which only goes to show that there is always a proper way to achieve goals when on a spiritual quest. When we do not go about it the proper way, we can have a real, what used to be called 'spiritual emergency', which can often be interpreted as mental illness of some sort. Facing and fighting the dragon without guidance and preparation can be dangerous.

Birscha, the archetypal nurse of our childhood, is the first (direct) mention of the feminine in this tale and she is also his first Teacher. It is the inner feminine wisdom which will aid Petru. She says that he will never reach the spring of the Fairy of the Dawn unless '*you ride the horse which your father, the emperor, rode in his youth. Go and ask where it is to be found, and then mount it and be off with you.*' When asked about the horse, the Emperor exclaimed '*By the light of my eyes! Who has told you about that?*' Fifty years have passed since I was young, and who knows where the bones of my horse may be rotting, or whether a scrap of his reins still lie in his stall? I have forgotten all about him long ago.' This time long ago – fifty years symbolises the great year, the jubilee, which comes after the forty ninth year (7 x 7 cycle). It is a return to the beginning, the primordial state; a time when the Emperor or Emperor Archetype was 'a student' of life, with his nurse, at the dawn of humanity.

As in other fairy tales, such as the ring cycle, the hero son has to either re-forge the sword of his father, or in this case find the horse that his father rode, that is the intuitive wisdom his father had as a young man, or perhaps to remake an Ideal of his Teacher. His exclamation '*Light of my eyes*' confirms that the Emperor is all about light and seeing.

The Emperor calls Birscha a witch, so he denigrates the feminine wisdom, and yet it looks as if she was also the Emperor's nurse all that time ago. After all in the beginning there was Sophia (wisdom). Petru is angry once again when he hears his father's words and returns to his old nurse and Teacher. She simply smiles on hearing this and says that if that is the way of things, all will go well. The Emperor has given the hint that a scrap of the old reins might be found in the stable. Indeed Petru finds the oldest, blackest, and most decayed pair of reins and brings them back to Birscha, who murmurs over them and sprinkles them with incense – in other words she performs a sacred ritual over them, and holds them out to Petru. '*Take the reins and strike them violently against the pillars of the house,*' she said. What did it mean to strike the reins on the pillar of the house? The pillar can be seen as the vertical axis which both holds apart (separates) and joins heaven and earth (*Axis Mundi*) at the same time it is a ritual world centre. The house is also a world centre - the sheltering aspect of the Great Mother, an enclosing protective symbol. To strike the reins on this pillar is surely a ritual and a powerful act in connecting directly with the heavens in a complex way. However, Murshid Nawab also pointed out to me that the pillar could symbolise the Kundalini – an energy which 'runs' along the spinal cord and is that part of us which, like a pillar, joins the base chakra to the crown chakra, in a way that joins and yet separates earth and heaven. To strike this with the reins, or our mastery of our ego, or small self is a major stage and is indeed a practice and form of initiation.

As Petru strikes the pillar, or raises the Kundalini, a beautiful horse stands before him, with a saddle of precious stones and a dazzling bridle. Splendid is used four times – a splendid horse, a splendid saddle, and a splendid bridle, all ready for a splendid young prince. Of course reins and a bridle are used to guide and control the horse, so this makes it even clearer that the horse is about inner guidance and mastery. Sitting firmly in the saddle is also important. Petru is being trained in a spiritual discipline, so that he can master the dragon on the edge of the conscious realm, and move into the next one.

'*Jump on the back of the brown horse,*' Birscha says and turns to go back into the house.

At this point the brown horse speaks to Petru telling him to sit firmly in the saddle for they have a long way to go and cannot waste any time. Brown is the colour of being dead to the world – 'to be in the world and not of it', as the Sufis say, and brown is the colour of some religious communities who are into renunciation or penitence. This horse can be understood as being the Spirit of Guidance (the teacher). When Petru sits on the horse his heart is braver and his arms feel three times stronger.

When they arrived at the bridge there was different dragon – one with twelve heads and even more hideous than before and shooting out more flames than the other. Now the dragon has twelve heads and twelve symbolises the complete cycle or cosmic order, and again it contains three and four (3 x 4), so the task is becoming more cosmic and archetypal, rather than personal. Petru showed no fear and rolled up his sleeves, so that his arms were free.

'Get out of the way,' he yelled, but the dragon only breathed out more flames. Petru was about to throw himself on the bridge when the horse spoke – '*Stop a moment: be careful and be sure you do what I tell you. Dig your spurs in my body, draw your sword and keep yourself ready, for we will have to leap over both bridge and dragon. When you see we are right above the dragon cut off his biggest head, wipe the blood off the sword, and put it back clean in the sheath before we touch earth again.*

To dig his spurs into the horse is something that would hurt the horse, but steady Petru and give him the energy to move forward strongly. All of this Petru did and so they passed the bridge. Perhaps the lesson here is to rise above our challenges and, at the same time, to cut off the largest head (as in 'head stuff') that we can. I think that this bridge could also be like crossing from left brain, rational, logical thinking to right brain magical and feeling – a place of no defined boundaries, which is why Petru wants to look at and see this new realm – he has never been there before and it is quite new.

Petru has journeyed through the physical worldly realm of the Emperor (consciousness), across the bridge into the realm of the unconscious. The first stage of his journey is now complete.

Petru's beautiful brown horse

Just as they are about to start the next stage of their journey, the horse offers Petru different speeds to choose from: The speed of the wind, of thought, of desire or like a curse. Petru says *'not too fast as to grow tired, and not too slow as to waste time'* to go at different speeds as they are required. Here is a hint of where and what this journey is, that is, inner space, when the horse talks about the speed of thought, which is the quickest, as it is instantaneous, and to desire, which is slower. Interesting he includes 'like a curse' here and I wonder what this is – does it mean that a curse is slowest? In the mind world, thought is the only reality.

He sees a desert before him, and they ride on for one day at the speed of thought, one at the speed of desire and one like a curse, till they reached the borders of the desert. Perhaps when we first go into the unconscious, in dreams or meditation, it feels like there is nothing there, just a barren desert.

Petru wants to walk around and see this new realm - before him lay a wood or forest made of copper, with copper trees and copper leaves, with bushes and flowers made of copper.

Hazrat Inayat Khan talks of a Copper Age; this a middle age; the age of cares, of worries, of anxieties and of responsibilities. There are even Copper Rules by Hazrat Inayat Khan:

COPPER RULES
My conscientious self:
Consider your responsibility sacred.
Be polite to all.
Do nothing which will make your conscience feel guilty.
Extend your help willingly to those in need.
Do not look down upon the one who looks up to you.
Judge not another by your own law.
Bear no malice against your worst enemy.
Influence no one to do wrong.
Be prejudiced against no one.
Prove trustworthy in all your dealings. [36]

---

[36] Hazrat Inayat Khan, *The Dance of the Soul: Gayan, Vadan, Nirtan, Sufi sayings,* p.142.

Petru has never seen or heard of anything like this forest before. Then he rides right into the copper wood – on each side the flowers began to praise Petru and to try and persuade him to pick some of them and make himself a wreath. Each flower offers something else – to give strength, to make him loved by beautiful women – they all tempt him. Just as he is about to pick a flower, the horse sprung to one side. The horse tells him not to pick the flowers as it will bring him bad luck. This is about not getting attached to phenomena and fascinated by the beauty of this realm, and not get stuck in that place where we are impressed by such things. For instance, we can discover that we have the ability of seeing, or hearing, or healing, or telepathy, but we must just move on, and not set ourselves up in the nearest market place. We must not pick the flower.

The horse tells him he will have to fight the Welwa of the woods if he picks a flower, but Petru in spite of making a huge effort not to be tempted, becomes weaker and weaker and, in the end, picks some flowers, which he weaves into a wreath or crown. Now he must prepare to battle the Welwa, which is really an aspect of the ego, perhaps the spiritual ego! When we first encounter the realm which we enter in meditation, or even when we begin on our practice, the temptation to use what we have learned for gain of our ego, is so strong. The mind or ego chatters to us and wants to distract us – then of course we have to do battle with yet another monster within us.

Out of a gentle breeze arose a great storm and darkness. The earth swayed and shook under their feet. The horse tells Petru not to be afraid and to use his bridle to try and catch the Welwa with it. The Welwa is indescribably horrible. Petru lays about him with his sword but can't actually feel anything. Sometimes we have to keep fighting even when we don't realise or even feel what we are fighting – we must not stop until it is done. The fight goes on for days and nights. Both the Welwa and Petru become tired but the horse tells Petru not to give up or stop. The story says that Petru planted himself firmly in his stirrups, which surely means that he steadies himself so he can make a stand, using his horse as a base from which to fight. After three days, again a long time, Petru manages to throw the bridle over the head of the tired Welwa. As soon as he does this a beautiful horse stands before him – he has released the horse from enchantment and now the horse rubs noses with his brother horse. When we overcome the inner monster demon by catching it using our mastery (bridle), the monster transforms releasing energy, which is added to that intuition that becomes that spirit of guidance. In other words, our inner voice or intuition becomes stronger. Intuition can be understood as inner tuition. Petru ties the Welwa to his own horse and rides out of the copper wood

When we enter a new realm, we often have to release an archetype, or inner figure, which has been enchanted – in other words an aspect of our life, which we fear and which prevents us from being our true selves. When released, this aspect becomes a helpful friend, or attitude, or instinct. A complex is really a bundle of energy which distorts our sense of the world around us – it is like seeing the world through a distorting prism, so when that complex is released or transformed, we have that energy to use in our life. It is very freeing.

Now they come to the silver wood, and Petru again dismounts the horse and looks around to see what he has never seen before. Hazrat Inayat Khan again talks of the Silver Rules:

SILVER RULES
My conscientious self:
Consider duty as sacred as religion.
Use tact on all occasions.
Place people rightly in your estimation.
Be no more to anyone than you are expected to be.
Have regard for the feelings of every soul.
Do not challenge anyone who is not your equal.
Do not make a show of your generosity.
Do not ask a favour of those who will not grant it you.
Meet your shortcomings with a sword of self-respect.
Let not your spirit be humbled in adversity.[37]

---

[37] Ibid p.141.

The silver age of the Hindus is like youth with a spring and delicacy and with its own responsibility. It is the age of treasures, but with its own trials.

As before, the flowers beg the young man to gather them, and as before Petru cannot resist them. The copper Welwa / horse now tells Petru not to pluck the flowers and although he knows by experience what this means, he cannot help himself and he gathers flowers and fashions himself a wreath. Then the storm wind howled louder, the earth trembled more violently and the Welwa of the silver wood came rushing on, seven times as strong as the Welwa of the copper wood. Note that this time the silver Welwa is seven times as strong as his brother (seven being the number of the cosmos and completeness as we have seen before). Again after three days and nights, Petru overcomes this Welwa by throwing the bridle over his head. Again the second Welwa thanks Petru for saving him from enchantment, and they journey on as before. So, from this we learn that having overcome our first inner demon and released it, we have a second one to overcome and this one is even more powerful than the first. Petru is still unable to resist the temptations of the flowers and has to fight the Welwa each time.

Now they come to the golden wood, even lovelier than the other two. Hazrat Inayat Khan has also written about the Golden Rules:

GOLDEN RULES
My conscientious self:
Keep to your principles in prosperity as well as in adversity.
Be firm in faith through life's tests and trials.
Guard the secrets of friends as your most sacred trust.
Observe constancy in love.
Break not your word of honour whatever may befall.
Meet the world with smiles in all conditions of life.
When you possess something, think of the one who does not possess it.
Uphold your honour at any cost.
Hold your ideal high in all circumstances.
Do not neglect those who depend upon you.[38]

---

[38] Ibid,p.140.

The Golden Age of the Hindus is like infancy – although dependent, the infant is sovereign, happy in the arms of mother, in the care of father, nothing to worry him, nothing to trouble him, no attachment, no enmity – happy as the angels in heaven.

Again Petru is warned not to stop and pick the flowers and again he cannot resist and weaves himself a golden crown. As soon as he has done that he feels something terrible, which he could not see coming near him out of the earth. A thick fog wrapped itself around him, so that he could not see his own hand or hear his own voice. He fought this with his sword but could not see what it was that he was fighting. On the dawn of the second day it vanished altogether. The horse told him it was the Welwa turned into a fog, but now she comes again. What does it mean that the Welwa appears as a fog? Fog is made up of the elements of air and water, but fog prevents one seeing anything and also muffles sound. It is frightening and is everywhere. After fighting all day and all night the fog suddenly vanishes. Notice the Welwa is a female this time. Now the Welwa comes at him again – it seems to be water - and yet not a river – a strange watery element. He is told not to stand still. The battle begins again. He is totally exhausted but grasps his sword and waits. The brown horse tells him to take a breath – and I wonder if this means literally a breathing practice? What attacks him is again indescribable and spoken of as a sort of paradox, that is 'a creature which has what it has not got, and has not got what it has'. It reminds me a bit of a Zen Koan, or perhaps an indirect method of self-hypnosis – to make the mind tired and to let go. Petru feels fear for the first time, but fights on. He is past fighting on his feet and is now on his knees. He settles himself in his saddle, grasps his sword and waits for the final battle. The water has gone with the dawn, but still he has to fight. The horse urges him to make one last effort and it will soon be over.

'Strike the Welwa on the mouth with the bridle,' the horse tells him.

What does this mean to strike the Welwa on the mouth with his bridle? The mouth is a symbol of the devouring aspect of the Great Mother. To strike her with the bridle is actually to strike her with his increasing mastery of himself. When he does this The Welwa utters a neigh so loud that Petru thought he would be deaf for life. It is interesting that there is a great and powerful, deafening sound that accompanies the release of the Welwa. Perhaps a release at this depth is accompanied with a sound or a great vibration which can overcome us and make us deaf.

Hazrat Inayat Khan says '*There is one thing in the whole creation which is like an alarm clock, set for a certain time to make a sound so that one may awaken. That clock sounds through all the activity of evolution, and when this is touched, man is awakened by the alarm.*'[39]

Soon the new horse is also trotting by his side. 'May your wife be the most beautiful of women,' she says, 'for you have delivered me from enchantment.'

I find it interesting that this new horse is a mare and that she talks about a wife for Petru –this shows that this story is about the integration of the feminine principle.

Petru now thinks about the crowns that he has woven from the flowers along the way, and what it has cost him. He decides to only keep the best and throws away the copper and silver crowns. The horse tells him not to throw them away, and that they may be useful, so he stops and retrieves the crowns. This really means that all the lessons along the way, everything we have gained, should be held on to, not put aside or discarded.

The second part of Petru's quest is now complete – he has journeyed through the copper realm, the silver realm and the golden realm and gained in mastery and 'hearing that inner voice', having gained three more horses in addition to his original brown one. Four is symbolic of the spatial scheme, or order of manifestation. It has a sense of wholeness and completion on earth – the four cardinal points, the seasons. The stage takes him through the unconscious mind from the copper realm, which is closest to our consciousness and the complexes which we overcome there, to the silver realm, which is further away and contains the issues and complexes from our youth, to the golden realm, which is preconscious, pre memory, but is in us at a very cellular level. The next stage takes him into the archetypal Collective Unconscious, in other words into the realm that we all share and are part of, but which is the realm of the Gods and Goddesses which are archetypal, not human. This is where we are all one at the depth of our being.

---

[39] Hazrat Inayat Khan, *The Mysticism of Sound and Music,* p.282

Now Petru sees a wide heath stretching out before him, but the horse stops as it fears that evil will befall them. The horse says that they are about to enter the kingdom of Mittwoch and that it will get very, very cold there. He is afraid that Petru will want to stop and warm himself by the fires along the way. Note that Mittwoch is a feminine form of Mercury it is also the planet closest to the sun, and is the day Wednesday in German. This seems to suggest a process in time and space. The position of Mercury / Mittwoch is centre.

However, this time Petru is able to ignore invitations from the men at the fires on each side of the road, even though the breath froze in his mouth. Petru makes his way through this frozen place where frozen rocks explode around him, his teeth chatter and even his eyelids are frozen. When they reach the dwelling of Mittwoch herself, he enters and greets her – the interchange is very 'ordinary' really, although he does recognise her as 'little mother'. He says 'Good-day little mother!' and she says "Very well, thank you my frozen friend,' but he waits for her to speak.

She tells him that he has done well and been brave and gives him a gift as a reward – a little box which has been lying around for ages waiting for the man who could win his way through the Ice Kingdom. He is told to treasure it and use it when he needs to. *'If you open it, it will tell you anything you want and give you news of your Fatherland.'* He has journeyed through the Ice Kingdom to find an aspect of the Goddess so that he can connect / communicate with his 'fatherland'. As Mercury is the Divine messenger of the Gods, and so of communication, the box which she gives him is a communication device to his fatherland and this is very important. We have to know what is going on at home, when we are on our quest.

After thanking her and riding away Petru opens the box and asks for news of his father. *'He is sitting in council with his nobles'* was the answer. *'Is he well?'* asks Petru. *'Not particularly, for he is furiously angry.'* *'What has angered him?'* *'Your brothers Costan and Florea,'* replied the casket. *'It seems to me they are trying to rule him and the kingdom as well, and the old man says they are not fit to do it.'*

The feminine Mercury has given Petru the gift of knowing what is happening at home with his father, the Emperor. This is how Petru realises that all is not well. This ability is developed in us when we reach a certain stage of evolution, in this case having survived the Ice Kingdom. This time Petru has not been tempted by the warmth of the fires tended by men. Here the opposites begin to come into play. The realm is feminine, but the beings tending the tempting fires are masculine. The gift she gives him relates to the 'masculine' Fatherland.

Petru rides away as fast as he can, but his horse wants to give him some more advice. He has known great cold, now he must endure extreme heat. He must not allow himself to be tempted to try and cool himself, or else evil will befall him. It is indeed so hot that his horses' shoes began to melt, but he continues and does not let himself be tempted by lovely maidens who stand by shady trees and bubbling streams. After a long time the heat suddenly seems to become less and in the distance he sees a little hut on a hill. This was the dwelling place of the Goddess of Thunder (in German Donnerstag or Thursday). This is the day of the Thunder God Jupiter. We have moved from Wednesday to Thursday, from Mercury to Jupiter, where we are again in the realm of a Goddess this time of thunder. Notice we are now faced with the extreme opposites – Heat (solar and masculine) versus cold (lunar and feminine) – these opposites must be integrated and this is part of the task.

When Petru drew reign at Donnerstag's door she came out herself to welcome him and invite him in. He tells her everything that has happened to him and then takes his leave, as he does not know how far it is to the Fairy of the Dawn. She asks him to stay as she wants to give him a word of advice. She says 'You are about to enter the kingdom of Venus, go and tell her as a message from me that she should not try and delay you.' On his way back he is to visit the Goddess of Thunder again and she will give him something that may be of use to him. This time he must wait for the gift until he has completed his quest and returned to her. The only advice is a message to Venus not to delay him, so it seems that this will be her tactic – to delay him there in her realm.

As Petru mounted his horse again, he had hardly ridden three steps when he found himself in a new country: a place which is just right – like the three bears – not too cold not too hot, but where the air is warm and soft like spring. However, the way runs through a heath covered with sand and thistles. This time the ambiance is just right but the way is through a very barren place, so we wonder what has happened here. At the far end of the heath he sees the house of the Goddess Venus. It took but a day to ride to the house and as they found themselves nearing it, Petru's heart leaped at the sight, for all day long he had been followed by a crowd of shadowy figures who danced about him from right to left and from back to front. Now Petru feels a thrill of fear!

The horse says: *'They won't hurt you they are just the daughters of the whirlwind amusing themselves while they are waiting for the ogre of the moon.'* I wondered what this meant and found that the whirlwind was regarded as a manifestation of energy in nature, rising from a centre of power associated with gods, supernatural forces and entities that travel on whirlwinds, or speak from them. The whirlwind thus becomes a vehicle for the divinity: 'The Lord answered Job out of the whirlwind.' So these entities (female) are waiting for the ogre of the moon – a female divinity – here with negative connotations! She is an ogre! But then female energy was regarded with fear in those times long ago, after the fall of the Goddesses.

As Petru is about to enter the house, his horse tells him to stop as there are several things he wants to tell him first. The house of the Goddess Venus is guarded by the whirlwind, so this energy in nature protects her. Petru is to take the copper wreath and go with it to a hill nearby and then say to himself. 'Were there ever such lovely maidens! Such angels! Such fairy souls!' Then hold the wreath high in the air and cry *'Oh! If I knew whether anyone would accept this wreath from me-----if I knew! If I knew! And then throw the wreath away from you!*

Scarcely had he flung away the copper wreath than the whirlwind flung itself upon it, and tore it to pieces. This is a gift which the whirlwind accepts in its own way and Petru can now leave. Venus is related to the West, and her day is Friday. She signifies the launching of the new moon on the sea of the night and defends the moon against all monsters of darkness.

The horse then tells Petru that there are other things that he wants to tell him. Now Petru is to take the silver wreath and knock at the windows of the Goddess Venus. When she says 'Who is there?' answer that you have come on foot and lost your way on the heath. She will tell you to go on your way back again; but take care not to stir from the spot. Instead be sure to say to her, '*No indeed I shall do nothing of the sort, as from my childhood I have heard stories of the beauty of the Goddess Venus, and it was not for nothing that I had shoes made of leather with soles of steel, and have travelled for nine years and nine months and have won in battle the silver wreath, which I hope you may allow me to give you, and have done and suffered everything to be where I now am.*' So he is to flatter Venus and tell her that everything he has done and been through is only to see her and be with her. He knows how to be, with the Feminine.

He approaches the house in the dark, the only light coming from the windows to guide him. At the sound of his footsteps two dogs begin to bark loudly. Venus asks which of the dogs is barking – which I find a strange question. The dog is a guardian of the passage; guardian of the underworld and keeper of the boundaries between this world and the next. Does it matter which dog it is? In any case Petru answers, '*It is I O! Goddess; I have lost my way on the heath, and do not know where I am to sleep this night.*'

'*Where did you leave your horse?*' asks the Goddess. Petru didn't know how to answer so Venus tells him to go away, as there was no place for him there. She withdraws from the window.

Petru then repeated what the horse had told him, and no sooner had he done this the Goddess opened the window, and in gentle tones asked him in. She asks to see the wreath and he gives it to her. She then invites him into the house and tells him not to fear the dogs, as they know her will. As he passes, the dogs wag their tails to him. So Petru has passed the tests and eventually answered exactly as the horse told him, so he has safely crossed that boundary to the next world and is able to converse with the Goddess. Venus needs to be loved and worshiped for her beauty and she also needs to know what the hero has undergone and suffered to be with her. Venus, as you know, is the Goddess of love and also represents the beautiful woman to be won by the hero lover in mythology.

He wishes her good evening and then sits down and listens to her speak – mostly about the wickedness of men, with whom she is angry. Petru agrees with her in everything as this is polite isn't it! He was tactful and respectful and of course this is the proper way to be with a Goddess. He has learned the Art of Personality[40].

The Goddess Venus was not what you would expect – she was so very old and had many, many wrinkles on her face, but Petru devoured her with his eyes and Venus was joyful when she saw his eyes fixed on her like that. Venus is happy to be adored as she should be. It is the wickedness of men who have turned her into an old hag. I think there is something about the Patriarchy which has denigrated one of the greatest most beautiful Goddesses to an old hag.

'*Nothing was that is, and the world was not a world when I was born,*' said she. '*When I grew up and the world came into being, everyone thought I was the most beautiful girl that ever was seen, though many hated me for it.*' Clearly Venus is an Archetype – a concept of the feminine, of the beautiful inner beloved of every man and perhaps an ideal for many woman. But her current aspect also reflects the fall of the great Goddess, matriarchal religions of old, and prior to the dominance of the patriarchal religions, which are still so powerful. When a man loves a woman he believes she is the most beautiful woman in the world. In the story she tells Petru that in every hundred years she got another wrinkle and now she is old. She goes on to tell Petru that she was the daughter of an Emperor and that their nearest neighbour was the Fairy of the Dawn, with whom she had a violent quarrel. With that Venus broke into loud abuse of her.

It seems that there is or was a split in the feminine principle here between the Goddess Venus and the Fairy of the Dawn. It also indicates that this split must be healed both within Petru, but also in the world, as much damage has been done by it. This split still exists I think – we idealise 'the mystical Feminine Sophia' but denigrate Venus the Goddess of love, beauty and sensuality.

Petru sympathises with Venus, agreeing that she must have been badly treated. He does this for politeness sake, the story says! Again he

---

[40] Hazrat Inayat Khan, *The Art of Personality, The Sufi Message Volume 3.*

is being tactful. Venus now gives him a task to perform. Close to the Fairy's house is a well, she tells him, and whoever drinks from this well will blossom again like a rose. She asks for a flagon of it, and tells him that the kingdom is guarded on every side by wild beasts and dragons. She gives Petru a tiny flute which an old man, perhaps her Teacher, gave to her when she was young, and whoever listens to it goes to sleep, and nothing can wake them. Petru is to play it as long as he is in that kingdom so that he will be safe. Petru then tells Venus that he has another task to fulfil at the well of the Fairy of the Dawn, and Venus is still better pleased when she heard his tale. I think Petru's quest pleases her because she realises that he will bring the feminine principle back to the world and back to his kingdom.

Next morning Petru feeds his horses well with corn and takes them to the well to water, so it is clear that our inner 'spirit of guidance' needs to be nourished, before this last great stage of the journey. Venus calls out to him from her window to stop, as he is ready to start, as she still has some more advice for him. He is to leave one of his horses there with Venus and only take three. Three is the number of forward movement and symbolises overcoming duality, so this is an appropriate number of horses for him to take. Four is a more solid static number. She tells him to ride slowly until he gets to the Fairy's kingdom, then dismount and go on foot. To go on foot means more freedom of movement, but also indicates willing service and humility or reverence. On the return journey he is to see that his three horses stay on the road, while he walks. But above all he must never look the Fairy of the Dawn in the face, for she has eyes that will bewitch him, and glances that will befool him. She is hideous!

It takes Petru two days and nights travelling through flowery meadows, to reach the palace of the Fairy of the Dawn. It was, neither hot nor cold, bright nor dark and Petru did not find the way a step too long. He saw the most beautiful splendid white castle which dazzled his eyes. The castle represents spiritual testing and something difficult to obtain. What is to be attained is enlightenment, as the symbolism of the Dawn is about illumination. In Buddhism it is also the clear light of the void and in Christianity it is the advent of Christ bringing light to the world.

He jumped down from his horse and began to play on his flute as he walked along, He had hardly gone many steps when he stumbled over a huge giant who had been lulled to sleep by the music of the flute. This was one of the guards of the castle. Interesting the comment here that Petru stopped to measure him! This gives some insight to his enquiring mind. We too have to measure the beings / things we need to overcome and then aid us. In a sense he gets the measure of the giant.

Before him were many strange and terrible creatures as well as dragons all stretched out before him fast asleep. Then he came to a river of milk and precious stones and pearls. The river ran around the castle. Milk is from the Mother Goddess and is the food of divinity for the gods – divine nourishment. Milk has also to do with initiation rites and ceremonies. The pearl is a lunar symbol representing the power of the waters, cosmic life, and denotes birth and rebirth.

Petru has to cross the river but how? This is another barrier to cross and it seems by the symbols, that this is done by powerful initiation rites, ceremonies and ritual. This is a very important process and he is getting toward the end of his journey. He decided to wake the giant but every time the giant woke up he tried to pick Petru up, as if Petru was a fly. Fully awake, the giant was dangerous to a very small Petru. The giant here means the brute forces of nature, or primordial power and forces. What Petru does is use this force to his advantage to get across the river. To do this he has to do battle with these forces first. Finally, the giant acknowledges that he is beaten at last and begs for mercy. The giant it seems to me is not as scary and difficult or perhaps dangerous as Petru's other combatants and this whole scene has a different feel to it. I think that this scene is an enactment of a powerful ritual. So that when after a while Petru tied up the two little fingers of the giant with his handkerchief and then drew his sword, it is purely symbolic. I suppose that with his little fingers tied up he would be unable to pick Petru up, on the other hand if we hold our hands with the two little fingers together we have two attitudes of prayer, one with the hands facing one another, and one with the hands together open and facing heavenwards. Petru promised to fight the giant fair and square if he would then take him over the river. The fight with the giant took a long time (three days and nights), until in the end Petru was on top with the point of his sword to the giant's throat. The giant gave up and agreed to take Petru to the other side of the river. Petru bound the giant's left hand to his right foot, tied a handkerchief around his mouth, to prevent him crying out, and another around his eyes, and led him to the river. Again, this binding of the hands to feet seem to be symbolic of this same ritual, which is in effect, to get Petru to the 'other side' of the river.

Once they reached the river bank the giant stretched one leg over to the other side and, catching up Petru in the palm of his hand, set him on the further shore. Petru then played on his flute and put the giant to sleep again. The flute and the music of the flute indicates harmony, but can relate to extremes of emotion – the flute of Krishna is the 'voice of eternity crying to the dwellers in time.' It can also relate to seduction. The flute is one of the instruments (like the veena) which is very conducive to meditation. Listening to this music can certainly transport you to altered states like sleep! When we get down to this level of the 'collective unconscious' we are using the right-side brain – the part of us which is feeling and emotion, so certain music can transport us to this realm. When this happens, the left brain goes to sleep or dormant so to speak. While in this space and dealing with some of these sleeping giants, whose aid we really need, we have to be quick and powerful enough to awake the giant and use it to our own ends – this is also a great battle for us. We have to harness its power so it does not hurt or hold us back in the task we are on.

Even the fairies who had been bathing a little lower down the river, heard the music and fell asleep among the flowers on the bank. It shows here that when we put the left brain to sleep, as it were, we are also putting beautiful and wondrous parts of ourselves to sleep. The Gods and Archetypes live in the collective unconscious; there is no room there for the human part of ourselves – we lose our humanity in a sense when we enter this realm. Petru wonders how, if the fairies are so beautiful, why then should the Fairy of the Dawn be so ugly?

Now he was in the wonderful gardens, but everyone and everything was asleep. He passed through the courtyard into the castle itself. It was an amazing place of gold and jewels and the stables, where the horses of the sun were kept, were more splendid than the palace of the greatest Emperor in the world.

Petru went up the stairs and walked quickly through the forty-eight rooms until he comes to the forty ninth – seven times seven! As we have said before: seven is the number of the universe and the number of completeness – a totality. It is also the number of the Great Mother, so Petru has to traverse this spiritual and temporal reality which is the realm of the Great Mother.

In the middle of the room was a very old well and by this well slept the Fairy of the Dawn, the Great Mother / Feminine Principle of Sophia herself. As Petru looked at her the flute dropped by his side and he held his breath. When he actually sees her he is completely mesmerized and does not notice her beauty or otherwise, only the atmosphere of the divine Feminine Principle, which has overwhelmed him. This is probably the reason why he was told not to look at her.

Near the well was a table on which was bread made from doe's milk and a flagon of wine. Doe's milk indicates feminine nourishment, as well as gentleness and meditation. It was the bread of strength and the wine of youth, and Petru yearned for them. This is clearly a ritual symbolic meal like the Christian communion, with the bread relating to the resurrection. He looked at the Fairy of the Dawn sleeping and a mist came over his senses. The Fairy opened her eyes and looked at him, and he lost his head still further; in other words, he loses himself when she looks at him – but he manages to remember the flute and with a few notes sends the Fairy to sleep again. He kisses her three times. He then lays his golden wreath upon her forehead, eats a piece of the bread and drinks a cupful of the wine, and this he did three times over. So he performed a very crucial ritual here at the well of the Fairy of the Dawn. This is where he attains enlightenment or illumination.

The fairy herself has a very passive role although she is so powerful. I wonder if we could see this in relation to the drop in the ocean. We as 'drops' find ourselves losing our 'dropness' and becoming one with the ocean – a total unity of Being with the Divine. If we lose ourselves in this process and get merged with the One completely, we are not able to get back to our real realm of consciousness. The fairy has to be put to sleep at this stage, so that he does not get so drawn in and not be able to function. This can lead to madness. Then he draws water from the well and vanishes swiftly.

As he passes through the garden it now seems different - more fresh and beautiful than before and this is because of the three kisses he had given the Fairy of the Dawn. Now he rode as fast as longing and at length dismounted, leaving his horses by the roadside goes on foot to the house of Venus. When we approach Venus we must always come on foot, ourselves alone, with humility. As fast as longing is a lovely phrase – longing drives us to the beloved and Venus is the Beloved of man. She is the Goddess that has been repressed and disparaged by humans since the advent of patriarchal religions. When we repress and ignore the Gods and Goddesses – the Archetypes within us, they come back to us in a very negative form, even as diseases. Venus knew he was coming and welcomed him. He holds out the flask containing the magic water and gives it to her. She receives it with joy. Venus helps us when we recognise her and do her honour and pay homage to her. Petru brought her the water of life and of beauty and regeneration: he has done this within himself in his own psyche and will therefore do the same in the world when he returns to his own realm.

Petru now stops off, as he had promised, with the Goddess of Thunder. As he is leaving she calls him back to warn him: '*Beware of your life; make friends with no man; do not ride fast, or let the water go out of your hand; believe no one; and flee flattering tongues.*' She tells him that he holds something very precious and gives him an enchanted cloth to help him – whoever wears it cannot be struck by lightning, pierced by a lance, or smitten with a sword, and arrows will glance off his body.

Petru now rides off and consults his treasure box to find out how things are at home. The Emperor was now totally blind, and Petru's brothers Florea and Costan are trying to persuade their father to give the government into their hands. But the Emperor would not, saying that he did not mean to resign from government until he had washed his eyes from the well of the Fairy of the Dawn. The brothers had found out from the witch and teacher Brischa that Petru was on his way home bearing the water. So we learn that our teacher always seems to know what is happening with us.

The brothers set out to meet Petru intending to take the magic water from him and claim as their reward the government of the Emperor and his Empire. Petru does not believe the box and throws it on the ground breaking it into pieces. He has not taken in the warnings of the Goddess of Thunder, not to trust anyone and also he is still naive and does not want to believe anything bad or negative about his brothers. I think that many on the path of the heart have this innocence or naivety in them and must learn to trust no one, but to use their inner knowledge to find their way in the world.

Now Petru is on his way home – he hears his brothers calling him. His horse tells him to go on otherwise things will go badly for him, but Petru wants to see what is going on and has again forgotten the warning given him by the Goddess of Thunder. When he sees his brothers he jumps off his horse and goes to embrace them. His horse stands by hanging his head sadly. When we ignore the inner voice of guidance, however well-meaning this deliberate avoidance may be, there is a part of us which does feel ashamed and we hang our heads metaphorically.

The brothers try and persuade Petru to give them the water to carry, but Petru naively tells them what the Goddess of Thunder said and about the magic cloth she had given him. Both brothers realise the implications of the cloth, and now know there is only one way to kill Petru. He has shown them his weakness as well as his strength, so they know exactly what they must do to get rid of him. They try to coax him with flattery to have a drink of water from a stream, so that they can then drown him.

The end comes suddenly. The horse neighs; Petru knows what this means and does not go with his brothers. He goes home to his father, cures his blindness with the sacred water, and his brothers are never seen again.

Petru has avoided the trap and enters his Fathers kingdom to make it his own. The Emperor was old and ready to give it to the bravest and wisest of his sons – the only one who had done the inner work and journeyed far into the unknown to come back with the water of life and light. And so his eyes laughed for evermore. We must remember that it is the wisdom of the Goddesses that he encountered, which gave him the gifts to help him achieve his purpose. He had to integrate the feminine with the help of his teacher.

Petru had to return into the world of consciousness –we all do. This is where we live but we bring with us the knowledge and experience that we have gained in that inner space.

This story is really a tale for the masculine process of enlightenment, but there is much to be learned from this by women also. Many women these days are almost forced to be 'animus' driven, just so that they can compete in this world, and many are trying to re-discover their feminine side. So, in this way, perhaps we as women can also find sustenance in this story.

THE LITTLE
HUMPBACKED HORSE

Part One

ur story is set in a rural Russian village, with an old peasant man who has three sons. As is common in fairy tales, the two older brothers are bright and hardworking and sell their golden grain to the Tsar, whose palace is nearby. However, there is also the youngest brother, Ivan, who is described as a 'fool'. Often in fairy tales the older brothers set off on a quest but fail, usually because of arrogance, or greed. On the other hand, the youngest son, who appears to be naïve and innocent, succeeds in the quest. This is because he has befriended the animals, and it is their assistance, which eventually leads to his success. The animals in myths can be seen to represent the instincts and/or intuition. We can already begin to see and understand much from this setting. The 'fool' represents the extreme opposite of the highest temporal power - the Tsar or King. In the Tarot, the fool is at the beginning and end of the inner journey; his number is zero (O), unlimited and eternal, which already gives us a clue to his character. He is simple and honest – not really of this world. In some tarot packs the fool is depicted with a small dog nibbling at his heels – perhaps to communicate something or warn of danger. In other packs the fool is blindfolded, which shows his ability to act by inner insight, or out of his animal instinctual nature.

In Russian folk tales Ivan Durak is known as Ivan the Fool, who typically works in a paradoxical fashion, doing what seems to go against common sense to achieve his goal; so this gives us a further insight as to the character and purpose of Ivan in this story. In all the extant Firebird stories the 'hero' is Ivan.

Then comes the inevitable disaster, in this case 'someone' has come in the night and trampled down the fields of golden corn. The golden corn symbolizes the fertility of the earth, awakening life, and growth through the power of the sun. This happens in our life; there are setbacks and we feel like 'someone' has trampled on our corn.

The inner story begins with the situation where the ego, or perhaps the patriarchy, loses its power over life and abundance, when 'someone' tramples the corn. I mention the patriarchy only because of the absence of the feminine principle in the background of the story. Often the feminine is lacking or not mentioned in a myth, and this is an important aspect of the tale. All the characters are male. The trampling of the corn could even reflect attitudes to the earth and the feminine – something to be used but not necessarily respected.

The brothers decide to stand guard over the fields at night in order to catch the villain who is doing this terrible deed. The first brother goes out to stand guard but he is soon 'overcome with fright' and dives into the nearest haystack where he spends the remainder of the night. In the morning, he douses himself with water and pretends to his father and brothers that he has been out in the rain all night, but that 'everything was all right'. His father is well pleased with him as he outwardly seems to have done the right thing, and has prayed and bowed to left and right before telling his tale. I wondered if the left and right sides relate to the inner feminine side of life and outer masculine side of life, or perhaps it simply demonstrates that they are outwardly 'Christian'. In the Roman catholic mass the priest bows to left and right over the offering where the offering is blessed and prepared for actual transformation. All through this tale there is an overt Christianity, which covers a deeper inner secret path. I wonder if this seemingly devout Christianity was superimposed onto an older pre-Christian myth, or whether it relates to the conflict between Christianity and the mogul invaders in Russia and the spread of Sufism from Bagdad to Bukhara and the southern Soviet Union, my feeling being that this is a Sufi teaching tale. This becomes clearer later on in the story.

The next night the second brother goes out to stand guard. A fearful frost sets in. He is cold and shivering, so he spends the night walking around his neighbour's fence. In the morning, he comes in very cold, prays, and like his brother bows to the left and then to the right. He tells how cold it was, but that 'everything's all right', even though, in fact, he did not stand guard at all. His father is once again well pleased.

During the previous night, when the older brother was supposedly out in the rain, the water symbolising emotions (aspects of the feminine), showed that he could not cope with the situation. The following night, the frost sets in, representing a freezing of the emotions, which of course relates to the feminine realm. This illustrates quite clearly how emotions which have been ignored, can become hard and cold.

The next night the youngest brother Ivan is sitting on the stove, singing of a dark-eyed beauty. I was very puzzled by the image of Ivan sitting on the stove, until I remembered the beautiful and magnificent 'Kachelofen' or tiled ovens or stoves which I saw in Austria as a child. It is certainly easy for a child to climb on top of the oven and watch the world go by, on the cosy warmth.

I remembered these same 'Kachelofen' in the homes of my family in Austria and understood that they were often very decorative and made for heating the home in winter, rather than for cooking.

Ivan was apparently oblivious of what is expected of him. Even in the love song, Ivan shows an emotional inner life, which is related to the feminine. His brothers coax and beg him to go out, but to no avail until his father asks Ivan to go out and 'bribes' him with food (beans and peas) and some pictures. The bribes are seemingly simple things, but the father perhaps knows that Ivan would not be interested in such things as gold and silver. Beans and peas are food or nourishment, perhaps related to the masculine (beans) and the feminine (peas), and the pictures are possibly related to beauty and harmony – which Ivan loves, or it could be that the father presented Ivan with a vision (a picture being worth a thousand words), which convinced him to accept the challenge. At any rate, all of this works. Ivan puts on his coat of russet brown, puts a lump of bread in his pocket and off he goes. His coat could symbolise the earth itself – mother earth. In most parts of the story Ivan is frequently seen with a crust of bread symbolising life, the food of the body and the soul and also a symbol of union, having many grains in one substance. The bread is also related to the feminine.

'Night fell and the white moon rose' – Ivan is under the light or the influence of the feminine principle, the spiritual aspect of reflected light in the darkness : inner knowledge; the irrational, intuitional and subjective. Ivan is not afraid – he is sharp and aware. He sits on the ground slowly munching his bread and counts the stars.

He first hears the neigh of a horse and then sees a mare 'whiter than the whitest snow' with a silken mane of long ringlets of gold. In myth the sound of a neighing horses foretells the coming of danger. It is interesting that he first hears the neigh of the horse; first there is the sound, almost as a warning of as yet unseen danger or conflict. This horse is a mare and therefore would represent the lunar or feminine power and fertility. As the horse is white, this would mean that it does indeed represent the moon. In India and China, the great Mother, Goddess of Mercy can appear as a white horse. There is also the idea of a nightmare – a mare that comes in the night to terrorise and disturb sleep! It is through this fight that he overcomes the negative feminine and undergoes a transformation, which changes his relation to the feminine. Without this the next stages of evolution cannot happen.

Ivan, however, only 'sees' the mare as the 'rogue', which has 'played tricks' on his family and trampled down their corn. He is not afraid, awed or intimidated. Ivan seizes the mare's tail and jumps on her back, facing her rear rather than frontwards. I have pondered what this could mean. There is something very 'foolish' about sitting on the horse facing the wrong way, and yet it does enable Ivan to hang onto the tail and not 'see' the dangers ahead of him. Had he faced the right way, he might not have been able to hang on as he did. Sometimes in life we simply have to hang on and have faith that all will be well, perhaps this is why it is called blind faith. The fool also is often depicted as looking or facing backwards, while moving forward, which has been described as a way of connecting the wisdom of the future with the innocence of childhood. His energy seems to be unconscious and undirected, seemingly outside of time and space, yet having its own purpose. The horse does everything in her power to dislodge him, she bucks, runs wildly over hill and dale trying to get free of him. But by holding onto her tail Ivan hangs on until the mare gives up, being by this time 'spent and trembling'. Often in such an inner struggle, we just have to hang on tight and not give up. Eventually the adversary becomes tired and gives up. This overpowering of the 'monster' allows Ivan, our hero, to restore his relationship with the archetypal Feminine or Great Mother. The transformation, which he undergoes during this tussle, changes his relationship to the feminine, symbolically expressed in the liberation of his own masculine power or energy.

Now we come to the 'deal', which often occurs in myth and folk tales. The mare submits to Ivan. He must care for her, but she warns him that every morning for three days, he must let her out to graze and after these three days, she will bear two handsome steeds and another little horse which will be only twelve hands high, with two little humps upon his back, ears a yard long and with two black eyes. The mare tells Ivan that he can sell the two beautiful steeds, but that he must not part with the little humpback horse, under any circumstances. This little horse will be his faithful friend, his everything! In return for this, he must agree to set the mare free. Ivan accepts these conditions and finds the mare shelter.

Again, there is this agreement that always seems to occur at this stage of the process, when the hero, or seeker, wins his first battle or achieves the first part of his 'work', and at this stage he is usually given something magical, which will help him in his quest, even though it appears strange, even ugly.

The horse clearly represents wisdom, nobility, light, power and fleetness, as well as innocence, and is usually ridden by heroes in the myths, so the two horses given to him by the mare, represent this development in his journey.

At this stage in the process, Ivan has reacted to the initial 'issue' of the trampled golden corn of his inner world and by successfully surviving his encounter with the 'night mare', has been shown his teacher and guide, the little humpbacked horse. This is an initiation experience, which is going to change his life completely.

Ivan finds the mare shelter in a shepherd's shack. He then returns home, singing the same love song as before. At the door of his cottage he yells, shouts and bangs on the door, giving his brothers a great fright, and making them angry. Ivan, in his usual carefree way, simply climbs back up on the stove and tells them his version of the story. Notice that he does not bow or pray, or make any outward pretence at a Christian ritual.

The story he tells is close enough to the truth, but told in such a bizarre way that he knew he would not be believed. In addition, he stops after his encounter with the beast or Satan as he calls it. There is no mention of the 'deal'. In many fairy tales there is a secret, which must be kept, so Ivan tells the story to suit his situation. When children discover that they have a separate 'self', that is they become self-conscious, (usually at about age five), they are able to understand and keep secrets, as well as withhold 'truth' or in reality to tell a lie to protect themselves. Thus Ivan, with a strong sense of 'Self', knows exactly how to tell his version of his adventure. Of course his brothers and father laugh till they cry, while Ivan simply goes to sleep on the warmth of the stove. It is interesting that all along Ivan touches the world lightly – there is no attachment or ego related to any of his actions. He simply is, and he does what is required of him.

Now when Ivan did his deal with the mare, that being that he should keep her for three days – this number (three) indicates creative power, growth, as well as 'everything', that is, the universal, which can also represent the soul. It can also simply signify a long time in fairy tales. Soul time is not temporal and indeed the poem here says that we cannot tell how much time has passed since the night of the encounter.

So, some time later, it could have been a year or three years, the older brother is tipsy, it being a holiday, and comes across the shepherd's shack where he sees Ivan's handsome pair of steeds with golden manes, and, standing beside them, the little humpbacked horse. I wonder whether the brother's tipsy state might indicate that he was not in his usual worldly state, but in another, perhaps altered state due to the effect of alcohol or 'spirit'. At any rate, it is in this state that he is able to 'see' the three horses. He immediately realises that this is the reason that Ivan has been sleeping here and races off to tell his younger brother. They both return and gaze at the horses – they notice the golden manes, silken tails and hoofs made of diamonds inlaid with huge pearls – horses fit for a tsar to ride. The brothers are immensely jealous and can't understand how their fool of a brother has managed to get such horses. Perhaps this shows also that, although one can have a sort of spiritual experience while under the influence of a 'drug' of some sort, the process is not lasting and does not have the same effect on the psyche, that is, evolution of the personality.

The brothers are still coming from a place of greed, jealousy, envy and of course fear, rather than from any insight. Often special psychic powers or phenomena are misused in this way, where a mystic would simply be silent and continue on his or her journey. The brothers plan to steal the horses, sell them at the market and enjoy the proceeds, while they gleefully imagine their brother searching for his horses in vain. Their plan agreed, they cross themselves – again Christian posturing, where their actions are far from Christian. They kiss one another and off they go to Sunday market. There is an interesting glimpse of background in the description of the market town, with mention of strange ships in port and the possibility of the Sultan come to enslave the Christian world. So again this tension, between Christianity and Islam, in that Islam spread into Russia via Sufism mainly by transmission from teacher to students, quietly but mostly without conquest.

We now find Ivan skipping through the meadow, again munching on his crust of bread, on his way to his horses. The little hump-backed horse, meets him, prancing in delight to see him, but Ivan 'weeps sore to find his two steeds gone'. He wonders what devil stole them. Here we begin to realise the potential of the little horse in the story, when he tells Ivan not to fret and who it was who stole the horses.

Ivan and his Little Humpbacked Horse

The little horse tells Ivan to hurry and get on his back and off they fly to catch the thieves. Here we discover that the little humpbacked horse is also a flying horse or winged horse like Pegasus. When Ivan overcame the mare earlier, as in the mythological slaying of the dragon, it could be seen as bringing about an ascent of his spirit or energy. The soaring creative forces are set free by overcoming the 'monster', in his case the mare, giving him his ally the flying horse.

The symbolism of the little humpbacked horse is interesting; Nawab suggests that a horse with two humps could well be a way of describing a Bactrian camel such as those that originated in Turkistan. To the Russian people of the Northern forests, a camel could well have been described as a horse with two humps. So, this story could have been imported to Russia from the Sufis further south. On the other hand, I was also told by Nawab that in Russia, 'Humpy-back horses have an identity with the centaur – half man, half horse – having knowledge of men and of gods and devils.' Sometimes a fabulous beast with a combination of different characteristics, suggests possibilities of creation and potentialities, as well as freedom from the conventional principles of the phenomenal world. That the little horse was to be only twelve hands high is also significant, as twelve symbolises a complete cosmic cycle, there are twelve months of the year, twelve signs of the zodiac and twelve hours in each day and night.

However, the long ears also remind me of an ass or donkey and this brings us back to the 'fool', who, as a jester, sometimes wears asses' ears. But the ass can also be the symbol of patience, humility and fertility. On the other hand, I was surprised to discover that ears are associated with the spiral, the whorled shell and the sun. The ear hears the 'word' of creation and so is also associated with the breath of life and the feminine principle. The energy of the Zikar can be experienced as spiral; the energy of the whole universe is spiral, and the primal sound of the universe heard with the 'inner' ear is the deep humming of the Hu. In truth, I feel that the little humpbacked horse is a metaphor for the spiritual teacher or master who, carefully and lovingly, teaches the student the ways of the inner journey and who is later internalised as the inner voice, or inner teacher, or even intuition. Indeed, the little humpbacked horse is more than that and could possibly represent the teachings themselves – like a trinity of Teacher, Teachings and the Student, or indeed the 'God ideal' or Spirit of Guidance. The teacher is everything to the student, just as the little horse was to be everything for Ivan. As with great teachers, there is no sign of an ego – no sign of any 'specialness'. Like the Dervish' he can be a beggar in rags, or the 'fool', or a little humpbacked horse whom nobody would notice or covet. Teachers will often describe themselves in a humorous way and don't take themselves too seriously. A little humpbacked horse would thus be a wonderful description of 'the teacher'.

So it is that on the spiritual journey, after the initial encounter, there is often a secret time of quiet and peace, spending our inner life and space with the gains we have made, such as the beautiful steeds and the little humpbacked horse. But then there is a time of loss and suffering brought about by the manifestation of ego in the outside world, which propels us into the next real stage of the journey. The fact that there are two horses here might indicate an impending manifestation, since all that is manifest in duality is in pairs of opposites. However, Ivan now has his little humpbacked flying horse to aid him.

His thieving brothers are confused and scared when confronted by an irate and angry Ivan. He declares that though they may be cleverer than he, he is at least an honest man. The brothers confess their theft, but plead their case for selling the horses and offer him 'high heeled boots and a hat with bells and feather' - the trappings of a 'fool' indeed. Ivan agrees to their plan, but says that he will accompany them to the market. They are not at all happy with this, but they 'feign goodwill'. So they all continue on their way to market. The weather turns cold and they find themselves in a forest, where they camp for the night, eat, drink and make merry. Again, affected by alcohol, the older brother sees a light in the darkness of the night; the brother points this out to Ivan telling him it is a fire and that they need embers with which to light their own fire on such a cold dark night and so he sends him off to bring back some embers. He hopes that Ivan will fail to return, so that they can forget all about him. It is interesting that it is the problems and suffering of the world which propel us to do the inner work. Like Dante, the seeker finds himself in the middle of a deep dark forest confronted by a 'beast burning bright'. As Dante is confused and terrified, he meets the archetypal 'wise old man' whom he understands to be the poet Virgil, who then guides him on his own descent into Hades. Our story of Ivan has similar features though not necessarily in the same sequence.

Ivan obeys his brothers and climbs on his horse to 'fly' to this next task, where he finds himself swiftly taken to a field which is as bright as day - plenty of light but no smoke or heat. He is astonished but the little humpbacked horse tells him that the light is from a Firebird's feather, and warns him for his own sake:

'Touch it not, for in its wake many sorrows, many woes follow everywhere it goes'

Ivan answers, *'You're telling me – woes and sorrows - we shall see.'* Ivan understands exactly what he is doing, and that the inner work is full of danger and suffering but he has found a trace, a feather of the Divine Light representing light and lightness and he takes up the quest or inner journey resolutely. He wraps up the feather in a rag to hide its glare, and puts it in his hat.

There is much symbolism in the Firebird and its feather. Firstly, the Firebird is symbolic of the sun, signifying divine royalty, nobility and uniqueness, and its feather signifies gentleness since it crushes nothing it alights on. As a phoenix (a universal symbol of resurrection and rebirth by fire), the Firebird could be associated with the consummation of the *'magnum opus'* the great work of regeneration in the process of alchemy. As fire it has two aspects - heat and light, but this Firebird in our story is shown as a being of light only, so its feather again represents light and lightness, as well as the soul and flight to other realms.

The brothers represent the outer world, the patriarchy, greed, fear, corruption, power, and of course the small self or ego. For the seeker, like Ivan, it is imperative that he hides anything to do with spiritual knowledge and inner power, as these would be rejected, distorted or mocked by the outer world, and could even be used by it for base purposes.

Ivan has hidden the feather in his hat, which could indicate that he is to take on the power of the Firebird, which would put him in touch with the transcendent, instinctual knowledge and truth of this bird, in that it is both next to the crown charka and the seat of life-force. The hat itself, as a head covering, could denote a protection of the inner life, so when Ivan hides the Firebird's feather of light and lightness in his hat, he is both integrating the inner knowledge and wisdom of other realms, and protecting his inner life.

Ivan rides back to the brothers, tethers his horse and tells them that all he found was a burnt out stump and that he could not raise a spark or ember from it. The brothers again laugh at him, but he merely goes off to sleep. This time Ivan does not bother with any semblance of the truth and simply 'acts the fool'.

Next morning, they enter town and we find the mayor, who with great pomp and ritual, is opening the fair. The mayor seems to me to be a symbol of power and corruption – he is wearing furs and guarded by a hundred soldiers. He mistreats the townspeople, with his soldiers 'cracking whips on backs and shoulders' to make way for him. He sees the great crowd and finds them around Ivan's handsome black horses, with their 'silken manes and flowing tails gleaming golden in the sunlight'. In alchemy, black signifies the absence of colour and is the first stage of the 'Great Work'; dissolution and the descent into hell.

The mayor races off to tell the Tsar of the fine steeds. The Tsar excitedly prepares to go and see them; he puts on the robes and crown of a king and is taken by coach, so that all the people may greet and bow before him.

The Tsar is charmed by the steeds, he praises and strokes them and asks who is master of these horses. Ivan pushes his brothers aside and now proudly claims his steeds. The Tsar asks if he will sell them, but Ivan says no – he will swap them and asks for 'twice five caps full of silver – and that makes ten'. This could indicate that there would be five caps full of silver for each brother; The Tsar adds a further five roubles for good measure. The numbers here have more meaning than that though, and Ivan is explicit in that twice five makes ten. Five is the number of man, forming a pentagon, with outstretched arms and legs, like a five-pointed star. The pentagon shares the symbolism of the perfection and power of the circle, a symbol of wholeness. Five is also the number of the *hieros gamos* – the sacred marriage of masculine and feminine in alchemy, as well as of meditation and spiritual aspiration. There are, of course, the five senses, five elements, five pillars of Islam and, interestingly, given the twice five above that, there were twice-five incarnations of Vishnu. Ten is the perfect number, the return to unity – based on the two hands (twice five); it is completeness and the number of the cosmos and the paradigm of creation.

It is interesting that Ivan asked for silver – the moon and feminine aspect of gold, given that there is still a total lack of the feminine in the story thus far, with Ivan being aware only of the feminine in nature such as the moon and the mare earlier in this story. So Ivan knew and understood the value of his steeds and what needed to be swapped for them. The Tsar also seemed to understand their value and complied; here was another 'deal' on the inner journey. It is interesting the difference between the feeling and concept of selling the horses, as opposed to swapping them. Swapping implies an exchange whereby each one gets something one wants, and needs, of equivalent value. Of course the 'fool' and the King are opposite poles of the same archetype and thus belong together. They remind me of the archetypes of the Puer Eternus (eternal youth) and the Sennex (the old king who fears to die). They are two sides of the same coin. In effect, Ivan and the King are now 'working' together on the inner journey.

The horses are led away by ten grooms in livery of silver and gold – notice once again the number ten. But the horses trip their grooms, break their bridles and run back to Ivan. The Tsar returns to Ivan and offers him the position of master of the horse, with gold brocade raiment. Ivan agrees with joy, but on condition that the Tsar will never treat him roughly and will always allow him enough time to sleep.

Ivan becomes part of the Tsar's court, just as it should be – unity: Fool and King together. I find it interesting that the only thing Ivan asks for is fair treatment and enough sleep, and wonder whether sleep is that time that the seeker needs for the inner life – dreaming, meditation, and contemplation. Also, in looking back over this first part of this saga, Ivan has always been asleep before and after his great adventures. Do we always make enough time for these things in our inner life?

Meanwhile Ivan's brothers take the silver, have a drink or two, and ride home to make a good life for themselves, marry and live happily ever after, praising Ivan. We do not hear about these brothers again – they are no longer part of the story and part one of our tale is complete.

However, we are told in summary at this stage, of all the events which will happen in the next two parts, and it is revealed that Ivan eventually becomes the Tsar. I wonder if this is to emphasise that it is the journey, which is important, and not the goal. We also now know that this is a story of transformation from Fool to Tsar, just as in alchemy when base metal lead (the heart) is turned into a heart of gold.

Given that this story is in three parts, this seems to reflect the three stages of life, as well as the process of inner life, each of which reflect the other. The first stage would cover early adolescence to late twenties and is about the making and success of the individual in the outer world and the overcoming of the negative 'mother'. The two brothers could symbolise this outer or ego driven stage of life, where in the end they are relatively well off, can marry and make a family, as well as caring for their elderly father.

The King, the highest temporal power in the world has united with his 'Fool' and opposite, and has gained the two magnificent steeds, who clearly have to be cared for by Ivan – symbolising perhaps the psychopomp, that is, passage from this world to the next. As the horses are black, they could represent the death before rebirth – to die before death. As there are two horses, this could signify duality as well as dynamic power, twofold fleetness and nobility. The ground has been prepared for the real magnum opus or great work, with the horses signifying the first stage of this work.

Part Two

The setting for this part of the story is quite different from the first. It seems to be in a magical or mythological realm, with emphasis on the little talking horse, as well as the paradoxical - a stallion flying toward the sun, goats grazing on the seas, Buyan Island floating on the wild ocean, a wondrous maiden sleeping in a casket, guarded by gentle forest beasts and nightingales making their music overhead. These are all symbols, which are important to understand before we continue with the story.

The horse is often mentioned as being clairvoyant and clairaudient in fairy tales and, as such, it has the capabilities of the 'psychopomp' – a leader of lost souls, as indeed the little humpbacked horse is for Ivan.

It is interesting that the first card in the tarot trumps after the Fool is the Magician, so this next stage is based in the realm of magic, or myth. Certainly the flying stallion represents the masculine aggressive solar power and fire. The winged horse of Greek mythology is Pegasus who opens the spring with his hoof, so for this reason, the capability of bringing the unconscious (water) to light is attributed to him.

Goats also represent vitality, creative energy, fire and creative heat together with a vibrant masculinity. Goats grazing on the sea would seem to link the masculine, fiery, creative energy with the qualities of the 'anima mundi' the Great Mother, the sea and potential of life, the source of all life, also representing the deep unconscious realm.

In Persia the religions of Mithras and Zoroaster have as their heroes (Mithras and Zoroaster) with the mother of Mithras, (Anahita) being the virgin Goddess of all the waters upon the earth and the source of the cosmic ocean. In Zoroastrian temples, water from the river was channelled into an underground canal to the temple, so that it actually ran under and surrounding the temple. The fire altar was positioned in the middle of the temple, with the water going underground all around it – the union of fire and water. The floating island could therefore relate to the coming fire in the story. An island can also be a place of isolation and loneliness, as well as a place of safety and refuge from the sea of chaos. The ocean always represents the unconscious and the first part of any deep inner work is often the 'night sea journey', or 'dark night of the soul'. The religions of Mithras and Zoroaster were the forerunners of Sufism in Persia and there are many parallels in their symbology and mythology.

So, as we have said, the background realm of this second part of the story has, as its base, the water of the great feminine cosmic ocean, which existed before the advent of fire and the masculine principle.

The wondrous fair maiden sleeping in a casket, reminds me of Snow White in her glass coffin, in the depths of the forest. Ivan's anima or inner beloved is deep in his unconscious, or the collective unconscious, so deeply asleep that there is no awareness in or of her, but the gentle forest creatures protect her; these represent the instincts within. This then is the inner realm or setting for this next stage in Ivan's process.

In reality, Ivan has left his home, his father and brothers, and has moved into the Royal Court, with lovely garments to wear and twenty-five chests full of caps and shoes to wear. He has plenty to eat and drink and sleeps as much as he wants to. Since twenty is the number of all the fingers and toes, it carries the significance of the whole man, together with the five which is related to the perfection of man, as in the five pointed star we saw earlier. This number is extremely significant of the inner spiritual state that Ivan is operating from. Twenty-five is, of course, also five times five and signifies a unity of unities, so, in fact a higher level of unity or Being. Caps and shoes would mean that the whole man is covered from top to toe, and indicates freedom since being bare-headed and barefooted was the sign of a slave. On the other hand, having lots of different caps to wear could also mean that he can play all the roles he needs to, and the many shoes could indicate that he has lots of different standpoints in the world – so that he is shown as flexible, open and dynamic. It is interesting that caps denoted the levels of initiation in the Zoroastrian mysteries.

Things are going well for Ivan, but the chamberlain, who was previously the Master of the Royal Horse, and who is of noble blood, was extremely jealous of Ivan and wanted him out of his way at all costs. So the chamberlain, feigning friendship, watches Ivan, and he notices that Ivan never groomed the steeds or otherwise was seen to look after them, although they were always beautifully turned out. The chamberlain suspects that Ivan is a goblin sprite and thinks to tell the Tsar what a wicked infidel and sorcerer Ivan is. The chamberlain hides in the horses' stall in the evening and waits in fear and trembling for what is about to transpire. At midnight, in the blackest part of the night, he sees the 'sprite' enter the stall and the horses pawing the ground in anticipation. Ivan enters, bars the door, takes off his hat and slowly takes the Firebird's feather out of his kerchief (which was in his hat). The light blazes from the feather, and the watching chamberlain almost screams in fright. Ivan puts the feather in a corn-bin and proceeds to groom the pair of horses with tender care, all the while singing his merry song. The chamberlain realises that Ivan is not a sprite and so he cannot tell the Tsar the tale he had meant to, but quickly thinks up another tale to tell instead. An unsuspecting Ivan meanwhile puts out the finest corn and mead, wraps up his feather and makes his bed by the horses and sleeps there with his hat under his head. So it is clear that Ivan nurtures his inner horses at night – in sleep as dreams, or in meditation, and keeps his inner life groomed and nourished, while sleeping with the divine light of wisdom at his head.

As Ivan snores loudly, the chamberlain snatches the feather from Ivan's hat and hotfoots it to the Tsar, who is still sleeping. As do all the minions in the court, like the mayor in the first part, the chamberlain whines and grovels to the Tsar, swearing he is telling the truth, while telling his tall tale, saying that everyone in court knows this to be true. How often have we heard this – everyone says so! He tells the Tsar that Ivan is concealing from him a Firebird's feather, and, not only that, Ivan has been heard to boast that, if the Tsar commanded, he could bring to the Tsar the actual Firebird itself. With this, the chamberlain approaches the Tsar's bed, on all fours, and drops the feather on the floor. The Tsar is enchanted and amazed, and interestingly bites the feather's tip. Then, presumably finding it 'genuine', puts it under lock and key and demands the fool to be brought to him. Of course in those days a feather was used to write with, and so can be seen as an instrument for ordering the Tsar's bidding, or will.

There is an amusing vignette at this point, which is illuminating. As the lords-in-waiting rush for the door to fetch Ivan, they collide and fall sprawling to the floor – the Tsar roars with laughter, so the courtiers' ham it up and do it again, much to the Tsar's delight. He rewards each one for this entertainment with a brand new hat.

They then hurry to Ivan, where they punch and kick him, pulling his hair, but he does not awake. This 'sleep' he is in is very unusual and deep – as if in some sort of altered state, as in meditation. He is finally awakened with the stable broom. I find it interesting that it is something from the stable, that is, his inner realm which can wake him up, and also something which keeps the space clean and well swept.

Ivan prepares himself to meet the Tsar and strides forth 'in pompous pride', with his horsewhip at his side. He certainly seems to be somewhat inflated, but as ever is unafraid. Although he courteously bows low before the Tsar, he also demands to know why he has been awakened. The Tsar jumps up furiously 'left eye squinting, seeing red' and roars that it is Ivan who must answer to him - why has he hidden the Firebird's feather – which is the Tsar's by right. The 'left eye' in a king seems to represent the inner sight or insight of the Divine, as this part of the story definitely focuses on the 'Divine Right of Kings'. Everything that is in the court or that belongs to Ivan belongs by right to the King. The Tsar is like the ego, really a tyrant or autocrat. Ivan again is 'bold' and denies everything – he cheekily asks if he had given his hat to the Tsar, and denies having the Firebird's feather, all this, of course, without realising that he has in fact been exposed. It could also be that the feather, which now is no longer in Ivan's hat in fact, has deprived Ivan of his insight to know that the Tsar is now in possession of the feather. The Tsar furiously shakes the feather in Ivan's face, and on seeing this, Ivan is absolutely dismayed and now grovels before the Tsar. The Tsar forgives him, but since he has heard that Ivan has boasted that should the Tsar but say the word, he could bring the Firebird to him, now demands that Ivan must bring him the Firebird. This he must do within three nights. Ivan does not deny that he had had the feather, but vehemently denies that he has boasted about being able to find a Firebird. The Tsar becomes furious at this, and orders Ivan not to argue; he threatens Ivan with impalement, should he refuse this task.

Ivan, who is now in tears, returns to the stable where his little humpbacked horse is waiting for him. Once again, it is the envy and greed of the outer world, which propels Ivan into the next part of his quest. At each stage in the inner quest, there is a time of peace and integration but then, inevitably, the next step has to be taken; it is like climbing a ladder, one cannot simply stop at any one point to enjoy the view, one must continue on the journey.

Once again the little humpbacked horse joyfully runs to greet Ivan but on seeing his tears, feels for him, when Ivan tells him what has happened. The little humpback horse reiterates to Ivan the warning of the consequences of picking up the feather, but he tells him that he should not worry and that the task is easy and that the path that lies ahead is that of service. Again, we have this hint that the path to enlightenment is one of service.

This story reminds me of an experience I had some years ago, under regression hypnosis. I found myself as the court jester, or fool, sitting at the feet of the King, who was huge, magnificent and very, very angry with me, because I had told him 'the truth'. I was so frightened that I ran away into the forest and hid in a hollow tree. Of course the King's soldiers found me, and I always assumed at this point that I had been killed. I thought at the time, somewhat wryly, that it was fairly typical of me to get into big trouble for telling the truth. In working with this present story, I realise that I had got it all wrong, in many ways. It was my duty to serve the King and in that I had failed. Firstly, I should not have made the King angry at my 'truth'. Had I been less afraid and intimidated by him, I would have had the tact and compassion, to show him the truth without making him angry. Secondly, that in having made him angry, I should not have been so afraid that I ran away. My duty would have been to face him and retrieve my position. By running, I had let us both down. I would have needed Ivan's fearlessness and confidence with the king, and it is this that I most admire about him. He is so cheerfully unafraid and confident. As I did not experience myself being 'killed' in that experience, I would now like to think that I was taken before the King and given a chance to continue in 'our' quest. Ivan was never afraid of the King, nor did he wonder who had 'dobbed him in'. He just got on with what he had to do. I wondered how I could have been tactful, and at the same time also have told the truth and then recalled this reflection:

'A tactful person is subtle and poetical; therefore, some wonder how one can be tactful and at the same time truthful, and others even say that to be tactful is being hypocritical. But what is the use of a truth with no beauty and no fineness that is thrown at one's head like a brick?'

So this was my answer.

The little humpbacked horse then told Ivan to go to the Tsar and ask for two troughs of the best grain and some overseas wine, and to say that it was needed by dawn. The Tsar saw that Ivan's requests were complied with and wished him 'God speed'.

Symbolically, the combination of grain and wine are both solar and divine in nature, and seem to be in the nature of a ritual meal. Wine also signifies fire and truth. In the Zoroastrian tradition, it symbolises Divine Love. I find it interesting that the wine had to be from overseas – perhaps this means the spiritual message has come from afar, or simply that it had to travel over the sea – the spiritual depths. The grain could relate to the seed of life and is the result of harvesting. So these are the 'tools' required for this stage of the quest.

At dawn the humpbacked horse arouses Ivan; and he tells Ivan that duty is calling him. Duty or service is a fundamental way of finding wholeness or unity with the Divine.

They pack the grain and wine into a sack, and off they go. They ride for seven days – now seven is one of those special sacred numbers, which really means the completeness and totality of the universe and the integration of the heavens and the soul with the earth and the body. This indicates that Ivan was on a deep inner journey and had achieved some level of individuation and wholeness.

When they arrive on the eighth day, the little humpback horse tells Ivan what he will see. If we understand the humpback horse as the 'spirit of guidance', as manifested in a teacher, then Ivan is being shown what to expect in this special realm that he has reached. They are in a dark, dense, greenwood in which there is a glade and 'in the middle of this glade stands a hill, of silver'. Every morning a flock of Firebirds arrive here before dawn to drink from the stream, which flows through the glade. Ivan upon hearing this, rushes to the glade and there he finds the most idyllic beautiful place.

'Blades of grass like emeralds bright and the breezes as they blew, scattered sparkles through the dew; Flowers sweet of beauty rare blossomed in the meadow there.'

'In the middle of this glade rose a hill, of silver made, like an airy tower' with its summit hid from sight and the sun, gilding it with its summer rays until the peak flashes like a beacon.'

The colour green / emerald seems to be important here – green is certainly a sacred colour. In some Sufi traditions green is the colour of the heart and related to water. The hill is rounded and silver, so it represents the feminine element, with the sun's rays meeting the silver brightness to flash forth as a splendid beacon of light. This is Ivan's experience of the realm of the Firebird and it feels like a mandala, similar in fact to the meaning to the number seven – a circle of enclosed sacred space with the central symbol of the silver hill, or tower, rising to meet the sky; it represents the feminine silver (queen) rising to meet the Divine sun (masculine, King) - the union of heaven and earth. The importance here is the union of the opposites; the coming together which is both creative and the perfection of wholeness.

The little horse and Ivan fly up the hill a long way, it is getting dark so they stop and the little humpback horse gives Ivan his next instructions; which are to mix some wine and grain, and to fill one trough with this mixture. Ivan must then hide himself under the other trough and wait, making no sound, keep eyes and ears alert and he is warned not to fall asleep. One of the important things about spiritual practice is to remain alert, focused and not to fall asleep.

Ivan is told that at dawn, flocks of Firebirds will come and peck at his grain; he is to ignore their chatter and grab the nearest one and yell for his humpbacked horse to come quickly. I find it curious that after receiving his instructions, Ivan asks if the Firebird will burn his fingers, and puts on mittens to protect himself. He does this without humpback telling him to, and I feel that this was not necessary, as the Firebird is a being of light, but not of heat – but Ivan was not to know this. Ivan does as he is told, catches a Firebird, and puts the bird in his sack. At this stage, instead of quickly going back to the King, Ivan cannot resist scaring off the rest of the birds, who are by now slow and intoxicated from the wine and grain. The mystical wine that comes from 'the Friend' intoxicates Sufis into Divine ecstasy, so this wine has intoxicated the Firebirds.

Ivan really does act as the fool or as the madman – for apparently no reason whatsoever. Perhaps there is a connection with the destructive energy of the fool, or simply that this is simply a sign of youthful exuberance. It is also interesting to connect the French word for fool Le Fau, with the word for fire, echoing the fool's connection with light and energy. Where the fool might say that he is light and travels light; the fire of the archetypal fool personifies the transforming power which created civilization and which can also destroy it.

Once the birds had flown away, Ivan returns to the Tsar with his prize. The Tsar asks Ivan if he has brought the Firebird, the Tsar being well aware of the chamberlain's anger at Ivan's successful return. Ivan asks for the court to be put into darkness, and pulls the Firebird out of his sack. The Tsar and all the courtiers are blinded by the light and think that a fire has broken out. Ivan laughs at them and tells the Tsar that it is the Firebird – a lovely plaything! Ivan does not seem to understand what this Firebird really is. However, the Tsar is well pleased and makes Ivan the royal groom. He is now elevated to a position closer to the Tsar, from master of the horse to royal groom – but still connected with the horses.

What can this part of the story really mean? The capturing of the Firebird for the Tsar? What do we know of the Firebird itself? They were said to have red feet and absurd tails not at all like chickens' tails. It is indeed the Phoenix, symbol of rebirth by fire and of the sun, regeneration in alchemy, with redness also symbolising the third stage in the great work. For the Tsar having the Phoenix signifies divine royalty, nobility and uniqueness and its appearance signifies peace and benevolent rule. After the black horse symbolising death, this stage of the work is then about resurrection, life and immortality. In early religions pre Buddhist (the Hindu Vedas and Zoroaster) the focus was fire and the sun, with light, as symbolic of the source of all Beings. So the first step on the spiritual quest is to attain the Divine light and fire.

The chamberlain is, of course, even more irate and jealous than ever because of Ivan's success and again plots vengeance on him.

As I was working with this tale, one of my sons came on a visit and was very concerned with problems at work – he felt that someone had been telling tales about him to the boss, and he wanted to find out who this person was and to justify himself. I told him this part of the story – how Ivan did not bother about who had told the Tsar the tall tales, but just did what he had to do, as best he could and that was the only way to dispel this kind of negativity. I also suggested that the tales were being told because of envy and insecurity in the teller, just like the chamberlain. My son was rather thoughtful at this point and then agreed that this was exactly how things were at his work. Sometime later he told me that he had done as I suggested, and that behind the scenes HR had been auditing him, as a result of the stories. He had come out of this with very high praise, so he felt like he had caught the Firebird for the Tsar after all and was surprised and delighted. I also think that like Ivan he did not really appreciate completely what he had achieved.

In the palace kitchens one of the servants (Yeruslan – he is named where the other servants and courtiers are not, and he can read, whereas the kitchen servants would not be able to read.), was reading some tales, especially one about a lovely Tsar-Maid.

He relates this story of a distant place, a strange ocean, which has never been sailed by Christians. There are blackamoors there, which seems to suggest North Africa or the Middle East – again perhaps Sufi lands? Merchants told of a beautiful maiden – daughter of the moon and sister of the sun, who sails in a boat of gold. She steers this boat with a silver oar and plays a silver stringed musical instrument as she sings. This is certainly overwhelmingly a vision of the Feminine Principle – daughter of a Tsar, but a 'Tsar' in her own right, in a golden boat, who is shown with these symbols depicting her as the Queen of Heaven, the Mother Goddess. As a moon goddess, she is the controller of the life-giving waters and the resurrection of its life; hence she is rowing her boat from shore to shore.

Upon hearing this tale, the chamberlain again rushes to the Tsar claiming that Ivan has boasted that he can catch this wondrous Tsar-Maid. As before, the Tsar demands that Ivan be brought before him. Although the chamberlain is always lying to the Tsar, these lies have a tendency to become true. In the world it so often happens that, although we do not know that we can do certain tasks, if pushed, we can achieve them, in spite of ourselves and others. When life is easy and good, we are not inclined to volunteer for difficult quests or tasks – we need a firm nudge!

Once again the Tsar demands that Ivan bring him the Tsar-Maid, on threat of impalement, and once again Ivan returns to the little humpbacked horse in despair. The little horse reminds him, that he has ignored his earlier advice, but that the task is quite easy and reiterates that all these tasks represent service.

This time, Ivan is to ask the Tsar for two large cloths, a tent of gold brocade, a dinner service made of gold from overseas. He is also to request sweetmeats to appeal to the Tsar-Maid. Whereas before, the wine had to be from overseas, this time it is the gold dinner service that must come from overseas. The Tsar sees that Ivan's requests are complied with and wishes him God-speed on his quest.

Once again the humpbacked horse wakes Ivan at dawn and tells him that duty is calling. Again it takes seven days to ride to the dark and dense greenwood. The ocean lies ahead – the abode of the Tsar Maiden. He is told that twice a year she spends a day on shore and that tomorrow is to be one of these days. I wondered at the meaning of this – what happens twice a year, which is related to the coming of the feminine principle, the moon? I discovered that there are usually two lunar eclipses in a year – I think this may well be a relevant interpretation.

When they reach the ocean shore, Ivan is told to pitch the tent of gold brocade, lay out the cloths and the gold dinner service together with the sweets. The shore is the place between land and sea, the conscious and the unconscious, the place between the realms. Ivan is to hide behind the tent, and after the Tsar-Maid has eaten, he is to seize her whilst she is playing her music. He is warned, once again, not to fall asleep and to keep his wits about him. Ivan does as he is bidden, and he makes a hole in the brocade of the tent, so he can observe the maid. At noon, the Tsar -Maid comes with her musical instrument in her hand and goes straight inside the tent.

When Ivan caught the Firebird – symbol of light, fire and the sun, it was in the darkest part of the night, just before dawn. The masculine Divine principle as represented by the Firebird was captured in the night under the influence of the feminine moon. We now see the reverse applying as the feminine Divine principle is to be 'caught' when the masculine principle of the sun is at his highest in the sky.

When Ivan sees the Tsar-Maid he is disappointed, he sees her as pale and skinny; this would certainly reflect the symbolism of the moon during an eclipse. Just as he could not see the beauty and importance of the Firebird, he cannot see the beauty and importance of the Tsar-Maid. At least he is not tempted to fall in love with her, as happened in the story of Tristan and Isolde, where Tristan was sent across the sea to Ireland to fetch the princess Isolde, to be the bride of his king. The princess does not belong with the commoner, but with the king, and tragedy follows when this principle is not followed.

The Tsar-Maid enters the tent without hesitation, tempted by the sweetmeats, she eats them and drinks the honeyed mead. I think that she is attracted to her opposite - the sun qualities of gold. The tent is enclosed, safe and beautiful – the feminine principle being about arts, weaving and crafts, the creative aspect of life. The sweetmeats and honeyed mead would be sweet nourishment to sustain her; the dinner service could be a play on the word service, which as we have repeatedly seen before is the way to the Divine Presence. The ancients in the cult of Mithras used to call the priestesses Mother Bees, they called the moon Bee and used honey rather than water in their purification rituals and initiations. So, to partake sweetmeats and mead made from honey is a natural sacred sacrament. Honey is associated with the purity and fertility of the moon. The moon, in ancient Persia, was believed to be the source of honey. Honey-moon actually means continued love and fertility in married life. Grain and wine were used to tempt and nourish the Firebird; here it is sweetmeats and honeyed mead, which are used to tempt the Tsar-Maid.

After she has partaken of the offerings, from the golden dinner service she then plays her music. The Tsar-Maid's powers are non-verbal, they are the primordial feminine power of emotions, feeling – music. Sound is the primal and first vibration of the universe – in the beginning was the 'word/sound' – it is the first connection we have with the outside world when we are in the womb, and it is the last thing we experience before death. Music is beyond language and speaks directly to the soul and consequently Ivan is lulled by the sweet music and falls asleep.

He is awakened by the little humpbacked horse, who is furiously neighing and kicking him. At this stage in the inner journey it is ever more difficult to stay awake. When Ivan was with the Firebirds he did not find it so difficult to stay awake and ignore their chattering, but now he is lulled to sleep by the sweet music. This can happen to us in meditation too – when we find ourselves close to the peace and beauty of the feminine and that oceanic consciousness, we find it easy to become 'unconscious' and miss crucial opportunities to catch some aspect of our soul that we need. I think it is also very easy for a young man who is first in contact with the divine feminine (in his first love perhaps) to fall asleep and miss the opportunity. Jungians believe that the soul is feminine - the words Anima and Soul being interchangeable. The ultimate life's work is to integrate the feminine or soul aspect of ourselves into the masculine aspect in a sacred marriage. I would add that after this integration or sacred marriage, we then need to integrate or perhaps dissolve into the Divine.

Ivan is frightened, realising that he has failed to stay awake. He promises not to fall asleep again, and the little horse tells him that all yet may not be lost. So it is that we are given another chance, and in reality we get another chance with our beloved, inner or outer. If we miss this, there may never be another opportunity again. Perhaps this second chance is related to the effect of the moon on the tides and the eclipses. The tides depend on how close the sun and moon are to the earth, due to the elliptical orbits of the moon and earth. So the tide will be both very high and very low twice on that day, allowing the Tsar-Maid to come ashore again. In many places there are two very high tides per year called King Tides in Australia. So when we are riding high, this second chance presents itself to us.

The little humpback horse warns Ivan not to sleep this time, otherwise he will really lose his head. So it is that even if we fail once, there is sometimes one more window of opportunity; we must take opportunity when it presents, not when we think we are ready. It may never come again. Perhaps during such an 'eclipse' of the moon, in an inner sense, we have another chance!

Ivan then searches the shore for flints and rusty nails from ship wrecks beached on the shore. He plans to use these to keep awake. I really wondered at the use of these items and found that flint can mean a hardening of the heart as in the expression – 'As hard as flint', and especially as flint is also related to the bringing forth of fire. A nail is used to hold things together; a rusty nail could be seen as a disintegration of such a binding. So this might mean that Ivan must allow his connection to the Tsar Maid to disintegrate and so would not come under the spell of her music.

This time the Tsar-Maid comes ashore in the early morning and does as before. As the shore is the place between land and sea, so the morning is the place between night and day. It is the place between realms. Ivan does indeed get sleepy, but he overcomes this by hardening his heart against the music and by not allowing himself to become attuned to it, in that he gets angry with her, as he did with the Firebirds. So he seizes her by her long hair and calls for the little humpbacked horse and off they go. As the hair is the crowning glory and also symbolises life's energy, it is by this means that the Divine Feminine has been captured.

When Ivan arrives back at the Palace, the Tsar actually runs out to meet him. The Tsar, who is enraptured at the sight of the Tsar-Maid, leads her to his royal throne where he proposes marriage to her.

She, however, turns away, and refuses to reply. The Tsar becomes even more entranced by her refusal. She then says that if he really loves her, he has to find and fetch her ring, which lies on the ocean floor, and this must be done within three days. The Tsar himself fetches Ivan this time and tells him he must bring the Tsar Maid's signet ring from the bottom of the ocean. If he succeeds he can ask for anything he desires. Note that this time Ivan is being bribed rather than threatened, and the Tsar himself has gone to fetch Ivan, so we can see that there is already a change in the Tsar's attitude. From here on the rest of the court and courtiers no longer play a part in our story. There is no need, as there is now a personal and direct relationship between the Tsar and Ivan.

Ivan protests that he has only just got back and needs a rest, but once again the Tsar gets angry and orders him off. The Tsar-Maid now gives Ivan yet another task to do. He is to visit her mother the moon, and ask her why she conceals her light for three nights and three days; he is also to ask of her brother, the sun, as to why does he shroud his face in gloomy clouds. Here it is interesting to note that if the Tsar-Maid's mother is the moon, and her brother is the sun, who then is her father? Obviously a Tsar, so this indicates that she is in herself a Tsar. However, she is not ready to marry the Tsar of our story. She has to test the Tsar to make sure he is right for her.

The questions the Tsar-Maid wants asked of her mother and her brother are questions about light and darkness. At the beginning of the cycle, the new moon disappears and we have a black sky for three days – at these dark times, things are hidden from us, as they are when clouds cover the sun. The Tsar-Maid wants to know why the light of both sun and moon are sometimes hidden. This is really about the inner light of our spiritual journey, and it is Ivan's task to discover this for himself. There are indeed always periods of light and darkness in our lives. But it is actually Ivan who is given the tasks to perform, not the Tsar.

Ivan returns to his humpbacked horse. He tells of the tasks he has been set and that the Tsar now wants to wed this skinny girl. However, this time Ivan says that he has questions that he needs answered. Next morning Ivan sets off early towards the sea, warmly dressed but, this time, with three onions in his pack. This is a change from his usual crust of bread. Onions would here be used as a potent protection against 'negative' lunar powers; such as he is destined to come into contact with.

And here ends the second part of our story. As we have seen, Ivan has quested to bring the Firebird to the Tsar, as a symbol of the nobility and solar power of kingship and of course Divine Light. He has also brought for the Tsar, the lunar Tsar-Maid – the Divine Feminine principal. However, the sacred marriage has not yet been agreed to by the Tsar-Maid – there is still much to do and further tasks lie ahead.

Part Three

The setting for this final part of our tale is in the 'real' world this time. The Divine Feminine, as the Tsar-Maid, has been brought to the Tsar in the second part of this story, but we are now shown the 'plight' of the feminine in outer peasant village life. Firstly, the horses have run away and the peasants have a tough job rounding them up; this seems to me to mean that the masculine energy representing reason, intellect and nobility is out of control and out of balance in the village. When the raven croaks in the treetop amusing the villagers, it represents an announcement of the fall of women, as of Eve.

We are shown 'woman' as wife, so that when all is well with her, the whole village is happy, but when all is not well with her, village life is disrupted. The newly-wed wife gets a beating from her husband's mother, is trussed up and tied to the oven, with her shoes taken away from her. The feminine principle is demeaned and abused in the patriarchy, especially when the patriarchy is out of control. The sacred feminine is not glorified or respected. It is the husband's mother who is the instrument of her abuse, just as so many women nowadays continue and uphold, and indeed continue, the patriarchal demeaning and disregard of other women. In other words, it is the crone who has been so harshly repressed by the patriarchy, yet this aspect of the sacred feminine needs to be honoured and respected for there to be a healthy balance in the world.

The glory of song, dance and the earthiness of the feminine are seen as dangerous and out of control – she has to be trussed up and not allowed to wander. This is the world that the Tsar-Maid is being brought into. The Tsar-Maid is really the female Tsar, she is not queen, as this would make her consort of a King, nor is she princess, as daughter of a King. She is 'King' in her own right, with no need for any other. It is very much like the Jungian meaning of virgin – whole in herself without the need for a masculine partner.

So it is that Ivan again flies off on the back of his little humpbacked horse, flying for twenty thousand leagues - a long, long way – perhaps in reality many years of inner work and journeying towards wholeness, to find the Tsar-Maid's signet ring.

They again come to the ocean shore – to the realm of the feminine and the place between the earth and the sea. There the monster whale has been lying for ten years, in pain and suffering, unable to beg the sun to pardon him. Pardon him for what I wonder. In those days the whale was seen as a monster which swallows beings whole – like in the story of Jonah and the whale.

In reality, the poor whale has been 'used' as an island; he is a mass of holes where the villagers had put in stakes and poles, driven their ploughs and a forest had even grown on the whale's tail – this wonderful creature of the depths, symbolizing the power of the cosmic waters, and so representing both cosmic and individual rebirth, was being thoroughly abused. In effect the whale was being used as if it was land, rather than being a creature of the deep ocean. Is this how the Divine Feminine is used these days – do we do this to ourselves too? The whale asks them where they are going – they tell him that they are going eastwards to the sun as envoys of the Tsar-Maid. The whale begs them to ask the sun why he must suffer such disgrace and for how long, - in return the whale promises to serve Ivan. Ivan promises to do as the whale asked.

They travel to the place between earth and sky, and then leaving mother earth, they fly into the blue sky itself – to the place where the sun sleeps at night and the moon sleeps in the daytime – the city where the Tsar-Maid's tower is. Here follows a most beautiful description of a sacred city, perhaps paradise. In fact, the description reminds me of a Mogul emperor's palace, with its gardens, birds of paradise, palace spires and pillars. And above all of this are stars burning with a holy fire, with the form of a Christian cross, which is setting the heavens ablaze. To understand this description, I have gone back to the teachings of Hazrat Inayat Khan, 'As man looks up from the earth he sees the sun in the heavens, he sees the most luminous body there without any support, bright, shining and warm.'

The Firebird and the Tsar-Maid

'In all places on the earth, God has been pictured in the form of the sun, so that the great masters and teachers are depicted with a sun disc around their head. This disk was called the 'Zardash' and the name Zarathustra has the same origin. A deeper study of the sun suggests the four directions of lines that are formed around the sun. It is this sign that is the origin of the symbol of the cross.'

'First was the word and then came light and then the world was created; and as the light is expressed in the form of a cross so every form shows in it this original sign. Every artist knows the value of the vertical line and the horizontal line, which form the skeleton of every form. From a mystical point of view there are two paths of attainment, both equally necessary for perfection. One is the expansion of the spirit from a single being to the whole universe, which signifies the horizontal line, and the other is the journey of man to God, from the limited state of being to the unlimited, which represents the perpendicular line; and in this cross is hidden the secret of perfection'.[41] This myth really represents these aspects of the form of the cross, as well as the inner and outer journey to wholeness.

Ivan and the humpbacked horse come into the presence of the moon. Ivan bares his head and bows respectfully before her. This is quite different to his interaction with the Tsar. He gives the moon news of her daughter and passes on the Tsar-Maid's question. The moon is at first angry that it was Ivan who stole her daughter away, but he explained that it was the Tsar who demanded this of him. The moon is now very happy to hear of her daughter and tells Ivan that it is because she was mourning and grieving the loss of her daughter and this is why she has withheld her light from the earth for the three days of the dark of the moon, and that this is also why the Tsar-maid's brother the sun has withheld his light and warmth in dark clouds and shedding tears for her as rain. Then the moon asks Ivan how her daughter is, and he replies that she is wasting away and is very skinny, only skin and bones. Here Ivan mentions that no doubt the Tsar-Maid will fatten up after she has

---

[41] Hazrat Inayat Khan, *The Gathas, The Sufi Message, Volume 13* Motilal Banarsidass Publishers, Delhi, 1990. p.93.

married the Tsar. The moon is furious and tells Ivan that her daughter will never marry such an old nasty toad, who is vain and greedy. Such an apt description of an un-evolved ego, rather like the Sennex archetype mentioned before – an old man trying to hold onto what he has got and not allowing any creativity, evolution or revolution in his realm.

Now Ivan tells the moon about the whale and asks her why the whale is in such a state of suffering and pain and what he can do to be pardoned. The moon tells him that the whale had swallowed thirty ships one day without permission from his Lord, but that should he free the ships, his pain will be taken away and he will be rewarded in his old age. What does it mean for a whale to have swallowed thirty ships? This is really about the abuse of power without permission, but an act that the whale committed in a state of unknowing. The Lord of the Whale is obviously the sun, even though the whale is the 'Lord' of the deep. In another story of the Tsar-Maid, she arrives with a fleet of thirty ships with a maiden on each one to meet Ivan. The ships symbolically carry the sun and the moon across the seas, and, as such, represent the fertility of the waters, with the ship also representing the sheltering aspect of the Great Mother. Since there are thirty ships (being three times ten), this means the multiplicity of creative power and the triad symbolizing wholeness – so there are ten triads – with ten being the number of the cosmos and the paradigm of creation. Thus it is this type of power, which has been abused by the whale. This aspect of the feminine has been completely swallowed by the whale, so that the whale itself becomes used and abused by the people, just like the earth has been used and abused since the industrial and technological revolutions. Creativity and the feminine are not valued, the only value is in the patriarchal production and reduction of everything for its use alone. We also find ourselves as part of this cycle, of swallowing our vessels of the sun and moon to find ourselves chained to the corporation.

Ivan now takes his leave – he kisses the face of the moon and embraces her. She thanks him and tells him to put her daughter's mind at ease, for the Tsar-Maid will never marry a toothless greybeard, but only a handsome young man.

On Ivan's return he stops off at the whale island and tells the people to leave immediately, or they will be drowned. The peasants leave and Ivan now tells the whale what the moon told him. The whale responds by immediately opening his mouth and releasing the ships, with their crews. The ships all sail happily away and the whale tells Ivan he can have whatever he wants from the ocean, but Ivan only asks for the Tsar-Maid's signet ring. So as Ivan has aided and released the whale, who in turn released the thirty ships with their crews, the whale now aids Ivan. Thus the whale summons a tribe of sturgeons to find the ring hidden within a chest. The sturgeon is considered the most noble of the fish in Russia.

Here the whale begins to act like a royal ruler ordering the various fish to do his bidding. He is the king of the deep. The sturgeons search near and far but cannot find the ring. They tell the whale that the only one who can find the ring is the perch, but he cannot be found. All the sea creatures look for him. It is strange that the only fish that can find the ring is a 'vagrant brawling perch'. The image of the perch that we get is of someone who enjoys a good fight and will take on anybody fearlessly. Just for the fun of it, he would kiss the girls and cause havoc around him. Really it seems that such a feisty, testosterone-driven, aggressive male is the only one who can find the casket with the Tsar-Maid's signet ring. This perch seems to be the opposite balance to the femininity of the Tsar-Maid – the inner work is really an integration of the opposites. So it is that the perch is finally given the task of finding the ring; The perch is to the whale as Ivan is to the Tsar.

The perch finds the casket easily, but it is very heavy, stuck fast and cannot be raised, even with the help of other fish. It is interesting that the Tsar-Maid asks only for her signet ring, but it is enclosed in a casket – just like the fair maiden in a glass casket described in the introduction of the second part of this story. The casket seems to represent a power or energy which has been trapped in the depths of the unconscious. An energy like this is very dangerous, when it is released; it requires great care and courage to bring it out into consciousness.

Finally, the perch has to ask the sturgeons to raise the casket. This they do quite easily. So the masculine active principle can, with its sharp cutting edge of intellect, like the sword of discrimination, find the ring contained in the casket, but it requires the group effort of the sturgeon to raise and take the casket with its contents to the Tsar. The sturgeon seems to symbolise a relationship with the mother goddess and procreation as associated with the water element, given that the sturgeon's eggs (caviar) are so famous as a rare and expensive delicacy both in Russia and all over the world.

It is the related feminine that must actually raise the casket and bring it to the Tsar for the Tsar-Maid. It is a combined effort from the depths of the unconscious cosmic depths of the divine masculine and feminine. The ring is such a well-known and powerful symbol in myths and fairy tales. We can see the power of the ring as a symbol even today in Tolkein's *Fellowship of the Ring*, and Wagner's *Ring Cycle* of operas. The ring represents power, identity sovereignty and completion – but as the Tsar-Maid's signet ring, it represents the power as 'king' to authorise, ratify and confirm her authority. The ring can also be seen as the hidden treasure, or 'the pearl without price' which is the knowledge of the soul's uniqueness, which lives in the depths of the primordial ocean – contained in the casket of the heart. It also represents the union of the masculine King or God and the feminine Queen or Goddess – the *Hieros Gamos,* or sacred marriage. Until we have raised this treasure in ourselves, from the depths of our being, we cannot relate as a complete human being with those around us. Until the Tsar-Maid has her signet ring / treasure, she cannot make the sacred marriage, as she needs this symbol of her power and authority. A signet ring is used by royalty to authorise legal documents, so we can see it is something which is required by the Tsar-Maid to rule.

In a sense, the casket containing the ring holds the soul or to put it in a more Sufi way – the soul within the space of the heart. Ivan has freed the captive and raised the treasure and so gained possession of his soul's treasure. He has found within himself the fruitful centre, the point of renewal and rebirth, upon which the creative Divinity and the continued existence of the world depends. Ivan himself is not yet aware of this, but the truth is that it would be impossible for him to find the treasure, unless he had first found and redeemed his own soul.

At the last possible moment, just at sunset, the whale emerges from the ocean with the casket to give to Ivan. Although Ivan himself cannot raise the casket, the little humpbacked horse does so with ease and off they fly to the Tsar. So it is that although we cannot, at this stage of the journey, hold and contain the 'wisdom' of the teachings, the Spirit of Guidance, in the form of the teacher, can.

As they arrive, the Tsar runs out to meet them and demands his ring, without even greeting them. Ivan gives the Tsar the ring and mentions that he also has a little casket or jewel box, but that it is extremely heavy. His guards take the casket away and the Tsar rushes off to present the Tsar-Maid with her ring and again offers his love and marriage. The Tsar-Maid only answers that she is but fifteen and will not marry an old man. She tells the Tsar that the only way she would marry him would be if he – the Tsar - could be reborn and become young again. If he has no fear of pain, she tells him, he can do this. Here is the great hint that the process of transformation is both painful and frightening. Notice that Ivan does not have to tell the Tsar-Maid what he has discovered from her mother and brother – this was information which was for himself to find out – she of course already knew. We are so often sent on a quest, which is really for our own selves to find out that is, the whole journey is really for our Self.

She then instructs the Tsar as to what he must do. He is to have three cauldrons, set up in the palace courtyard. The first one to be full to the brim with chilled water, the next full of hot water with a fire under the cauldron to boil the water and keep it boiling. The last cauldron must be filled with milk and heated till the milk boils. The Tsar is told that if he wants to be young and handsome, he must first undress and plunge naked into the boiling milk, then into the boiling water and lastly into the cold water, then he will be transformed. The Tsar does what he always does when he wants something – he calls for his groom – poor Ivan. Ivan protests that he does not want to be sent off to some distant shore again. The Tsar then tells him what he has to do regarding the three cauldrons. Ivan is horrified and says that he is not a chicken, a pig or a turkey to be scalded or boiled. The Tsar threatens Ivan with being drawn and quartered if he does not obey. So once again Ivan creeps up to the hayloft to tell the little humpbacked horse of his plight. The little horse as usual tells him that he should have listened in the first place and not picked up the feather of the firebird. However, the little horse offers his friendship and swears that he won't leave Ivan in the lurch. Ivan is told what he must do the following morning.

When he strips off his clothes on the lawn next morning, he is to ask the Tsar to send him his horse so that he can say good-bye to it. The groom will fetch the little humpbacked horse that will wave his tail about, dip his snout in each cauldron, and then he will squirt Ivan twice. Ivan is to whistle loudly three times and then quickly dive into the hot milk and then the hot and cold waters. Ivan goes to sleep and next morning things happen just as the little horse has told him.

Now what does this process really mean? First of all, there are to be three cauldrons to be set up in the palace courtyard. Three as we have seen before, is about the soul, wholeness and creative power, and indeed there are always three tasks or tests for the hero. The cauldron represents the feminine power of transformation, renewal and rebirth, so that three cauldrons could mean there are three powers, like the magic cauldron, of regeneration, inspiration and abundance.

The first cauldron contains milk, which has been used in initiation ceremonies as a symbol of rebirth – it is nourishment from the mother goddess and the food of paradise. In Sufi terms, milk is sometimes seen as representing wisdom. There is a prohibition against 'boiling the kid in its mother's milk.' Things are not prohibited unless there has been a practice of doing it, so in this case the boiling of the seeker in the milk is actually a metaphor for an initiation ritual, which was in fact prohibited.

Milk and water are combined as the milk of spirit and the water of matter, or even the heavenly milk of the mystic bride. The symbol of the fire here is also extremely important and follows on the Firebird theme. The kindling of fire is, in effect, the re-enactment of the act of creation, of birth and re-birth, of integration and reunion by means of sacrifice. In alchemy, fire is the central element – the great work begins and ends with fire, and it is interesting to note that fire is fundamental to the whole process - the heat has to be applied constantly, and if the 'process' is allowed to cool, then the fire has to be kindled all over again and the process restarted.

So it is with our practices and inner work – the fire has to be kept going and certain energy applied constantly to complete the process of 'enlightenment'. So both the milk and the water have to be heated and kept 'on the boil', so to speak. Whereas the Firebird presented light without heat, the fire heating the milk and the water in the cauldrons represents and is heat without light. In the Zoroastrian tradition the fire was the Sacred Centre, the place of divinity and the divine light in the soul of man.

Water and fire are two conflicting elements, which eventually penetrate each other and unite; they represent all sets of opposites in the elemental world, so that 'burning water' is the ultimate union of opposites – the union of the Sky Father and the Earth Mother. In psychoanalytic terms, 'if a union is to take place between opposites such as the inner masculine and the inner feminine, this union will come about through a *third* thing which will represent, not a compromise, but something *new*, an entity which can only be described in paradoxes --- like gold that is not gold.'[42]

Water is symbolic of the Great Mother and associated with birth and baptism. Water 'washes away' and regenerates. To dive into the waters is to search for the secret of life, the ultimate mystery; it is death to the old life and rebirth into the new.

Thus the process is of the ultimate union of opposites, resulting in transformation and enlightenment. This process can be extremely painful and frightening, as can be seen in the stories of Moses and Mohammed.

Ivan too is terrified and reluctant, but his little humpbacked horse gives him advice. Ivan is to strip himself naked before the process begins, which really means that he is giving up and striping off all his outer trappings, attachments, and ways of being – it is a complete renunciation. Then the little humpbacked horse is to wave his tail about, which means that he is giving Ivan guidance and balance – it feels like

---

[42] Molly Tuby, 'Opposites and the Healing Power of Symbols', in *In The Wake of Jung,-A selection of Articles by Jungian Analysts*, Molly Tuby (ed), Coventure, (np), UK, 1983, p.100 (out of print).

an initiation really. The little horse is then to dip his snout in each cauldron; the snout is of course related to the sense of smell, which in the Sufi system symbolises power, will, fire and transformation. When the little humpbacked horse, who is the Spirit of Guidance, is dipping his snout into the cauldrons, it means that he has been there before – he has trodden this path of initiation and evolution and knows what to do, like the Teacher who has been there before us. The little horse is now preparing the way for Ivan using his will and power by infusing the cauldrons of milk and water with these feelings knowledge and attributes. This makes them 'safe' for Ivan and at the same time squirts Ivan twice with this 'magic portion,' or mix of the milk and water. This is like an anointing or even a baptism of fire, but there is also a sense that this is a transmission of knowledge and wisdom from Teacher to Student. Being squirted twice simply means the opposites of sun and moon / masculine and feminine principles, but also perhaps that it is doubly powerful.

Ivan is then to whistle loudly three times and jump into the cauldrons. In the earlier part of the story, the firebirds' chatter and the Tsar-Maid plays her silver instrument to distract him, but this time Ivan is to make a sound – a whistle three times. Sound and hearing are related to the element of ether in the Sufi system, where ether is a very high and fine vibration, which leads to the bringing of a new religion and peace. Here is the number three again, symbolising completeness, but also the third and new entity, which emerges when there is this union of opposites, as we have previously seen.

All the court is there to watch the spectacle, the Tsar with the Tsar-Maid make an entrance. Ivan bids his little friend good-bye and does as he was told. When he emerges from the last cauldron he is transformed into a wonderfully handsome youth. Ivan bows to the Tsar-Maid. The transformation is complete.

The crowd and indeed the Tsar himself are full of wonder at this transformation. The Tsar now decides to go through the transformation process himself, so that he can be reborn young and handsome and then marry the Tsar-Maid. The Tsar undresses, crosses himself and dives into the hot cauldron, where he is boiled on the spot. The Tsar cannot undergo the transformation without having done the 'work' and being supported in this by a teacher, like the little humpbacked horse. The old King/ego must die before the new can take his place.

At this the Tsar-Maid stands up and calls for silence, unveiling her face. She asks the crowd who, now the Tsar is dead, would they have her marry instead – and then points to Ivan and asks that they recognise him as her beloved husband. The crowd are all too willing and for her sake they recognise Ivan. So the beautiful Tsar-Maid and Ivan, her consort, are married amidst great merrymaking. The transformation is complete and the Tsar-Maid and Ivan rule together, in a state of union, as Tsar.

So it is this contact with the 'higher' aspect of the Feminine, (in the 'captive princess'), which draws our hero 'upward and on' and also 'into' the totality of himself as a Being united, this changes him from a callow youth into the consort of the Tsar-Maid. The Tsar-Maid is the ruling feminine principle. She is a female Tsar in her own right. She is not the wife or consort of a Tsar. It is in fact Ivan our hero who is her consort but becomes united with her. This is what makes this story so remarkable.

GOLDEN CHISEL AND
THE STONE RAM

s with any good myth this Han folktale starts with 'Long, long ago...'-a bit like 'Once upon a time...' This puts the story in that other realm, the space within; the land of Fairy. The setting of the story, as with a dream, presents the problem or situation it is dealing with. In this case, there was no sweet spring water in the community; the only water the people in the village had was salty and bitter and their organs were saturated with its brackish flavour. Here water, especially spring water, can be understood as a metaphor for "the water of life," or spiritual nourishment. Hazrat Inayat Khan often uses water as a metaphor for spirit. In *Sufi Teachings,* for example, he gives this image:'...a spiritual person's life in the midst of the world is like the life of a fish on the land. The fish is a creature of the water; its sustenance, its joy, its happiness are in the water.' And in "Friendship," in *In an Eastern Rose Garden,* he says, 'Love is life, and life is symbolized by water. When one wants to bring water up out of the ground one has to dig for it...' We could imagine that these villagers in the story were deprived of life's pure energy and spiritual nourishment, or even that their spirit was contaminated by the earth, the base material self.

There was an ancient prophecy that had been handed down among the villagers and they all knew of it but could not understand it. I wonder if this means that in every culture there have been prophets and teachers who know and have spoken of the way or path to finding pure water/spiritual enlightenment. These teachings are cryptic insofar as they speak of esoteric knowledge. In other words, they can only be understood by someone who is a seeker, who is on the path. This cryptic prophecy was:

Hearken ye all
Who now for water thirst:
From Stone Ram's lips
The purest spring shall burst!

Golden Chisel is the seeker, that part of ourselves, the higher Self that is searching, longing for 'something,' which in this case is the stone ram of the prophecy. He is also the creative, artistic part of ourselves - he can chisel animals, birds and plants in stone and make them appear lifelike. He is able to make millstones to grind pure, white flour. Although a millstone may seem mundane, flour, being fine and white, could mean purity, sun, light, sacredness, redemption or illumination. In alchemy white is related to the feminine principle, the moon, the purity of undivided light, and the second stage of the "Great Work" or inner process of finding the heart of gold. The ram, although often thought of as a sacrificial animal, was originally connected with the sun (gold) and creative and generative power. So there is already a connection between Golden Chisel and his creativity, and this ability to provide the means to make the fine white flour with which to nourish the people. Perhaps also he was called Golden Chisel because he had a 'heart of gold,' as it is understood in the process of alchemy. He was the one who was constantly on the lookout for the stone ram of the prophecy. This search was not purely for himself but to relieve the suffering of the people in his village.

In his daily work Golden Chisel was always aware somehow of the search for the 'stone ram'. In spite of great hardships, he was forever searching. Late one evening, when returning from a remote mountain, he saw in the darkness a spark of light shining in the centre of a dried pond, south of the village. This sentence seems to contain a lot of information. First, he was returning from a remote mountain - perhaps he had gone to a remote, high place within himself; mountains are often thought of as the place of the spirit. Secondly, it was night-time or dark, which could mean that he had been meditating or that perhaps it was a dream - certainly it would mean that he was in another realm. So from that place he saw a light over a dry pond. It is interesting that again there is that image of the dry pond. Why south of the village? When doing Tai Chi (in China) the Chinese always bow to the north, where the enemy, the Mongol invaders, came from, and then towards the south, to their teacher. Of course it could also mean that south was towards the heart of China, the ancient capital having been Xian, which is south of the Yellow River. Could it be that the teachings themselves had become dry and contaminated? Golden Chisel could perhaps have seen a light in those teachings after coming back from the "remote mountain" place within himself.

The next day he began digging at the centre of the pond where the light had appeared. He dug through red clay and black sand and then suddenly there was a flash of light and he dug out a dazzlingly bright stone, somewhat resembling a ram. At Summer School the one and a half feet between head and heart was mentioned—perhaps this is what was meant by that digging. The red clay - dense earth, red like blood, and it is said that God made Adam from moistened red clay. Black sand - not so dense, unable to hold water, negative - an inability to focus and concentrate? Again there is a possible connection with alchemy, as white with black and red depict the three stages of initiation into enlightenment.

Golden Chisel had found the stone and he knew that he could make it into the ram of the legend. First he carefully observed it and contemplated its form, so that he understood the task that lay ahead, the form or image that he would create. Contemplating the stone could be like the creation and contemplation of our Divine Ideal - the ideal that we attempt to emulate in our practice. When I first heard the story I imagined a black stone but the story says it was a dazzlingly bright one - perhaps like a diamond.

The next stage in the process or story is the carving of the stone ram; this is very hard work. The carver's tools became blunted, (indicating that it could well have been a "diamond" or the "diamond heart") and it took a long time; nine days and nights - again there is much symbolism in this. Seven or nine usually means a long time in teaching tales, but nine here is also a sacred number—three times three. And when he was finished, the little ram came alive! It is interesting that it is on completion of the last hoof that the ram comes to life, and later it is in the hoof that the ram is wounded. Usually we are born head first, the feet being the last to emerge into the world. The hoof is then a sign of completion or birth. Stone here can signify stability, reliability, immortality, the indestructibility of the "Supreme Being." In alchemy, uncarved stone is the *prima materia,* the feminine principle, and is associated with the male symbol of the chisel, which gives shape to the *prima materia.* The carved or polished stone denotes the character that has been worked upon and perfected.

I feel that this 'work' of chiselling the ram is like our inner work. It takes a long time, and it takes everything we have got. The tools being blunted may even refer to overcoming our *nafs* or small self in the process of polishing the heart or creating a heart of gold or polishing the diamond.

When the ram came to life, he appreciated the effort that Golden Chisel had made and he offered Golden Chisel gold or silver but Golden Chisel asked for something even more precious: pure spring water so that every household could enjoy the "true taste of tea and food." Thus instead of personal gain, Golden Chisel chose a way to aid the whole community, a service that would be everlasting. This was a more difficult task for the ram. Sometimes when one achieves a certain level of growth, like bringing the ram-ideal to life, we might be tempted to be satisfied with the personal gifts of gold or silver, perhaps representing phenomena or powers that we had not dreamt of, but there is always a next step upward for the seeker. On the ladder reaching towards enlightenment, we should not stop at the step we have reached but should keep on going. The ram agreed to try to find water but he extracted a promise from Golden Chisel: he must never divulge their secret to a soul. If a stranger should spot him and "tell the world," that would be the end of the magic. This is much like working with dreams, that if we tell our dreams they lose their magic, their energy. We should not speak of our inner journey to strangers, or in other words those not on the path. Esoteric truth or mysticism is, by definition, hidden, a mystery, not to be divulged to non-initiates, because it would not be understood properly, it could be distorted and even be dangerous to our psyche.

Of course, the hidden stone could also represent the philosopher's stone of the alchemists, representing the supreme quest for the reconciliation of all opposites; the attainment of unity; regaining the Centre; perfection; absolute reality; spiritual, mental and moral wholeness in man; the *spiritus mundi* made visible. The carved or polished stone denotes the character, which has been worked upon and perfected.

The little ram scampered away—thirty miles to the Yellow River, sucked up a bellyful of water and disgorged the water into the dried pond, back and forth three times each night. Again, as a multiple of three, thirty miles symbolizes a sacred number; it is significant that the river was very far away and that he made three trips each night. The Yellow River for the Chinese is a very sacred river, it is near this river that many royal tombs have been found and it was the centre of early Chinese civilization. In other words, the water of life is found at a sacred place at night. The colour yellow is solar, the light of the sun and golden, again connecting the story to "gold." As Murshid Nawab pointed out in our Summer School, the river could also represent the kundalini flow, also symbolized by the serpent or dragon, and indeed the river gods in China were thought to be serpents, which could become dragons as they rose to the heavens in search of enlightenment.

The pond became full of 'sweet, limpid, blue water'; the villagers were happy and thought that blessings had been sent to them from heaven; they now had sweet water to drink and cook with. Only Golden Chisel really knew how the pond was replenished each night.

One might think that this is the end of the tale, but no, there is more!

Often when we reach a certain stage of evolution, when we connect with the 'water of life' in our meditation or in the night in our dreams, we think that is as far as we can go, but Hazrat Inayat Khan constantly teaches that the necessary application of our inner work is in the spreading of the teachings.

A hundred days passed, or in other words a very long time, during which the water was replenished every night by the ram. Then one morning the ram did not return. Golden Chisel searched along the road to the Yellow River and eventually found the ram lying 'among rank weeds, moaning.' The wicked god of the Yellow River had cut off one of his front hooves and the ram could no longer run.

What does this signify, the ram with his front hoof cut off by the god of the Yellow River? Who is the god? I think that in this case he represents our greedy, jealous ego or small self, which can become inflated after a long period of subjugation or of having been tamed. The stone ram (the ideal) has been bringing water to the village nightly. We use this ideal for our inner work; we perhaps emulate our teacher in the process of *fana-fi-shaikh,* our ego slowly becoming smaller until it disappears into the ideal. In alchemy, the process of keeping the ego tamed is like the fire on the crucible, it must be kept constant. The god was jealous; he resented the ram "stealing" his water, and had determined to stop this.

Perhaps this jealous god also represents some archetypal aspect of the collective psyche that wanted to stop the water being taken each night. During the Australian Summer School there was discussion about the wall we sometimes encounter after doing our practices for a long time; in the beginning the practices are easy and we get tremendous energy and light from them, but then they seem to get more and more difficult. The ego throws up all sorts of difficulties. We can't move easily in and out of the "other" realm, and the energy does not flow smoothly any longer - and that could be like having our hoof cut off. This front hoof could also signify our connection with the earth and our direction— the front hoof could be the one which points to where we are going, or indicate how we stand on the earth, our "standpoint." With this gone we are paralyzed. The river god wounds the ram, and so it is that the limited individual, the ego, mars the perfection of the ideal.

Golden Chisel's heart was filled with sorrow and great concern as he carried the ram home in his arms. The water in the pond dried up and the villagers were at a loss as to what to do. When the ideal has been damaged, the water of life or spiritual awareness does not flow any more.

214

As the story continues, Golden Chisel, in his distress and anger, vowed to avenge the attack of the god. He carved a new golden hoof for the little ram. So the seeker has to mend the ideal, which has been damaged and wounded by the demon in ourselves. This new hoof is made of precious gold!

One moonlit, starry night Golden Chisel took out the sun-and-moon talisman that had been handed down to him through his family, mounted the stone ram and rode to the Yellow River. It is the ideal which carries us to do battle with our demon.

The god of the Yellow River is here described as "brooding, with his head lowered, squatting on the riverbank like a huge rock." To me this feels so much like a depression. Years ago, I was in a therapy group in which one of the members gave the same impression as this "god"- he sat rock-like and brooding, and with his words and actions he "killed" us. The energy of the group stopped flowing and we became completely stuck. Nothing happened at all and we mostly just sat there, uncomfortable and unable to do anything. On one of our weekends away, our facilitator tried to break this impasse. She brought in a cardboard box and an axe, which she placed before the man in our circle. She told him that if he wanted to kill, he could kill what was in the box. We sat frozen in horror, as out of the box came the small quacks of a duckling. She encouraged him to kill it, while the rest of us wept. In the end after what seemed like a long time, he put away the axe and the little duck and wept with us—he could not kill it.

The story says that 'It was as if an evil wind blew in the forest.' Could it be the god was depressed and tormented? The forest could represent the lack of spiritual insight in the god of the Yellow River, who was lost in the darkness. This negative god could be the dark side or shadow of the stone ram - our divine ideal. C. G. Jung, in his book 'Answer to Job,' discusses the idea of Satan as the dark side of God.

Then the fight was on between Golden Chisel and the god. Golden Chisel was in danger of being frozen by a blast of air from the mouth of the river god, but Golden Chisel calmly took out the sun-and-moon talisman and tapped it a few times, whereupon it suddenly gave out a golden light and a purple haze spread from it like a raging flame.

The sun-and-moon talisman is very important. It symbolizes the reconciliation of the ultimate archetypal opposites, which is the 'great work' of the alchemists. Sol and Luna are gold and silver, king and queen, soul and body. The sun has always represented the supreme cosmic power, the yang, jelal principle, the all-seeing Divinity and its power, the centre of being and intuitive knowledge. The moon represents the great feminine power, symbolic of the rhythm of cyclic time, universal becoming, as well as the spiritual aspect of light in darkness. It is the essence of the yin, jemal, feminine principle in nature but also of immortality. The full moon signifies wholeness, completion, strength and spiritual power. The sun and moon together represent the *'Hieros Gamos'*—the sacred marriage of heaven and earth.

I am fascinated by the way the sun-and-moon talisman is merely mentioned in passing in the story and yet is so important and significant. Without it Golden Chisel could not have overcome the god of the Yellow River. The talisman had been handed down through his family; he knew he had access to this intuitive knowledge and power, which we all have. It is at one and the same time the tool and the goal of the "great work."

In the ensuing fight Golden Chisel used the sun-and-moon talisman to overcome the frozen petrifaction and darkness of the river god. He did not kill him; the ego or small self must not be killed but must be overcome, as it conceals the pearl without price in its mouth. The heat or warmth of love perhaps melted the freezing wind—the frozen emotions and feelings. Ice and snowflakes, coming from the breath of the river god, symbolise frozen water, the emotions which do not flow any longer. The sun-and-moon talisman, as Murshid Nawab put it, is Golden Chisel's family heritage, or in other words, the power of light and love from the Father/Mother 'above'- this is what defeated the jealous and frozen god of the Yellow River. This power overcomes the frozen structures and dark places in ourselves which can be encountered during the inner work. A. H. Almaas writes about our being born with our Essence intact but surmises that as our "personality" or small self develops, it takes parts of our Essence, which then creates holes, and that by shining light into those holes—understanding our weakness and defenses - we restore our Essence and become complete again.

The point is that this demonic part of ourselves has to be confronted and overcome, or we are lost. Anger and outrage helped Golden Chisel in his task. The energy of anger can be useful.

A friend who is a Christian minister found this part of the story very useful in his work, saying it helped him "take on" the hierarchy of his Church, which had become bogged down. He had been dreading a forthcoming meeting but found the inner power to do what he needed to do, when contemplating this archetypal battle.

The god had no answer when Golden Chisel told him that the Yellow River flows on earth and belongs to everybody, that it does not belong to the god. "We will not let you keep it for yourself," he said. The small self wants to hold the spiritual power, the water of life, for itself, rather than letting it flow for all beings.

The defeated river god then offered to atone for his error. Of course the completion of the transition, of the self-sacrifice, is seen when the ram (the Ideal) and Golden Chisel (the seeker) both say together that they want water for the village, for others. This is the ultimate service.

The river god gave the ram a round pearl, sparkling and crystal-clear. When the ram would hold the pearl in his mouth, pure water would flow forth like a fountain forever. The pearl is the lunar power of the waters, the essence of the moon, and the life-giving power of the great mother. It is interesting that the "pearl of perfection," together with the dragon, can be seen as the spiritual essence of the universe, and as enlightenment. It can also signify the unfolding and development of man in the quest for enlightenment. In the Chinese culture the pearl can also indicate genius in obscurity, which relates to the idea of not allowing others to see one's accomplishment. Real esoteric teaching is done in obscurity and not with phenomena and 'magic' works.

I wondered why the pearl was to be held in the mouth of the ram for the water to flow. The mouth appears as the gateway between the deep inner realm and the outside world but it could also relate to the power of speech or the utterance of words of power.

Now Golden Chisel and the ram had to get back to the village before dawn, but the fight with the river god and the golden hoof from the ram's previous wound slowed them down. It is interesting to note that the gold hoof and the fight with the demon do slow us down. This slowing down seems to be necessary for the next stage of the process. A young cowherd had risen early and was driving his cattle out to pasture when he saw a bright light shooting towards him from a distance. He cried out for everyone to look at Golden Chisel riding a stone ram.

When the ram heard this he was immediately transformed into a heap of rocks, out of which flowed a limpid sweet spring. The village now had fresh running water without the need for the ram to make the journey to the Yellow River.

Someone asked me what this young cowherd signifies in our own psyche. I have wondered about this, especially as he is so necessary to this story. Perhaps it is that young grounded part of our self, who is up at sun-rise, the part that cares for the cows, which feed us and provide us with milk, all of which are related to the great mother and the feminine principle, the one who *sees* the light and knows what it means. Again the symbol unites the solar masculine and the lunar feminine principles.

On being observed, the ram breaks into pieces, and from the heap of broken stone arises a constant spring of fresh water. As Murshid says in the Gayan, 'I have found Thee at last as a pearl, hidden in the shell of my heart.' In other words, the heart has to break into pieces before we can connect with the divine Beloved and live in that connection or oneness. Perhaps this means that it is hard to let go of the structure we have created, we do not even know that this too has to be left, destroyed—it becomes dust, and then the soul/spirit gives us eternal life. When someone *sees* it and names it, then it becomes nothing. Spirit and matter is an uneasy partnership until matter is 'transformed'.

I think that the disintegration of the stone ram signifies the next stage of evolution, to fana-fi-Allah, for the ideal too has to be annihilated into the Divine Being. Then the water of life and love flows forever, directly from the soul of the seeker to all those around him. The teachings continue to flow and nourish all who contact them.

Source

The story of 'Golden Chisel and the Stone Ram', in *Favourite Folktales of China*, translated by John Minford, Graham Brash, Singapore, 2000.

APPENDIX

Ponderings on the Unstruck Sound

Nuria Daly[43]

For a long time, I have been fascinated and mystified by the story of the Zen monks whose task it was to understand the koan, "the sound of one hand clapping." To me it seemed impossible, but in some of Hazrat Inayat Khan's Sufi teachings I found hints of something similar, a practice in which one tries to listen while closing the ears. Here was a great mystery, and I felt drawn to it. I felt like the monk of my early imaginings but I discovered that there was indeed a practice to do with withdrawing breath and awareness from the outer material world, and directing it inwardly. In so doing the senses are drawn within until it is possible, we are told, to hear an inner sound, see an inner light, and even smell the fragrance of the inner essence of our whole being. It seems to me now that this is in fact the ultimate mystery and the basic tenet of all mysticism. Indeed, Hazrat Inayat Khan states that "The mystery of sound is mysticism;" and it is on this aspect, sound, that I am directing my thoughts.

There is a close parallel between hearing and vision because both involve the sensing of the frequencies of certain vibrations. Indeed, some people can hear light and colour, and see sound.

From the spiritual point of view, light and sound are really one.

---

[43] First published in *Toward the One: A Journal of Unity*, Volume Eight, Spring 2007.

We humans are generally not capable of sensing vibrations outside the ranges of physical vision (vibrations with a wavelength between 400 and 700 nanometers) and hearing (frequencies between 20 and 20,000 cycles per second). However, we can see and hear in our dreams when our physical senses are asleep, and accounts of "out-of-body" or "near death" experiences speak of people seeing and hearing from this disembodied state of being. I have heard a blind woman tell of a near-death experience where she was actually able to see and describe what was happening to her "body" from far above it.

Even the sense of smell can be felt in dreams and in out-of-body experiences. One mureed tells of an experience when she was undergoing an operation. She remembers meeting her long dead father, whom she recognised initially by the fragrance of wood and wood shavings. Her father's hobby had been carpentry and woodwork. In her experience he was wearing a woodworker's apron, as he had often done when alive. She nestled in his arms, comforted, before being told to go back as her time had not yet come. During the operation she had indeed died for a time and been brought back to life in this realm.

Spirit has been described as "God-in-Action," so spirit can be understood as a non-material vibration of God-in-Action. The whole world—the sun, the moon, the earth and the stars—are all sustained by Spirit, which can also be said to be the "Word." To quote Hazrat Inayat Khan

We find in the Bible the words: 'In the beginning was the word, and the word was God' and we also find that the word is light, and when that light dawned the whole creation manifested. These are not only religious verses; to the mystic or seer the deepest revelation is contained within them. ...It teaches that the first sign of life that manifested was the audible expression, or sound: that is the word.

Hazrat Inayat goes on to say, 'All down the ages the Yogis and seers of India have worshipped the Word-God, or Sound-God, and around that idea is centred all the mysticism of sound or utterance. Not alone among Hindus, but among the seers of the Semitic, the Hebraic races, the great importance of the word was recognised.'

This Word has, of course, intent behind it—pure Divine intelligence.

Every major religion refers to creation as having been brought about by a word, or a saying, or a name. It is the sound that precedes light, which in turn, precedes manifestation.

Hindu (Upanishads)

Accordingly, with that Word, with that Self he brought forth this whole universe, everything that exists.

Taoist (Tao Te Ching)

The nameless is the beginning of heaven and earth. The named is the mother of ten thousand things.

Jewish (Book of Genesis)

And God said, Let there be light: and there was light.

Christian (Gospel according to John)

In the beginning was the Word, and the Word was with God, and the Word was God.

Islamic (Quran)

Creator of the heavens and the earth from nothingness, He has only to say when He wills a thing: 'Be,' and it is.

Sikh (Adi Granth)

One Word, and the whole Universe throbbed into being.

Hazrat Inayat Khan quotes Shams-e-Tabriz, that 'the whole mystery of the universe lies in sound.'

So, this Word is ringing in every atom of creation, and it is to 'hear' this Word that we do our practices and meditation. It is the Hu that we can perhaps hear after Zikar when we close our ears.

As our Murshid says: 'Words themselves have the power to vibrate through different parts of man's body.' They can affect us powerfully, as we can know from chanting or saying Wazifas, and as Hindus and Buddhists find in chanting mantras. 'The power of the word is in accordance with the illumination of the soul…. that word comes from some mysterious part that is hidden from the human mind.'

This recalls an interview with an English woman, an academic, who had come to Western Australia to work in the prison system. There she formed a close relationship with a young Aboriginal man who was in prison. She eventually married him, went to live in the remote bush and compiled a dictionary of his language. When she was asked how he had "attracted" her or formed the initial connection, she said that he told her that he "sang" her from his cell. It says much about this man's spirituality.

The soul can be thought of as a ray of the spirit, just as a ray of sunlight is part of the sun, is of the same essence as the sun but is not the sun. The soul is spread in our whole body. Really the difference between soul and spirit is the level of consciousness, or the level of vibration of that sound or Word. Hazrat Inayat Khan tells of the legend 'which relates that God made a statue of clay in His own image, and asked the soul to *enter* into it. But the soul refused to enter into this prison, for its nature is to fly about freely, and not be limited and bound to any sort of captivity. The soul did not wish in the least to enter this prison. Then God asked the angels to play their music and, as the angels played, the soul was moved to ecstasy. Through that ecstasy—in order to make this music clearer to itself—it entered this body.' So the soul has entered the body to experience the music of life.

For the soul to experience this music, we have to unite it with the all-pervading conscious energy of spirit, and this may be done by repeating words such as wazifas which relate to aspects of the Divine non-material realm. This takes our mind away from the outer material world and towards the inner world. So we ride the wave of spirit as an audible vibration, not heard by human ears but by a faculty of the soul.

The soul then hears the Divine music which it longs to hear. Hazrat Inayat Khan has said:

Abstract sound is called saut-e-sarmad by the Sufis; all space is filled with it... The knower of the mystery of sound knows the mystery of the whole universe. . . The sound of the abstract is always going on within, around, and about man. As a rule, one does not hear it because one's consciousness is entirely centred in material existence... Those who are able to hear the saut-e -sarmad and meditate on it are relieved from all worries, anxieties, sorrows, fears and diseases; and the soul is freed from captivity in the senses and in the physical body. The soul of the listener becomes the all-pervading consciousness...

The soul takes great pleasure in hearing what has been called Divine music, or "the music of the spheres." In southern Africa the bushmen of the Kalahari desert are said to be able to "hear" the stars and this celestial music. There is a story circulating that the astronauts can hear the sound or vibration of the earth in space and that this sound vibration is similar to the sound made by the Aboriginal didgeridoo. This may be a modern myth but if myths are the dreaming of a people, then there could indeed be some truth in this tale. This deep vibration can also be felt when hearing Tibetan monks chanting or playing their horns.

Two years ago my husband and I were visiting Cologne and he wanted to film the cathedral in the evening without all the tourists and noise. That evening we found ourselves in the audience of a most amazing organ recital in the Cathedral. For us the sound of the music and the atmosphere of this sacred space was a numinous, unforgettable experience. The vibration of the organ resounding in the dome of the cathedral was profound.

Of course the glorious chanting of the monks and nuns in the Catholic Church has been used in the same way, and in the Eastern Orthodox Church the chanting of the gospels is part of the service. Similarly, the Quran is chanted in the mosque. In all spiritual practice, sound or song is used to connect to or communicate with God, the source of all.

The film Baraka, a beautiful visual work without dialogue, shows peoples and tribes from many parts of the world using song and music as a way of connecting with the sacred. In the film we see a tribe sitting in the jungle chanting and moving together in rhythm like birds, in ecstasy— a sort of participation mystique; we see a lone monk walking slowly through the streets of Tokyo, ringing a small bell rhythmically and oblivious to the frantic rush around him, a still island amongst the mayhem; we see the ecstatic whirling of the Dervishes; and we hear the voice and power of a volcano erupting.

The Australian Aborigines use song in their most sacred and secret "men's and woman's business." There are song lines which convey the relationships from the dreamtime or creation myths with the land and all the tribes and peoples of the land, including the animals, waterholes, rocks, and all of creation. The aboriginal languages are completely different from modern languages like English. The words and phrases convey the feeling, history, source and relationships of the particular "words" and their relevance to everything around them. As Hazrat Inayat Khan has said, in ancient languages "every name reveals to the seer the past, present and future of that which it covers." So these ancient languages are powerful in their sound and meanings, and that is probably why many of the sacred names of God in many traditions are chanted in the original language, like Sanskrit, or Aramaic. Once, during a short course on the Epic of Gilgamesh, our professor read parts of the epic in the original, ancient Sumerian. It was wonderfully onomatopoeic: the volcanoes rumbled and the text could almost be understood without translation just from the sound of the words.

There are outer sounds which are somehow associated with the inner sounds, sounds like the vina, the flute, distant bells, the buzzing of bees, thunder, or the running of water, until the sound finally becomes *Hu*, the most sacred of all sounds. These sounds are heard with the ears of the soul.

In this material, physical universe we mostly live in, conscious energy is vibrating at a very low rate — it is the first level, the bottom floor of creation, so to speak. In our material world our physical ears cannot sense these sounds which can be heard by the soul. Our perceptions and consciousness are pulled outward and away from the higher realms of spirit. So we reach up to ever finer levels of vibrations by doing our practices, so that we can eventually begin to hear that "unstruck sound" which belongs to these higher realms.

The second plane of existence, next to our material plane, is commonly called the astral plane, because here the soul takes on the covering of the astral body which is said to sparkle with millions of little particles resembling star dust. According to Brian Hines in his book *God's Whisper, Creation's Thunder,* the sound related to this plane is said to be like a resounding bell or distant church bells. As this is the first nonmaterial region we become aware of, it perhaps explains why bells are used in churches and individual practice.

The third plane or realm is that of the mind, often referred to as the realm of the Jinns. This is the last level of creation and can be understood as the 'causal' region, because it is the effective cause of everything that lies below. The sounds related to this realm are said to be of thunder or the beating of drums.

According to Hines, the flute or harp is said to be the instrument or sound associated with the fourth level or realm. This realm could be said to be that of the angels, so it is interesting that angels are often depicted playing a harp and the Lord Krishna is always depicted playing the flute.

Srila Govinda Maharaja, explaining the Gayatri mantra, writes in Krishna's Flute, 'Like the trumpet of an elephant, it is a sound so great that it captures the heart and attention of everyone. But that sound has no material form—it is pure spiritual sound. And that divine sound descends into this world from the flute of the Lord Krishna.'

In Hindu spirituality devotees are told to chant mantras, as well as to meditate. Baba Muktananda once told one of his devotees to chant and to meditate. Two years later the man came to Baba and told him that the practices did not work. Muktananda could see that he had not done any chanting but had only meditated. He said that to meditate only is not enough, that we need to chant to give *us* the vitality and juice *of life* which leads to the Divine realm.

The sound related to the fifth and highest plane, the realm of ultimate reality or the home of the Supreme Being, is said to be that of the vina. In this realm, the domain of the Universal Spirit, says Hines, there are no divisions; it is a place of unity outside of time and space, the source of All, full of love, 'knowledge' (pure intelligence) and energy.

The vina is a very ancient instrument associated with the Hindu gods. There is for example the Saraswati vina, Saraswati being the goddess of music, knowledge and wisdom, as well as the goddess of speech, the power through which knowledge expresses itself in action. She is always seen playing her instrument, the vina. The vichitra (or unique) vina, originally called the Shiv vina, is associated with the god Shiva, the god of transformation, who preserves the world through meditation, and who dances the cosmic dance which sustains the cosmos.

Hazrat Inayat Khan tells a story of spending some time alone in a haunted house. He writes 'Whenever I played upon the vina at night, sitting on my bed, the bed would gradually begin to move as if levitating, and to rock to and fro. It would seem to rise for an instant some way into the air, but the movement was so smooth that there was no shock.' After some time, he had to send his vina out to be repaired. "One night to my great horror I heard a noise as if all the windows of my house were being smashed. For three days this went on, and I could not sleep. I had no peace at night until my vina came back. The spirits seemed to be so much interested in my music that they rejoiced in it and showed their appreciation by lifting me up; when the food of their soul was not given they rebelled." This shows how much the unseen beings also love and long for the music of the vina.

Our Master does not relate the various inner sounds to particular planes of existence, as far as I know. However, he does describe the process. *Some train themselves to hear the sawt-e-sarmad in the solitude, on the sea shore, on the river bank and in the hills and dales; others attain it while sitting in the caves of the mountains, or when wandering constantly through forests and deserts, keeping themselves in the wilderness apart from the haunts of men. Yogis and ascetics blow...a horn, or...a shell, which awakens in them this inner tone. Dervishes play...a double flute for the same purpose. The bells and gongs in the churches and temples are meant to suggest to the thinker the same sacred sound, and thus lead him towards the inner life.*

This sound develops through...different aspects because of its manifestation through...the body. . . until it finally becomes Hu, the most sacred of all sounds.

So, it is that through this understanding of the mystery of sound, I have a deeper resolution and direction in my practice. I know the practices that we have been given have the purpose of raising the level of our consciousness or vibration, so that the soul may be able to hear the music of Spirit, to hear the Divine Word and so that happiness and joy can be a part of all life. Indeed, my own practice has been heightened during the process of writing this article.

Sources

Brian Hines, *God's Whisper, Creation's Thunder Echoes of Ultimate Reality in the New Physics,* Threshold Books 1996.

Hazrat Inayat Khan, *The Mysticism of Sound and Music.* Shambhala 1996.

Hazrat Inayat Khan, *Tales.* Omega Publications 1991.

Srila Bhakti Sundar Govinda Dev Goswami Maharaja; http://dailydarshan.com/darshan/flute.html

First published in Toward the One: A Journal of Unity; Volume Eight, Spring 2007

ACKNOWLEDGEMENTS

This book was inspired by Murshid Nawab's teaching from the ancient Chinese story of *Golden Chisel*, at an Australian Sufi Summer School many years ago, so my deep gratitude goes to Nawab for his inspiration and guidance, as well as his 'knowing' which stories were the ones I should work on next. Five is a magic number for Hazrat Inayat Khan – there are sets of five in many practices, so it is an amazing coincidence that there are five stories that I have worked with in this book. It was not conscious. My gratitude also to Nawab's wife, Nirtan, who gave me many insights into *The Frog Princess* and Russia.

I would like to thank my beloved husband, Azad, for his patience and fortitude in reviewing early manuscripts of the stories as they were evolving. For dealing with what he called, my curly sentence structure, which seems to have come from German having been my first language, and for being my best critic.

There have been a series of amazing synchronicities (miracles) which have helped and guided me.

Firstly, my thanks to my Jungian friend of many years, Peter Ross, for giving me Henry Corbin's beautiful and insightful book *Alone with the Alone: Creative Imagination in the Sufism of Ibn 'Arabi*, at the precise time that I needed it. This feeling of experiencing the creative imagination, opened the veils which led me right into the weaving of the stories into life and living.

Some years ago, I was invited to join an august body of philosophers and thinkers, which I now call 'The Philosophers' Lunch Group'. Just how this came about is another story but my great thanks go to Dr

Nicholas Coleman for giving me the opportunity to be part of these lively, entertaining and often mind blowing (for me) discussions. My thanks also to Rev. Helen Summers for introducing me to Dr Coleman at a Melbourne Interfaith gathering and for her advice and support over the years. My special thanks to these fabulous, wonderful people: Dr Felicity McCutcheon, Professor Will Johnston, Professor David Tacey, Professor Greg Restall, as well as Dr Nichols Coleman and Rev Helen Summers of course. They have been so encouraging, helpful, and supportive.

My thanks and gratitude to my dear Sufi sister, Bria Zora Floren, herself a writer, who has encouraged me and taught me so much about writing. She also struggled with my strange sentence structure.

Then our Sufi brother, Dr Martin Arif Leckey 'found' Hannah Beak Wha reading Marie Louise Von Franz's book, *The Feminine in Fairy Tales*, in the park. After a lovely email interchange with her, I discovered that she was an illustrator! She has the wonderful ability of taking herself into the fairy realm to find the images which were just right for each story.

And finally, and perhaps most importantly, a very great Thank You, to my friend, Christine Godfrey, for reading and so skilfully editing this manuscript. Her insight into the tales was deeply personal and profound, especially for *The Frog Princess*, and it was delightful for me to see the effect of this on her life.

Thank you also to the team at Balboa Press for their professionalism and support.

BIBLIOGRAPHY

Sources

Minford, John (translator), *Favourite Folktales of China, Golden Chisel and the Stone Ram,* Graham Brash, Singapore, 2000

'The Fairy of the Dawn' in Lang, Andrew (ed.), *The Violet Fairy Book,* Longman Green and Co, London, 1901

The Frog Princess, <http://www.artrusse.ca/fairytales/frog-princess.htm> at 19 December2016

Giambattista, Basile, 'Cenerentola in *Stories from Pentamerone* <http://www.gutenberg.org/files/2198/2198-h/2198-h.htm#chap06> at 4 January 2017

Yershov, Pyotr, *The Little Humpbacked Horse,* Progress Publishers, USSR, 1957, <http://lib.ru/LITRA/ERSHOW/horse.txt> at 4 January 2017

Articles

'Fairy tale origins thousands of years old, researchers say.' in *BBC News,* UK, 20 January 2016, < http://www.bbc.com/news/uk-35358487> at 4 January 2017

Books

Corbin, Henry. *Alone with the Alone. Creative Imagination in the Sufism of Ibn 'Arabi*, Bollingen Series XCI, Princeton University Press, Princeton, New Jersey, 1998

Figes, Orlando. *Natasha's Dance: A Cultural History of Russia*, Penguin, London, 2002

Hawk Wing, Pansy, 'In Relation', in *The Unknown She: Eight Faces of an Emerging Consciousness*, Hart, Hilary, The Golden Sufi Center, California, 2003

Helminsky, Kabir, *The Knowing Heart: A Sufi Path of Transformation*, Shambhala, Boston, 2000

Hines, Brian, *God's Whisper, Creation's Thunder Echoes of Ultimate Reality in the New Physics*, Threshold Books, Vermont, 1996

Khan, Inayat Hazrat, 'The Art of Personality' *in The Sufi Message*, Volume 3, Motilal Banarsidass Publishers, Delhi 1989

Khan, Inayat Hazrat, The Dance of the Soul: Gayan, Vadan, Nirtan, Sufi Sayings, Motilal Banarsidass Publishers, Delhi, 1993

Khan, Inayat Hazrat, 'The Divinity of the Human Soul' in *The Sufi Message*, Volume 12, Motilal Banarsidass Publishers, Delhi 1990

Khan, Inayat Hazrat, 'The Gathas' in *The Sufi Message, Volume 13*, Motilal Banarsidass Publishers, Delhi, 1990

Khan, Inayat Hazrat, *The Mysticism of Sound and Music*, Shambhala, Boston,1996

Khan, Inayat Hazrat, *Sufi Teachings, The Sufi Message Volume 8*, Motilal Banarsidass Publishers, Delhi, 1994

Khan, Inayat Hazrat, *Tales.* Omega Publications, New Lebanon, 1991

Johnston, Robert A, *He: Understanding Masculine Psychology,* Harper & Row, New York, 2002

Lessing, Doris, *Briefing for a Descent into Hell,* Jonathan Cape, London, 1971

Rumi, Jalaluddin 'When a Madman Smiles at You' in *Delicious Laughter,* interpreted by Coleman Barks, Maypop Books, Atlanta, Georgia, 1990

Nightingale, Steven. *Granada: The Light of Andalucía,* Nicholas Brealey Publishing, London, 2015

Tacey, David, *The Spirituality Revolution: The Emergence of Contemporary Spirituality,* Harper Collins, Australia, 2003

Tuby, Molly, 'Opposites and the Healing Power of Symbols', in Tuby, M (ed.) *In The Wake of Jung,-a Selection of Articles by Jungian Analysts,* Coventure, (np), UK, 1983, out of print